DANCE INTO HER HEART

DANCE INTO HER HEART

What They Don't Tell You about Ballroom and Latin Dancing

PAUL BOUDREAU

GSPH

GENERAL STORE PUBLISHING HOUSE
499 O'Brien Road, Box 415
Renfrew, Ontario, Canada K7V 4A6
Telephone 1.613.432.7697 or 1.800.465.6072
www.gsph.com

ISBN 978-1-897508-70-1

Cover art, design, formatting: Magdalene Carson
Printed by Custom Printers of Renfrew Ltd., Renfrew, Ontario
Printed and bound in Canada

Library and Archives Canada Cataloguing in Publication
Boudreau, Paul A., 1953-
    Dance into her heart : what they don't tell you about ballroom and
Latin dancing / Paul A. Boudreau ; Jane Karchmar, editor.
ISBN 978-1-897508-70-1
    I. Karchmar, Jane II. Title.
PS8603.O9269D36 2010   C813'.6   C2010-901015-9

For Jill

CONTENTS

PROLOGUE

My ballroom dance adventure began with a private lesson. Many people start by signing up for a group class with other anxious people. I took my first step as a birthday present to myself.

My life started in Kingston, Ontario, born to parents who instilled in me a strong sense of ethics and a healthy dose of competitive spirit. My father was in the Canadian military, and we moved frequently, based on where and when he was told to go. When I was quite young, we left Kingston for Barrie, Ontario, then to Moncton, New Brunswick, the hometown of both my parents. From there we went to Fredericton. Then we spent three years overseas in Germany in the mid-1960s as part of the Canadian Forces presence. I was a skinny kid suffering from both allergies and asthma that kept my body thin and my muscles weak. I attended eleven schools in thirteen years, which turned out to be a healthy intellectual challenge. However, being highly introverted, my social skills developed far more slowly than average. Playing sports became a passion and an outlet. I found that I had good coordination and a strong desire to do well in sports, which became very valuable when I entered the world of ballroom dance.

I am in my late forties and still considered to be a decent-looking man. Standing five feet nine inches tall, my body is at a normal weight for my height, probably more on the slender side. There is plenty of dark brown hair on my head, and people often comment that I look younger than my true age. I have a moustache that once took forever to grow but finally looks full. Excessive strain and overuse through many years of competitive sports have worn down my joints. As a result, my activities shifted to lower-impact exercise such as roller-blading and swimming. (I often joke that I want to wear out all my muscles before I pass away because they will be no use to me after that!)

My office job is well suited to me and intellectually demanding. My marriage of twenty-three years having ended, and with my children grown up and pursuing their own activities, I find myself looking for a new diversion in the evenings. My self-esteem and confidence are low as a result of a stressful divorce, and it is time to focus on something else. I need a challenge and an activity to help me return to a positive and healthy path in life. I am about to enter the unfamiliar world of ballroom dancing. This is the city of Ottawa, the nation's capital, known for a solidly frozen canal in the winter and tourists tossing coins into the Centennial Flame fountain on Parliament Hill in the summer. In this region of 1.1 million people, there are no less than ten ballroom dance studios and countless other venues such as school boards and community centres that offer lessons or weekly dances.

And so, my journey into dance begins with taking private lessons once a week, attending one or two group lessons, and eventually, as my confidence increases, joining the student practice dances that are called "parties."

And I end up hooked for life.

PART ONE

GETTING HOOKED

1

GETTING STARTED

THE FIRST STEP

It is a bitterly cold January day as I huddle in the driver's seat of my car, looking across the parking lot. Piles of snow are unevenly stacked around the edges of the black pavement encroaching on the available parking space. In the early evening darkness, my body shivers, not from the cold air but from nervous tension. The door leading into the building in front of me is the entrance to a ballroom dance studio. Several weeks ago, I phoned the dance studio in response to a small, yet inviting, advertisement in the local newspaper to schedule my first ballroom dance lesson. I crave learning, and dancing seemed fascinating even now as I unsuccessfully try to convince myself that it is going to be fun. I am an introvert, and the prospect of close physical proximity and making polite conversation is a big hurdle to overcome. Frost from my breath coats the inside of the car windshield. My fingers wiggle inside the gloves to ward off the chill, and my cheeks feel the cold. After summoning up a bit more courage, I leave the car. My steps are tentative, and I move only because someone from the dance studio called earlier in the day to remind me of my commitment. I reluctantly walk across the parking lot and up to the studio door, wondering about the uncertainty that lies ahead. There is a fear of embarrassment and the awkwardness of starting something completely new and different.

I open the door, and a young, blonde, female receptionist looks up at me with a beaming smile. "You must be Paul. We are expecting you."

After directing me where to put my coat, showing me where the washrooms are, and making me feel like she is already a dear friend, I sit in the designated chair to wait for my teacher.

The dance studio has a large, rectangular, shiny, wooden floor. There are large windows along one long wall and a continuous row of full-length mirrors along the opposite wall. The sound system consists of speakers hanging from the four corners of the ceiling and a high-quality CD player that no one except teachers is allowed to touch. A water cooler sits in a corner, and there is a bulletin board beside it. Tagged to the board are a few small notes describing people seeking dance partners, a flyer for a store that sells dance apparel, and a poster about an upcoming dance show. In the studio, a few people stand very straight and walk around confidently. These are the teachers. Several other people of various ages are at one end of the studio attentively listening to someone who is giving them instruction. The men are lined up on one side and the women are lined up opposite the men. Music fills the room and I start to tap my foot.

My teacher is a dark-haired, slender woman, probably in her late twenties, and has been teaching dance for about six years. Melanie exudes confidence in the way she walks and presents herself without being cocky or arrogant. She is a grounded and intelligent person and is excellent at putting me at ease. This is exactly what I need in a dance instructor, and we quickly develop a rapport.

"If you know how to walk, you can do the Foxtrot!" my dance instructor exclaims assuredly. We foxtrot around the floor, and she adeptly avoids getting stepped on by my untrained, awkward feet. I look at them while dancing, as if to provide increased incentive to force them to go where I intend. My instructor persuades me to look up, over her right shoulder. Dancing with my teacher feels reassuring, although I know it has to look awful. I quickly become frustrated as new steps are introduced and I cannot repeat them easily.

Men like me who are new to dance lessons are recognizable by our big, seemingly oversized dress shoes or sports shoes instead of well-fitted, soft leather dance shoes. We lift our feet a bit higher or have a tendency to exaggerate a heel lead. As uncoordinated as we first appear, at least we have the courage to start a new activity. Progress can be realized very quickly for beginners if they apply themselves. At times I find the amount of information overwhelming, and yet deciphering instructions and turning them into a coordinated physical movement remains a true source of pleasure.

As difficult as it is to start, I am determined to continue and I am completely unaware that it will eventually lead to the discovery of a well-suited dance partner and, more than that, to something even more exciting than a great dance partnership.

Taking lessons alone with my instructor works out especially well because I am a man and she is a woman, which is the most common pairing for a ballroom dance couple. I also attend group lessons listed in a schedule that takes the form of a printed single-page calendar for the month and are for a specific dance and level of ability. They consist of ten men and ten women lined up on opposite sides and facing each other. The instructor walks us through a step separately until we look comfortable, adds music for some practice on the correct beat, then adds dancing the new pattern with a partner. I find that performing the new dance step alone is a challenge but acquired quickly. Dancing the same step to music actually makes it easier for me. The rhythm enters my ears, is interpreted by my brain, absorbed in the muscles, and eventually encourages my feet to move. Dancing with a partner is where it all falls apart. We look like bowling pins that are tottering back and forth.

At the dance studio, the student population is a grand variety. There are tall people, short people, very thin people, and not so thin people. Most of the dance students are middle-aged, perhaps a reflection of the aging adult population. There are only a few children and a few very elderly. There are as many couples as there are single people enrolled in lessons. Everyone is polite, and there are far more single women than men. Several students are figure skaters and take dance lessons to augment their training. There is a dentist, at least two doctors, several schoolteachers, and numerous government and technology industry workers.

I quickly realize that ballroom dancing is far more physically demanding than it looks. The best dancers make it look easy, whereas in reality it is not. All the major muscle groups are at work in dance. Above the waist, the arms and shoulders hold the proper frame. The stomach muscles are tight to provide good posture and frame. Below the waist is where all the movement originates. Obviously the legs and feet move to get around the floor, but the ankles, calf muscles, thighs, and hip muscles are all very active. In Latin dances, hip movement is a key styling ingredient, and it takes some gentle practice to get there. I find that my first attempts to perform Latin hip motion result in sore muscles. In the smooth dances, the legs have to work hard to propel the body so gracefully that it looks like the dance couple is floating.

Learning to dance follows a similar pattern for most beginners. The man has a tough challenge at the start because he needs to learn the steps, start and move to the beat of the music and lead the patterns. Beginners do not realize that social dancing is all leading and following, with the leader making decisions during the dances as to what pattern or series of steps will be used. It can take a while to feel good about doing a dance step. In social dancing, the pattern or sequence of steps is decided by the man, and this has to be communicated to the partner, even if it happens at the last second. Women face the challenge of having to learn the steps, listen to the music, and follow the pattern being initiated by what seems at times to feel like pushing on a big pillow. The learning curve is different for every dancer, and I observe several younger people and some determined women who learn very quickly at the beginning.

Considering the diverse learning curves, there is a recipe for fireworks between dance partners that can lead to interesting conversations between them. The level of ability may even out later as a couple moves to higher levels. The woman's part appears more difficult at higher levels, especially in the Latin dances, where they are expected to always look good and catch the eye with technically well-executed steps and a strong measure of confidence. A good guideline to avoid civil war between partners is to respect each other and know that no matter how bad you think your partner may be, there is always something that you are doing that could improve how both of you look on the dance floor.

As a beginner, I learn some good tips:

- Don't look at your feet.
- Stand up straight.
- Step to the beat of the music (especially men who are leading).

I learn that my feet are capable of moving without being watched every second. Otherwise, more people would bump into each other as they walk down the street passing each other on a sidewalk. It is important to place the feet in the right place, and the brain should be capable of directing the muscles appropriately. Some degree of trust is required. If a man looks at his feet instead of his female dance partner, it might convey the message that his feet are more attractive than her face. If a woman looks at her feet or all around the room instead of at the man she is dancing with, it strongly suggests that she would rather be dancing with someone else.

Good posture is an essential ingredient to proper dancing, and my posture is not ideal. It has always been a problem for me, from buying a well-fitted suit to making a good impression. My shoulders curve in and my neck extends slightly forward diagonally at an angle from my body. At least my chin normally tilts upwards, which is helpful in dance and looks natural. Standing up straight is an essential element in order to do any step properly. Leading a dance partner improves enormously when performed with good posture. A tall person initially tends to hunch over a smaller partner, or perhaps the shoulders sag forward. For good posture, the chest and rib cage should extend upwards as if the person has just taken a large breath and is holding it. Then the shoulders are pulled back and down. This applies to both men and women.

Music is the key to all dancing. When I hear music that quickly instills a feeling for the beat, it elicits much better dancing and helps my feet move at the right time. I rapidly discover that stepping at the wrong time or off the beat is frustrating to a dance partner. Some women simply go along, while others stop and try to correct it, which creates the sort of skirmish that has the potential to escalate. To alleviate any anxiety about when to take a step, men have to count the beats of the music in their heads and learn to do so without moving their lips. In the beginning, it seems as if the brain counts loudly and drowns out the music. Then gradually the music gets louder and the counting moves to the background but is still there. Eventually the brain will become trained to count the beats of the music and not even notice it.

I attend a group lesson with ten men and ten women in two separate lines facing each other. The teacher shows us a series of steps that we will be learning today. We all fumble with the pattern. After a couple of attempts, it finally looks somewhat close to the desired result. We dance it with a partner for about thirty seconds, then the women move one partner to the right, and we try it again with a different partner. I think I know it after the third partner switch. The teacher plays some music, and I forget everything. The women switch again, and I have a new partner. Some women have good posture, while others do not. I try not to look at my feet as they get tangled up with each other. Thank goodness I have only two!

At the studio, I meet a lot of other dancers during group lessons, and we are delighted to discover our common struggles and flaws. Some of the single people flirt and smile. Others are completely dedicated and serious beyond comprehension. Some dancers are already in a relationship or married and dance as a couple. They tend to learn more quickly, having a regular partner to practise the steps whether they are at the studio or at home. Some of the couples argue over whose fault it is when something goes wrong. There are a lot of mistakes made when learning to dance, and not being able to easily correct them is a common frustration for new dancers. Being new to the studio is awkward for me. I am anxious about the possibility of stepping on someone's toes during a dance. I question myself on what to wear. What do I talk about while dancing? Will I ever dance so poorly that I fall over?

Like many beginning dance partners, when I dance with someone, we resemble one of those robotic vacuum-cleaning devices that looks like a Frisbee on wheels. We head off in one direction, stop at an invisible barrier, then shift weight and head off in another direction. The music that fills the room while we dance could be playing somewhere else, and I am often completely disconnected from the beat. In the early stages, each partner hears a beat in his/her head and follows that with predictable, uncoordinated consequences. This is followed by the next stage of dance development where the man and woman finally have a few steps mastered and begin to work on their connection to each other. As they move around the floor, they take on the appearance of an accordion, or sliding doors that open and close, with each partner moving close to the other then moving apart then close again. This continues until they feel like their arms are about to fall off.

At a Saturday morning lesson, I dance a Merengue with my instructor. This official dance of the Dominican Republic is the easiest of all dances and only requires me to count to two in my head. We start off and I step with my left foot then with my right. The woman dances the natural opposite starting with the right foot. It is like a march to very fast music and looks so simple that the hips are eager to move, sinking the hip before the foot is placed. Rotation of the dance steps to the left, or counterclockwise, also helps it look less like a beginner dance. It is so easy that anyone can learn it in a few minutes as long as the steps are taken in time to the beat of the music. We do spins and waist rolls and soon I am bored with the simple steps, yet happy that I have learned a new dance.

Since I am gaining confidence dancing the basic steps in Waltz, Foxtrot, and Rumba, my instructor decides it is time to tackle Swing dancing. Unlike other dances where the couple mainly moves in the same direction, in Swing dances the couple moves away from each other in a step back. This can be very disconcerting. How does my partner know where she is going and why is she trying to get away from me? The answers are forthcoming. It starts with a good connection. We begin the journey with Single Swing and start it with a step back called a back-break. Swing is started with either a side step or a back-break, depending on how it is taught. The man's right hand is held in normal dance hold position, but the left hand is waist level, held with the palm facing up. The woman places her right hand, palm down, on top of the man's hand, and the curve of the fingers by both partners creates the small amount of tension required for the hold. We call the back-break a "rock" step because it is similar to a rocking chair: the dancer rocks back, then comes forward. I have to change the weight on each foot or I lose the beat very quickly. Gradually this progresses to a point where I learn Triple Swing, which has a more complicated side step than Single Swing. Eventually, from the basic hold, we add throw-outs, underarm turns, kicks, and a number of other fascinating steps. I start to love the Swing.

I attend more group lessons as well as my weekly private lessons and soon become competent at the basic steps of about half a dozen dances. My teacher encourages me to attend the beginners' practice party, which I have so far avoided.

Knowing that I am single, she slyly says, "Paul, women are asking me why you are not attending the beginners' practice party. You are good enough and they are looking for dance partners."

I pump up my courage and start attending the studio parties for beginners. Thankfully, the music plays for only thirty to forty-five seconds per song, which makes it easier to get through, using only the rudimentary steps in my current repertoire. They play the basic dances—Waltz, Foxtrot, Merengue, and Swing. Most of the people are very nice, and I begin to make friends. I also quickly realize that if I am to truly enjoy these practice parties, I have to get better.

At the parties, there is a mixer to select different dance partners to get the dances started. Soon I know the names of most of the other beginners and feel a gentle camaraderie in being so uneasy with an activity that should be as natural as walking. After the mixer, it is easier to ask for a dance from different partners. It is a brutal beginning, since I know only a few steps and therefore have no patterns to lead the woman through. However, as I learn more, it becomes fun. Also, it becomes a good opportunity to meet single women. This is not a blind date. I have the opportunity to dance and talk with someone and look for a special feeling or at least a decent personality before attempting to ask her out. For some reason, I find that it is the married women who are kinder, more forgiving, and more enjoyable during the beginner dances. The ratio of women to men in ballroom dance studios is said to be eight to one. I am also told that women love men who know how to dance, and evidence of that comes quickly.

Since the women outnumber the men, my dance card is always full. I dance non-stop for a full hour at most practice parties, getting a good physical workout. Men normally ask women to dance, but as people become familiar with each other, it becomes effortless. Soon, all I need to do is make eye contact with a woman and raise an eyebrow, and she knows that means we will be dance partners for the next song. My dancing improves gradually but consistently, and the next step in my learning is to attend the full-blown regular student practice parties. They play the basic dances, such as Rumba, Waltz, and Foxtrot and add the more complex ones like Tango, Swing, Salsa, and Cha-Cha. At the end of the evening, they have a Viennese Waltz, which terrifies me, so I always leave before then.

Another interesting facet of the party is that some women get tired of not dancing or waiting for men to ask them. They grab the closest man when a dance starts and become his partner. Dancing with the more experienced women is intimidating, but I hang on as best as I can, knowing that every dance makes me a better dance partner. My muscles start to feel comfortable and far less tentative with the steps, an observation that the teachers refer to as "muscle memory." I dance a Triple Swing with a woman, and in the American Spin she does two and then three complete revolutions. Thankfully, my part is to stand there and watch, then catch her hand when she is finished.

Waiting for a lesson is about the only time the men get to talk to each other. It is uncanny how much we have in common, especially our fears and mistakes in ballroom dancing. I start to talk to more people, and we share experiences. During one of the practice parties, I notice that Doug is also quite shy around women. He has an innocent playfulness that masks his shyness.

He asks a woman to dance: "Would you like to dance?"

"Yes," she replies.

Then he adds impishly, "With me?"

This subtle humour endears him to many women.

Dancing requires courage when a person does not have a regular partner. There is a lot of touching in dance, and there are a lot of introverted people. It can be unnerving to ask someone you never met before to dance, grab her with two hands and be close enough to feel her breath on your face. However, touching is a natural human need. At least that is what I remember from basic psychology courses in university. I remember the study where the baby monkey would rather snuggle up to a fur-covered wire figure and starve than take nourishment from a bottle wedged in a metal frame. It is a basic need and makes us human. Dancing is a social activity, and I am soon immersed in the culture. It is becoming more and more important to me and is very fulfilling.

I meet two men around the same age—Doug and Jim—and we become friends. Doug, of the self-deprecating wit, works for a private sector technology company where he decides how to set up e-mail computer servers in large organizations. He looks fit, dresses well, and tends to be very attentive in lessons. He has black hair, well trimmed, of course, and a square face. Doug's greatest weakness is his desire to please. He has limits but can be taken advantage of when he is not careful. Jim works for the federal government, has a natural outgoing and warm personality, and is interested in meeting women. His brown, slightly curly hair frames a kind face with eyes that twinkle. He is from Newfoundland and is very easygoing.

Two of us are divorced, and Jim is a widower, thus making us three single, available men. At the practice dance, when Doug accidentally steps on a woman's foot during a dance, he immediately apologizes, his face turning crimson. He avoids the woman for the rest of the night. When Jim steps on a woman's foot, he also apologizes and, if she is single, will offer to make amends by taking her out for lunch or for dinner. We three amigos share our thoughts on the easiest or toughest steps in the dances we are learning and sometimes trade assessments on which women at the studio make the best dance partners. We all talk about why we are here. We want to learn not only how to dance but how to dance well.

There are many reasons why people take dance lessons. The figure skaters want to have better balance, as well as to learn the steps, spins, and turns. I meet a few people who tell me that they are trying to increase the amount of exercise they do. This probably means they want to lose weight. Some people dance for the social aspects of meeting new people and getting out to organized events with their friends. Some single men of all ages simply want to meet women.

THE BENEFITS OF DANCING

There are so many good aspects to ballroom dance that it can be challenging to capture, list, and explain them all properly. Dancing is both mental and physical exercise. It is this combination that is responsible for all the claims that dancing can lead to better health. For any athlete or active person, dancing teaches the body how to improve balance and muscle control. An extended duration of continuous dancing will improve aerobic capacity, strengthen muscles, and provide mental challenge. I read one study that claimed there is a possibility of burning around three hundred calories for every thirty minutes of higher-tempo dancing.

Benefits:
- Cardiovascular fitness
- Mental alertness
- Increased strength
- Stronger muscles and muscle tone
- Decreased blood pressure
- Strengthened bones in legs and hips
- More stamina
- Increased flexibility
- Improved circulatory system
- Increase in calories burned, which supports maintaining proper weight

Here are even more reasons to get actively involved in learning to do ballroom and Latin dancing:
- Great exercise for the brain
- A way to meet new people
- Increased comfort level at social events
- More quality time with your life partner (or a new potential partner)
- Great entertainment
- Increased balance, grace, and poise
- Lower stress
- Decreased shyness and increased personal confidence

In addition to all this, there is at least one study, reported in the *New England Journal of Medicine*,[1] that suggests dancing may reduce the risk of Alzheimer's disease and other forms of dementia in the elderly. Dancing was a correlated factor, but other activities that involve the same level of physical exertion and mental stimulation should yield similar results. The study went further with dancing and suggested that dancing may be a triple benefit for the brain. Not only does the physical aspect of dancing increase blood flow to the brain, but also the social aspect of the activity leads to less stress, depression, and loneliness. Further, dancing requires memorizing steps and working

---

1   Joe Verghese, M.D., et al, "Leisure Activities and the Risk of Dementia in the Elderly," *New England Journal of Medicine* 348 (2003): 2508–16.

with a partner, both of which provide mental challenges that are crucial for brain health.

Some people harbour a misconception that they can never learn to dance. The concept of having two left feet is false. As long as you can walk, you can dance—and that is really all the coordination needed. If your physical coordination is weak, then it may take a few extra lessons to feel more comfortable. There are many activities in life that take coordination aside from walking, and people manage to do them. Anyone who has played any sport on a regular basis will have no problem learning to ballroom dance. If you know how to ride a bicycle without falling off, then your coordination is fine. If you play a musical instrument or love listening to music, then you will love to ballroom dance. The toughest challenge in teaching someone how to dance is when he/she has difficulty hearing the beats in the music, but even that can be easily overcome with a little practice.

Who would *not* want to learn? Life offers so many choices and so many adventures. You learn to ride a bicycle; you learn how to swim. Learning how to ballroom dance is one more feature of life that you need to learn, do, and enjoy to the fullest.

I am hooked on dancing because it is truly satisfying to add movement to music in a way that makes it feel natural. Dancing makes me happy. It also provides challenges and encourages me to set goals as I take lessons. I enjoy the music, atmosphere, and wonderful people. It is mentally stimulating and physically healthy. Dancing strengthens both mind and muscles. Beyond that, dancing is an adventure, and I am about to become submerged in more than learning simple beginners' basic steps.

ROLE MODELS FOR MEN

Some people still attach a stigma to ballroom dancing as not being macho enough for men to participate in. Nothing could be more untrue. Ballroom dancing is very physically challenging, and male professional dancers are as muscular as other athletes. When I was in elementary school, the boys who were teased were the ones who signed up for choir or singing lessons. Those singing boys are the ones who formed a band and became rock stars in high school, attracting an endless line of girls.

In Europe, ballroom dancing is taught in most schools; in Canada, physical education rarely includes ballroom dancing, and in Latin countries it seems as if everyone dances all the time. It may be changing, as more single men are signing up for ballroom dance lessons as a way to meet women, and more couples are looking to enjoy a new activity together. Also, I saw a recent sports show where a rather huge football player was interviewed. He noted that for players on football scholarships, ballroom dancing was one of their favourite college courses. The success of Emmitt Smith and Jerry Rice on the TV show *Dancing with the Stars* put male dancers in a new perspective. For anyone who still thinks that men cannot or should not dance, I have a short list of notable dance highlights.

John Travolta in *Saturday Night Fever* (Hustle) and *Pulp Fiction.* (Who cares what he was dancing—it was good!)

Arnold Schwarzenegger in *True Lies* (Tango)

Emmitt Smith, Jerry Rice, and all the other male athletes in *Dancing with the Stars*

Patrick Swayze in *Dirty Dancing* (Mambo) (especially interesting when he leads Baby into the room where she finds all the staff doing "dirty" Mambo dancing)

Sean Connery as James Bond dancing with Kim Basinger at a charity ball in *Never Say Never Again* (announced as a Tango but danced with a variety of unusual moves)

Antonio Banderas in *Take the Lead* (a predictable movie, but Antonio Banderas can move!)

Richard Gere in *Shall We Dance*

Tom Cruise in *Risky Business* dancing to Bob Seger's "Old Time Rock 'n' Roll"

Michael Douglas with Annette Bening in *The American President* (Waltz) ("I don't know how you do it," she says, meaning having so many people watch everything he does. "It's Arthur Murray. Six lessons," he replies, thinking she was impressed with his dancing.)

HANDS, STANCE, AND POSTURE

The dance hold or frame

The dance hold or frame refers to how the partners connect to each other. Teachers talk about points of connection, pressure, and muscles. For the smooth or standard dances, there is open and closed hold. In the open hold position, the couple is slightly apart with a space between them and that space should never change in size as they dance. Closed hold is where the couple may be touching with some parts of their bodies, mainly the right side of the man's rib cage to the woman's right side. There is little to no space between the couple, although their heads are still apart and looking over the right shoulder of the partner. Most teachers will have the woman stand slightly offset to the man's right side so that the couple does not step on each other's feet. That's probably good for beginners, who tend to bump into each other a lot. It gets more complicated for advanced partners. Standard dances have one type of hold position, and Latin dances have a slightly different one. Tango has a slight variation of the standard hold. All are fairly similar with subtle differences with arms or hands.

Dance hold: space between partners

Many women have difficulty with the dance hold. "How do I make him keep his distance without being rude?" If you have a regular dance partner and there is a relationship beyond dancing, then it might not be a problem. In any case, when a woman dances with a man there can be times when the man tries to move closer than what is truly comfortable. The woman decides how close to dance when she steps into the dance hold. From there, it is the man's responsibility to respect the distance, and the woman's job to maintain the space. Here is where the woman's left arm is important. The V-shape formed by the index finger and thumb of the woman's left hand should be firmly on the man's upper arm between the upper bicep and shoulder muscle. To permit a closer position, the woman can bend her elbow, and to create more distance, the elbow is straightened by pushing on the man's right shoulder. Once the distance is decided, the elbow needs to stay locked to maintain a consistent space while dancing.

However, the elbow should never be completely straight, and if the woman's left shoulder moves away without moving the right shoulder with it, then the frame will be awkward. This entire description is called the "dance hold." It works for the smooth dances such as Waltz, Foxtrot, and Quickstep. As a dancer improves his/her skill, more refinement can be added to the hold by a good teacher.

The woman has another extremely important role on the dance floor. The gentleman has the lead role in navigating traffic and other obstacles, all while maintaining his head in the proper dance position. However, there are occasions when the man moves backward or performs a step that does not allow him a good line of sight to the next direction. When there is a potential for a collision, the woman needs to send a warning, and that is done by firmly squeezing the man's upper right arm with her left hand. Some women overreact and simply yell, "Watch out!" which is of no use, since it may be drowned out by the music, and the expression does not really convey much information. Shouting "Watch out behind you!" takes too long, and two collisions can happen before that warning is acknowledged. When the man feels the squeeze, his proper reaction is to pause or take a much smaller step until he understands the availability of the space around the couple, and where they intend to move next. Another approach open to a woman who is aware of a possible collision is to stop moving. With a solid dance hold, the man also will stop, and the couple can move again when space is available.

Under no circumstances should either partner confront another couple aggressively after a collision. The dance floor is a polite place, and accidents happen, since ballroom dancing can be a contact sport. It is best if dancers remember to be gracious and hold their emotions in check.

The Claw

While there are so many other things to remember, there is a simple habit that men can develop with their right hand that women will appreciate. It is especially obvious in beginners but is also noticeable in a few experienced dancers. The man's right hand goes under the woman's left shoulder in a dance hold. The fingers of the right hand should be tucked nicely against one another and the thumb pressed up against the index finger. An open hand with the fingers spread wide apart is often referred to by teachers and women dancers as "the claw." An open hand resembles a claw instead of a warm, gentle embrace. At worst, the fingers may individually dig into the woman's back when the man gets tense or does an unbalanced spin turn, for example. Not only can the claw leave pressure marks, it also looks unprofessional. It is good to align the fingers and thumb against one another and make it a habit early on so as to avoid this practice from becoming something to worry about and have to try to correct when it is more ingrained.

A cousin to the claw is the "hitchhiker." Some men get their fingers tightly together but leave the thumb at a right angle to the rest of the hand. If the woman were not in the man's dance hold, it would look like he is trying to hitch a ride somewhere. A good clean look is to have all fingers and the thumb tightly together, although it is much more difficult to do consistently than one might expect.

BALLROOM DANCE STYLES AND STEPS: FOXTROT, WALTZ, AND RUMBA

There are challenges, unfamiliar terms, and a lot of surprises in the ballroom and Latin dance world. Dance students or fascinated spectators can find a lot of interesting information scattered in various locations: books, the Internet, dance studios, the minds of teachers, and the memories of many other dancers who are willing to share an experience or two. As an excited student of ballroom dance, I begin to gather information from wherever I find it and try to put pieces of the puzzle together. My knowledge as a dance student starts from knowing nothing about ballroom dancing and grows as I become curious and seek out more information pertaining to all aspects of dance.

The Box

The first step taught by most teachers in what is known as Social style for Waltz and Rumba is the basic box. It is also a step that is used with different timing in the Foxtrot. The box is simple to learn and is good practice for matching the timing of the music to the steps taken by the feet. While it is a good start, students have to learn more patterns for dances that move around the floor—such as Waltz and Foxtrot.

- The man takes one step forward with the left foot, then the right foot goes diagonally to the right side.

- The left foot closes beside the right. This is done to the basic count of 1-2-3 for the Waltz, taking one step on each beat.

- Next, the man takes a step straight back with the right foot then moves the left foot diagonally back and to the side.

- The right foot is moved beside the left, and this completes the box.

- The woman takes one step backward with the right foot then the left foot goes diagonally to the left side.

- The right foot closes beside the left. This is done to the basic count of 1-2-3 for the Waltz, taking one step on each beat.

- Next, the woman takes a forward step with the left foot then moves the right foot diagonally forward and to the side.

- The left foot is moved beside the right, and this completes the box.

Once the basic box is mastered, the man can take steps in a way that the couple moves gently to the left, making it look more like a real dance, and giving people watching the false impression that the dancers know what they are doing. Keeping the basic forward and backward steps straight, the man makes the side steps greater than a right angle, and this will be a turning box. The Waltz and Foxtrot use the same dance hold, which is the proper way to stand and place the arms when dancing with a woman. In the Waltz, the forward steps are heel leads; side steps and back steps are toe leads, which refers to which part of the foot touches the floor first when taking a step. This is a simple explanation for beginning steps. As a dance student develops more skill, a good teacher will explain the concepts of follow through and leg swing, as well as explaining that a toe landing usually refers to the ball of the foot.

Line of dance

Once a sufficient number of steps is memorized, the Foxtrot and Waltz will move around the floor, as I quickly find out when other dance couples move past me on the dance floor. The dances that move around the floor do so in a counterclockwise direction. This is known as the "line of dance" or LOD. Some patterns will not work well in the line of dance, so they should be initiated in a way that takes them along the centre of the dance floor. The couple can then rejoin the line of dance for other steps.

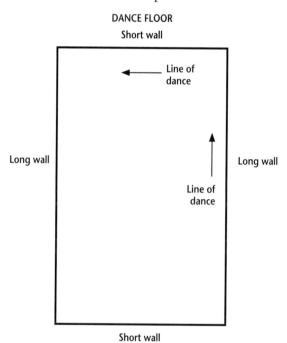

DANCE FLOOR
Short wall

Line of dance

Long wall   Long wall

Line of dance

Short wall

Ballroom and Latin dance styles

I discover that there is a variety of dances performed in the ballroom and Latin world, and there are two differing styles. The American Social style categorizes dances as smooth or rhythm. This style has a lot of fascinating features. The basic steps have been converted into simple patterns, making it easier for new dancers to get started quickly. Also, there are steps and sequences to help a dance couple move around the floor and navigate more easily in a social setting. At the more advanced level, American Social steps are very showy and have an appealing visual effect, which is why they are used in movies or television shows. In the smooth dances, this style, unlike the International style, includes dips, lifts, and separation of the partners.

American Social style
Smooth: Waltz, Tango, Foxtrot, Viennese Waltz
Rhythm: Cha-Cha, Rumba, East Coast Swing, Bolero, Mambo

Similar to the approach of a sporting organization that has gotten together and agreed on a single set of rules for the whole world, such as FIFA for the football/soccer world, the International style has its own set of rules. International style competitions in Canada are open to all and tend to have participation from a great variety of different dance studios. It gives amateur couples a chance to test their skills and also provides an opportunity for more advanced dance partners to perform and possibly represent their province or country internationally. In the standard dances for International, the partners are always dancing together without the separation that occurs in American Social style. There are also many other differences, such as the timing of the steps in some dances.

International style
Standard: Tango, Foxtrot, Quickstep, Viennese Waltz
Latin: Cha-Cha, Samba, Rumba, Jive, Paso Doble

There are also many other dances performed for fun and sometimes included in competitions, such as Merengue, Salsa, Bachata, West Coast Swing, Argentine Tango, and Hustle.

To make it easier to understand, I find out that if I am dancing boxes in Waltz, then this is American Social style. If the woman does a walk-around turn in Waltz, Foxtrot, or Rumba, then it is American Social style. American Social style music tends to be faster than International and that becomes more noticeable in a Foxtrot or Rumba, where I find it more difficult to get the full movement completed in the faster pace of a faster song. If the man leads his dance partner by taking three walking forward steps in a Foxtrot, and the timing is slow-quick-quick, then that's probably International style. This style has the couple remain together in closed hold position through the standard dances.

As a beginner, the first three dances that I learn are the Foxtrot, Waltz, and Rumba. They are normally taught in American Social style, unless the dance studio specializes in International style or the goal is to start competing immediately in International style competitions. In Waltz and Foxtrot, the Social style is geared toward getting couples around the floor easily and preparing them to navigate effectively so that they will be able to attend a dance event, have fun, and look and feel good about it. Social dancing includes giving the woman spins and dips, which I find both exhilarating and dangerous.

Beginner Foxtrot

I think that Foxtrot is one of the first dances taught because it is so easy to explain. If I hear Big Band music that makes me want to walk with a little bounce in my step, arms swinging back and forth at my sides and humming the melody, then that's probably a Foxtrot. I immediately think of a song like "Fly Me to the Moon," by Frank Sinatra, or "I've Got the World on a String," by Michael Bublé. This dance actually starts with a walking motion.

- As a man, I take one walking step straight forward with the left foot, then another walking step forward with the right foot.

- To finish the pattern, the left foot goes diagonally to the side, and the right foot moves beside the left, or "closes" the pattern.

    That is the first pattern. It is so easy, yet the simplicity is so under-stated. Can a person leave the studio knowing how to do the Foxtrot after one lesson? It might be possible, but not very likely because there is a lot more to it than just the steps. The first step needs to start with the man facing the wall on the long side of a dance floor at a forty-five-degree angle, known as "diagonal wall" position. Also from a man's perspective, he needs to know the step flawlessly and decide in advance which step is landed on the heel or the ball of the foot. The steps taken have to match the beats of the music that is playing. A man has to lead a dance partner so that she knows what the heck is being danced, and movement has to be in consideration of other dance couples, so that he and she do not collide with someone else who only knows the same step. This is why it takes a few more lessons.

- The woman takes a walking step back with the right foot, then another walking step back with the left.

- To finish the pattern, the right foot goes diagonally to the side and the left foot closes beside the right.

For both partners, the forward walking steps require that the heel of the foot touch the floor first but not by much. On the side steps, the foot lands on the ball of the foot, or as it is referred to in the dance world, a toe. The back steps require the toe to hit the floor first. It may seem obvious. However, there is always someone who wants to be different. For added technique, as the forward and backward steps are taken, the inside of the moving foot should mildly brush the inside of the standing foot.

The Foxtrot count

I always loved listening to music and used to play beginner guitar, mainly chords. I know that music is played in a series of regular beats. Dance steps follow those beats, and dancers take each step based on the designated timing for each dance. For Foxtrot, there are "slows," which take two beats, and "quicks," which take one beat. When the man steps forward on a "slow," he uses two beats to complete the step. The second forward step is also two beats. The side step and closing step are one beat each. So the rhythm of the Foxtrot in the steps above is slow, slow, quick, quick. To match the exact beats of the music, the timing is 1–2 for the first step, 3–4 for the second step, 5 for the third step, and 6 for the last step.

As a general rule of dancing, the man starts with his left foot and the woman starts with her right foot. Dancing the Foxtrot confirms my belief that no one has two left feet. Anyone can learn with a positive attitude and the willingness to put forth the effort required. In the end, it will be very rewarding.

It was the American Vaudeville actor Harry Fox who created the Foxtrot and first danced it publicly in 1914. It is typically danced to Big Band music. It was popular during the 1940s and, over time and with the emergence of Rock 'n' Roll music in the 1950s, it split into two versions, a slower dance, the Foxtrot, and a faster dance, the Quickstep. Currently, dance instructors shudder when people think they are similar. The Quickstep is a different dance and not simply a faster version of the Foxtrot. In International standard vocabulary, the Foxtrot also became known as the "Slow Fox." For musical context for Foxtrot, I think of singers like Frank Sinatra, Dean Martin, and Ella Fitzgerald at the height of their popularity.

The Foxtrot dance hold: open position

One of the first challenges of any man starting to learn how to dance is, "Where do I put my hands?" Of course, it is important to be careful. A lot of people are shy, and dancing has a lot of physical contact. In order to dance properly, the partners have to get close to one another.

- For the man, the right hand goes under the lady's left arm, with his palm on the upper part of her left shoulder blade. The area between the base of the man's right thumb and the wrist is pressed gently upward on the muscle under the shoulder.

- The left hand is held out somewhat, as if you were trying to signal a cab, and clasps the woman's hand gently. Both palms touch each other, and the fingers are together. The thumbs wrap around each other. The clasped hands should be held equally between the two dancers so that both elbows are in front of each dancer.

- The elbows are bent and the man's left hand is held outward at about the height of the man's head, although this depends also on the height of the woman.

- For the woman, her left hand is placed on the man's right arm with the area between the base of the thumb and base joint of the index finger pushed gently into the place between the bottom of the shoulder arm muscle and the bicep.

- At the start of the dance, each partner has the feet together and facing the same direction. There is no space between the left and right foot.

Beginner Waltz

Waltz is a dance taught early to new dance students because the steps are simple, and it teaches them to listen to the music, as the count is very distinctive. Waltz is one of the first dances where I learn to appreciate the gentle flow of music from a different era. When I hear music in 3/4 time that makes me want to float around the room without having my feet touch the ground, then it's probably a Waltz. It has a classy, elegant style to it. The origins of the Waltz can be traced back as a couples dance to 1750 in Europe. It became popular in Vienna in the late 1700s and moved to England in the early 1800s. Faster versions of the Waltz in Vienna became known as the Viennese Waltz.

Waltz music has a distinctive 1-2-3 beat for every bar. It is easy to learn the basic steps because the foot moves on each beat. My dance teacher loves Johnny Mathis and Nat King Cole. We waltz to "Around the World," by Nat King Cole, during one lesson. I am also captivated by a more modern-day Waltz, "Come Away with Me," by Nora Jones.

The Waltz count is in 3/4 time, and that 1-2-3 beat should be clearly heard in the dancer's head. When counting the beats while dancing, it is wise not to do so out loud. That is another sure sign of a beginner and might scare the heck out of any partner!

DANCE FLOOR — ALIGNMENTS

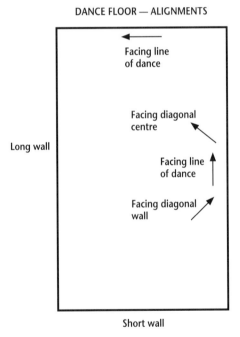

The dance hold for Latin

The dance hold for a Latin dance is slightly different than for the Waltz or Foxtrot. The arms are held in front of each partner. The man's left arm from the elbow to the wrist is perpendicular to the floor. The left arm from the shoulder to the elbow can be parallel to the floor, depending on the height of the woman. As a general rule, the clasped left hand should be at the woman's eye level. If the woman's height is close to that of the man, then the elbows should touch. The heels of the feet are together but the toes are slightly apart on two diagonals. The body leans lightly forward to exert a mild pressure on the partner.

Beginner Rumba

When I hear slow music with a Latin flavour that makes me want to move my hips regardless of what my feet do, then the chances are it is a Rumba. People who know very little about dancing often mistake the Rumba for a Waltz, because they are both slow. The Rumba has four beats to the bar and is danced with a series of slows and quicks, or two beats for one step and one beat for other steps. In American Social style, the most common timing is counted as slow-quick-quick, or 1–pause–3–4. James Blunt recorded a great Rumba, "You're Beautiful," and many artists have recorded the lovely song "Spanish Eyes." In International Rumba, the count is slightly different, with no movement on the "one" for most steps, and movement on all the other beats.

The first step people learn is the basic box.

- In American Social style Rumba, the man takes one step forward with the left foot and holds it for two beats of the music, and then the right foot goes diagonally to the right side.

- The left foot closes beside the right, with the two previous steps taken on one beat of the music each. The count is slow-quick-quick.

- To finish the box, the man takes a step straight back with the right foot then moves the left foot diagonally back and to the side.

- The right foot closes to beside the left. The most important style point is the hip movement, which requires the hip to drop slightly before each step is made and straightened at the end of the step.

- The woman takes one step back with the right foot and holds it for two beats of the music, and then the left foot goes diagonally to the left side.

- The right foot closes beside the left with the two previous steps taken on one beat of the music each. This is done to a count of slow-quick-quick.

- To finish the box, the woman takes a step straight forward with the left foot then moves the right foot diagonally forward and to the right side.

- The left foot closes to beside the right. The woman's hip motion is what gives the dance added appeal.

Rumba is danced in a defined space and does not travel around the room like the Foxtrot and Waltz. Every step is a toe or ball of the foot lead, which is probably why official Latin dance shoes have a higher heel. It encourages the front of the foot to land first. The Rumba is a Latin dance in which the hips move, thereby adding a pleasing visual effect to the dances. True Rumba music is slow and sexy. Women tend to love it because of the romantic music and they can move their hips easily, since women's hip joints are designed differently from men's. They move their hips to all the Latin dances and are still smiling. Men move their hips half as much for one or two dances and have sore muscles for the next three days.

2

DANCING AND SOCIAL SKILLS: ETIQUETTE

Some ballroom dance studios actively promote proper etiquette to complement dance skills. Since dancing can be both an intimate and intimidating experience, due to all the contact and closeness, some rules are advisable. The basic guidelines are similar to those for life in general. Dancers are expected to treat others with respect. Etiquette also extends beyond actions and provides some insight into appropriate clothing, personal appeal, and how to interact with other dancers.

CLOTHES

A dress code will depend on how formal the studio considers itself to be and can be ascertained by checking with the teacher or the studio manager. For lessons, some studios permit dancers to wear jeans, as long as they are clean. Other studios request dress pants for men and skirts or dresses for women. Dirty jeans with holes across the fronts of the knees are not appropriate. For student practice parties, it is appropriate to wear clothes that are considered a bit more formal. I usually wear dress pants and a dressy short-sleeved shirt, which tends to reduce the perspiration considerably compared to a long-sleeved shirt. For women, a skirt or dress is probably a wise choice. For charity dances or grand balls, a suit or tuxedo may be required for the man. An event described as "black tie" means that the man needs to wear a tuxedo. I rented one in a rent-to-own arrangement and bought it after the first event. I wear my tuxedo three or four times a year, which makes it a very worthwhile purchase. For women, a ball gown or fancy dress is required, full length in the winter, and perhaps a shorter cocktail dress for a summer event. At a grand ball, women's gowns and dresses are sometimes more revealing, which makes it tougher for the man to concentrate. The men have to remember to look over the woman's right shoulder.

Dangling metal belts are hazardous in spins, when they rise up and out, having a good potential to hit a dance partner. Awkwardly cut dresses may limit the ability for a proper dance hold or movement. For example, a knee-length tight dress on a woman could limit her ability to take big steps in a Foxtrot. Some women have long, flowing hair down their backs, making it more difficult for a man to place his right hand on the woman's shoulder blade. I generally try to get my hand under the hair instead of on top of it.

At some Swing dance parties, the mainstay is jeans. At other times people dress up or dress according to the Swing era styles. At a Salsa club, the dress code may look like a Caribbean shirt party. When a dancer gets used to different places, the dress code will be more obvious, and clothing can be selected to be comparable to everyone else unless the intention is to be unique.

LOOKING GOOD

Dancing requires close contact with a partner, and, like most other social activities, personal appearance and overall impression are important. An attractive appearance requires good personal grooming, meaning that hair should be kept clean. Men should shave regularly or trim anything that grows too long.

Dancing requires a lot of movement, and people perspire when they exercise. The more energetic dances like Salsa and Swing can certainly be considered exercise. Even if a person does not have a wetness problem, there can be an odour problem. In a format where the partners are so close together, it is important for a dancer to smell clean. Taking a shower and using deodorant are recommended but somehow not always achieved. It may sound patronizing, but it is unbelievable how many people thicken the air with unpleasant smells on the dance floor. On the other hand, there are people who attempt to cover it up with powerful perfumes or aftershave. Sometimes these scents can be just as unpleasant. For a single person who is trying to attract someone, a subtle amount may be more effective than several litres.

There are probably many experts in this field who give advice for people with a serious perspiration condition, but here are some tips from the dance world:

- Get a good antiperspirant deodorant.

- Carry a cloth handkerchief to dab perspiration off the face and hands when needed.

- Wear clothes that breathe. That polyester top might look great, but a cotton one might be more effective.

- For men, try wearing a short-sleeved shirt unless attending a formal party. It can make a big difference.

- Try adding an undershirt. This trick works for some men. The concept is that all the perspiration is contained in the undershirt and nothing gets to the outer layer.

- Another tip is simply to bring a second shirt and change at some point during the dance.

- Women should try wearing sleeveless tops and dresses and avoid heavy fabrics.

You may love garlic but if you eat so much that the smell oozes from your pores, then consider reducing the amount. Bad breath is a real dance killer. If people rarely want to talk, are hesitant to accept a dance request, frequently look away—staring at the ceiling or way to one side—then it may be time for a breath check. For a fresh breath, I make sure to brush my teeth and then have a breath mint, which I prefer over gum. Mouthwash is also good if you are planning to dance with a lot of different dance partners and want them willingly to return for another dance. If you love to eat beans, you may need to try Beano to avoid other unpleasant odours.

Chewing gum while dancing can be very distracting to a dance partner, especially if making noises while chewing. Apart from being unattractive, it can seem to indicate a lack of interest in the partner. When I dance with someone who pops gum while dancing, it startles me because I think the noise is one of my aching knee joints finally giving up!

REQUESTING A DANCE

The common practice is for men to ask women to dance. In some settings, women are also allowed to ask men to dance but they should not be overly aggressive in doing so. Some dance parties will have a "ladies' choice" dance, where the women ask the men.

When asking a woman to dance, a man walks over to the woman, asks her to be his partner for the dance, and holds out his left hand. If the woman places her hand in the man's, he walks her to the place on the floor where they will start the dance. The key is to be courteous. Yelling at someone, waving your hand like a traffic cop and expecting her to run across the floor to where you are standing, is not good dance etiquette. Wiggling hips suggestively at the start of a Latin song and pointing brazenly at yourself is also a less than desirable way to ask someone to dance.

Women should try to refrain from stampeding toward their chosen man in a ladies' choice dance. It is not polite to grab an arm with both hands as if staking a claim on a piece of property. These are not fictitious examples.

A nice start to requesting a dance is:

"Shall we dance?"

"Would you like to waltz?"

"May I have the pleasure of the next dance?"

It is wise to be careful when approaching more than one woman in a group in order to avoid having several of them reply at the same time. Making eye contact with the woman being requested to dance and extending the hand directly toward her are good habits. Do not grab the hand and pull it. Waiting for a reply will leave a much better impression. In the case where two men ask the same woman to dance at exactly the same moment, then the woman should politely accept one and offer a "rain check" to the other.

Some men have a knack for knowing when a woman is interested in dancing by reading her body language. She may be sitting on the edge of her chair, gently tapping her foot to the music or simply looking excited and happy to be there. Other men have no idea how to read clues, so the women have to be more proactive. Women can try making eye contact, hold it, and smile. If a man does not understand these actions, then he may not be from this planet. On the other hand, if a man is really attracted to and wants desperately to dance with a particular woman who has her arm around the man next to her and has her hand resting on his knee, it may not be the best idea in the world to ask her to dance. It is always good to read the clues and get to know people. The easiest way to know who is going to be a willing dance partner is to have already danced with him or her previously.

Dance etiquette encourages a variety of dance partners in order to develop better dance skills. Looking for a dance partner at an event can present different scenarios. There are situations where a couple prefers to stay together. Perhaps they are not ready for other dance partners yet or maybe they need to work on routines and steps they are struggling with from lessons. Other couples dance willingly with a variety of partners but reserve the first or last dance for each other. Single people are encouraged to ask a variety of dance partners, and the general rule, assuming a large crowd, is not to dance with the same person twice in a row.

It seems natural for dancers to seek out partners at their own level. However, dancing with people from all levels is more appropriate and garners respect. Dancers who continually seek out and monopolize only the best dancers on the floor are frowned upon. Good dancers should be able to make any partner look better. It has been said that good dancers seek out only the best dancers as partners in order to hide their own inadequacies. Some men believe in the expression, "What goes around comes around," and when their skills improve they tend to shun women who were hesitant to dance with them when they knew much less. We are all beginners at some point in time. We can all be proud of our dance ability, and the experienced dancers should be willing to donate a fraction of their time to those who can benefit.

When asked to dance, the anticipated response is "yes." There are reasons in extreme cases where someone refuses politely, and in these cases the person who refuses should sit out the dance and not accept another offer. That would be rude and a personal insult. There are valid reasons for declining a dance—such as when you need a rest or have promised the dance to someone else who is about to come out of the washroom. In this case, you can offer the choice of a dance later that evening. The other valid reason for turning down an offer is to avoid being monopolized by someone or, in some cases, to discourage inappropriate advances and avoid sending the wrong signals. For example, single women should avoid dancing with the same male partner for two or more dances in a row unless they want to send a message that they are no longer available to dance with other men. In one situation, I turned down a woman who requested a dance because I had just danced several demanding dances in a row and needed a rest. I politely offered a rain check.

If your request for a dance is declined, it is important to be polite and withdraw. Ask someone else and don't be discouraged. If your requests are frequently declined, it may be time to check your grooming, or ask a close friend for honest feedback on how you are perceived.

When getting onto the floor after the music has already started, the couple should check for oncoming traffic before beginning. If the dance is not a line of dance style, a good open space should be selected. When the music ends, the couple should thank each other and walk off the dance floor together at a reasonable pace. It is not good to tie up a partner, as it limits the opportunity to find a new partner for the next dance.

It is good practice to thank a dance partner, and the partner should be gracious in response. If the dance truly went well, a partner may give praise for any aspect that went particularly well. I was often thanked for having a nice lead and navigating well through a crowded floor. It takes a special person to understand what the other partner has to do to make the dance successful.

It is polite to end a dance by saying to your partner, "I would like to dance with you again," and listen to the response.

"We'll see," or "Maybe" is inconclusive at best.

"I would like that" is a sign of interest.

ON THE FLOOR

Sharing the dance floor is another important etiquette concern. Any patterns that move against the line of dance should be performed in a space that is free from other dancers. A reverse corte, for example, can be a nice touch in a corner but can be more than annoying in the middle of a long wall. Stopping or reversing direction in a dance provides a navigational challenge that may be frustrating to others. There are many reasons why people stop in the middle of a dance. Sometimes they forget a step. Or perhaps they feel off balance or lose the beat of the music. When a couple is following the line of dance, it is comparable to travelling along one side of a divided highway. Who would stop the car in the middle of a lane to discuss his or her observations with a passenger? Of course, there is space for people to go around you, although it is preferable for both safety and consideration of others to find an alternative. There are times when stopping is unavoidable. However, at those times the couple should quickly move off the dance floor or to the side, unless they can start dancing again quickly. When other dancers are all whizzing by along the line of dance, it is a good idea for a couple to save the more complicated steps until they can be attempted in the middle of the floor. When dancers are off the beat, a good suggestion is to try to do a hesitation step then continue to move again. In some cases, people stop because they are doing a choreographed routine and cannot start from where they stalled. If that is the case, the couple needs to immediately move to the very edge of the floor and walk with the line of dance to the next convenient corner.

More advanced dancers need to be considerate of the differences in ability of other dancers. They should not take over a floor as if it were a show and everyone should be watching them. At one dance I attended, a fast-moving couple gathered up a head of steam at the beginning of a long wall during a Viennese Waltz and moved quickly along the floor, nearly bowling over any other dancers in their path. Most dance couples scattered to avoid them. Unfortunately my partner and I were not so lucky. We were turning to head along the short wall when the collision occurred, and it was a bruising experience. I was unsure if they paused to apologize or merely to catch their breath before starting again.

Another tip on sharing floor space on a crowded floor is to take smaller steps. This can be frustrating but is necessary so that all couples can have fun and avoid getting stepped on.

ARM EXTENSIONS

Women love doing graceful, full-arm extensions that add a more advanced look and feel for the dance. These add a lovely touch when performing a turn or spin. However, on a crowded dance floor, extended arms become a weapon. I have witnessed a few people being smacked in the face or neck with a lovely hand from a woman's graceful arm extension. Unfortunately, in many cases, the hand had a sizeable metal ring on it, which led to gruesome results. Arm movement is beautiful in practice and good when a dancer is fully aware of the space available and of nearby dancers. Otherwise, a dancer needs to learn alternate options to move the arms and still look good.

AERIALS

Flips and throws are breathtaking when danced well and outright dangerous if they are executed when other people are on the dance floor. There is no reason to do these moves during a general dance with other dancers nearby. I saw throws in a Jive number at a practice dance and came within a few inches of getting a spiked heel in my ear. The unexpectedness and inability to predict them creates a huge problem for other dancers. A good rule of thumb is for dancers to keep aerials in a show or practise them alone, if they must be performed.

ATTITUDE

Who is to blame when a step goes wrong? The usual answer is no one, and, at the same time, both partners. Accidents happen and it takes two to ballroom dance. Regardless of what happens on the dance floor, good dancers merely smile and move on. If the couple is required to stop, then a good leader will make sure the woman knows what foot he is on before taking the next step. This requires a full weight shift to another foot before moving. Highlighting a mistake with a comment such as, "What the heck was that?" is not appropriate and can fluster and embarrass a partner. I have seen a couple walk off the dance floor and heard them talk quietly about mistakes they had made during a dance; yet while I watched them, they looked flawless. Couples that move well cover up any missteps in the flow of the dance, and mistakes go unnoticed.

It should not matter if a person does not have a regular dance partner; there is nothing to be ashamed of as a beginner dancer. Everyone starts that way, and practice is the only way to improve. If someone is a beginner and does not have a regular dance partner, then every dance will make him or her better. The same holds true for a couple. Dance improvement requires practice, so a single person should never hesitate to dance with someone new. Dance students will typically be scattered at various levels of proficiency and have different levels of ability in different dances. Every dance improves the skills, trains the muscles, and provides an experience to build on.

A dancer should be sensitive to the partner's limitations and preferences. One woman I danced with had a sore back and was grateful for the steps I used and was especially grateful that I did not attempt any dips. Not all women enjoy doing neck rolls in Salsa. I danced with a very large woman who could not perform the American spin in Triple Swing. Her ankles could not handle the torque in the change of direction. She was quite happy with regular underarm turns, waist rolls, and kicks. If a partner has physical limitations, it is appropriate for the man to accept them and lead steps that make it an enjoyable dance. If your partner requests restrictions due to comfort or other reasons, then make her glad that she danced with you. Similarly, if a man has difficulty leading certain patterns due to physical limitations, the dance partner should graciously enjoy the dance as if the limitations were of no consequence.

The best dancers stand out on the dance floor due to attitude and personality. These are the smiling, energetic people who make every dance fun. Considering all the potential stress in life, dancing is like a vacation to many people. Listening to great music and performing good movements, it is possible to get lost in the moment. Also, a smile or a polite comment will be appreciated. It increases the desire for people to share another dance together. Positive comments can increase a dancer's confidence and reflect well on the person who delivers them. People should be allowed to enjoy their time dancing and look forward to coming back. It is wise to avoid gossip and negative criticism of dances, dance styles, teachers, dance schools, or students of other studios. Everyone has his/her own path in life, and positive energy has the ability to multiply. Negative energy goes around and comes back at the initiator like a boomerang.

HELPING EACH OTHER

An all-too-common violation of etiquette at a dance event is stopping in the middle of a dance to correct a partner. This takes the fun out of the dance, like popping a balloon, and makes both partners look odd. If a step is missed or a mistake is made it is best to ignore it. In some cases, the couple may decide to try it again later during the dance, or it might be wise to avoid that pattern until a dance teacher can be consulted to correct it. When dancers are trying to perform a sequence they learned at a recent lesson, it will not always work, and they should practise more at another lesson or at home before using it on the floor in the middle of a dance.

Sometimes a dancer asks someone to show her a dance step or pattern so she can learn it. Caution should be taken so this does not disrupt other dancers. A number of factors need to be considered. Is there a space on the floor that will not disturb others? Can the instruction be given without having to speak over the volume of the music? Is it appropriate to take on this task, having enough knowledge to explain the step properly? I have been asked to explain Bachata, for example, and gone blank because my feet seem to move on autopilot once Bachata music starts. I can dance the Bachata, but I might not be able to explain it. Also, in the case of a man giving direction, this involves explaining the woman's step, which is naturally different from the man's part. It may be the mirror opposite or could be completely different, as in a turn.

A more polite approach would be for the dancer to indicate what he or she is interested in and ask if the person would be willing to show him or her at a convenient time. This could be prior to a lesson or before a student dance practice. This way, the request is not imposing a hardship. If you are looking for help on a step, or on a particular dance, a good time to ask is when the person is not busy dancing. If someone is sitting out a dance or during any other break in the music, he might be approachable. Most people are very willing to help.

3

STEPPING OUT

SHOW DANCE NIGHTS

The dance studio is holding a dance routine night at the studio. This is when the students dance with their teacher or, for those who have partners, as a couple, in front of an audience. In addition, there is a stern-looking judge who will stand or sit at the side of the dance floor with a clipboard for taking notes. The judge evaluates the performance, gives a generous score to encourage the dancers, and offers tips in writing on the score sheet regarding what the student needs to work on in order to improve.

My first "spot dance," as they are called, is a Waltz that I do with my instructor, Melanie. I am wearing the prerequisite neatly pressed black dress pants, white shirt, and black necktie. My teacher is wearing a black dress that is flared slightly below the knees. The performing students and their partners line up in a designated area, with the woman on the man's right arm, waiting for their names to be called. I notice that one woman locks her left arm securely through her partner's right elbow so that she can discreetly drag him onto the floor if he decides to rethink why on earth he is doing this in front of the entire dance studio, teachers, students, relatives, and friends!

My name is called, and we walk onto the floor proudly, as if we have performed this dance so many times in the past that it is a great honour for all the people in the audience to come and watch us. We walk to the middle of the floor. Melanie takes a position a few feet away and facing me, looking as if we are dancing the finals at Blackpool. Her black hair is pulled back neatly without a single strand out of place, and her impeccable makeup is appropriately overdone for a performance. I try to stop my legs from shaking and strain to remember what I am supposed to do next. I am sure that some of my hairs are standing straight up. Her face takes on an expression that implies this dance is the highlight of her life, and I am thinking, "What am I doing here?"

The music starts, we walk into a dance hold, and the waltzing begins. We do our choreographed routine well, with one exception where my uncontrollable foot bumps her foot and almost bowls her over. Otherwise we finish unscathed, and I relish the fact that it is over. Chatting with other dancers, I scoff at being nervous and, pretending it was easy, I start to relax, then cheer on the other terri-fied dancers when their names are called and they start their routine. A few days later, during my regularly scheduled lesson, I receive the results. My mark from the judge is a charitable 93 percent for a raw novice Waltz and enough to fuel a desire to learn more. Not bad for a beginner.

I start to enjoy group lessons enormously, as they follow a straightforward formula and allow me to meet and get to know a lot more people. I am now proficient at the basic steps of many dances, mainly because I practise them in my kitchen almost every day while I cook dinner. I also practise at work when a small lunchroom at the end of a hallway is empty. I waltz or samba around the empty tables and chairs. As soon as I hear someone, I freeze and pretend to be looking out a window, contemplating the latest business crisis, sternly rubbing my forehead with an index finger and thumb in a pincer movement. In reality, my brain is challenged far more with dance sequences than with work.

After a group dance lesson on a warm summer evening, I begin my drive home, and shortly after entering the curved highway entrance ramp, I have to stop. There are two or three police cars and lights flashing in front of me. It is impossible to back up on the narrow one-way road, so I sit patiently and wait. A few minutes go by, a car moves forward then I move a short distance. It is a R.I.D.E. (Reduce Impaired Driving Everywhere) Program roadblock to check for people who have been consuming alcohol. My turn arrives and I roll down the window. An enormous male police officer shoves his large, square head inside my car and places it in front of my face to get a good whiff of my breath.

"Have you been drinking tonight, sir?" he asks from this nose-to-nose position.

"No," I reply, "I have not been drinking. In fact, I am returning from a class."

He withdraws his head and smiles knowing my response to be truthful. He must be well over six feet tall, has the physique of a football lineman and looks ahead to see police officers involved in discussion with drivers ahead of us. None of the other cars are moving.

He looks down, now making casual conversation, and asks, "Do you mind if I ask what class it was?"

"Well, actually, it was a ballroom dance lesson."

The formal expression on his face disappears and now he squats down beside my car, his head at my level but outside the window. In almost a whisper he says, "And how did you like that? I am really interested."

"It's great," I reply encouragingly to The Hulk. "It's really great."

The cars in front of me are suddenly gone. Realizing the discussion was over, the police officer reluctantly stands up. I drive away pleased with my decision to get started in dance while others only wish they had.

On Thursday, I go to a small student practice party and I dance terribly. My brain actually goes blank on a Mambo, forgetting which direction to move my feet. This must be surprising to my randomly chosen dance partner for the Mambo, because she is fairly new, but still knows how to do the basic steps. We have a tiny dispute over which beat is the two-count that we have to step on. I maintain my opinion in the ensuing discussion only to realize later that she is right. For most of the night, I encounter some sort of brain fatigue in trying to navigate around the room and try not to think about what happens on the two-count in the Mambo.

In spite of progress, there are so many dances and so many steps to remember, there will always be some bad days. These are learning experiences and validation of the fact that everyone is human. The important point is not how badly a dance, a dance lesson, or a dance practice goes, but how a person responds. Will it be an experience that prompts greater determination to improve?

BALLROOM DANCE STYLES AND STEPS: MAMBO, TANGO, AND SALSA

Mambo

The current ballroom style Mambo is similar to the Salsa in some ways and very different in other ways. Socially, most people dance a Salsa to Mambo music. The big difference musically in Mambo is that the man's forward step is taken on the second beat in the bar of music. The first beat of a Mambo is usually very distinctive or heavy. Some teachers get people to take a side step, or a starter step, on the one-count so that they will be ready to follow it up with a forward step on the two-count. Stepping on the two-count is the most difficult aspect of the Mambo, and maintaining it through the song is a challenge. To fully appreciate the difficulty, it is necessary to watch the movie *Dirty Dancing* and listen to Patrick Swayze as he tries to teach it to Baby. The Mambo is danced heavier on the floor compared to the lightness of a Salsa. The Mambo pause step is visually more distinctive because it is held on the heavy one-beat and allows more time for development or movement of the hips.

Conversations

It becomes obvious that I have a lot more to learn about navigating around the dance floor. At a student dance party, I inadvertently brush one woman's back against a mid-floor post with a fancy cross-body lead during a Cha-Cha. Another time, I am thrilled that I remember the parallel walk pattern in Waltz. My pleasure is short-lived, because the wall is a lot closer than I expect, requiring a quick turn to the left. I dance a Hustle with a young blonde schoolteacher. She has already taken the next level of Hustle and knows the syncopated step, which I have not learned yet. What we end up dancing is not really something that could be called a dance. It might look like we are dancing but not with each other. For the next dance at this practice party, I do a Waltz with a woman and she starts talking about her ex-husband and failed marriage. She uses that f-word that rhymes with duck several times as well as other colourful language. My face grimaces and, being polite, I pretend to listen but am not happy with the foul language, especially during a Waltz. It might have been acceptable while doing a dramatic Tango, but not a lovely Waltz. My next dance partner is also divorced. She looks at me blinking her eyes and says that she thinks all the men are "hot," only to retract it less than a minute later by saying that most men are assholes and that she is fed up with them. I discreetly glance at the clock, waiting for the music to end, and think about how to improve my technique in the Tango.

Tango

Tango is a smooth dance originating in South America. When danced well, the Tango is sultry and suggestive. It has smooth, flowing movements punctuated by sharp changes in direction. Tango is probably most recognized for quick head turns where the head is facing one direction and moves in an instant to face a new direction. Although dramatic and fun, the Tango is rarely heard at weddings or general public dances. The dance hold for Tango is similar to the regular hold for smooth dances but instead of the man's wrist being under the woman's shoulder, the forearm goes under the shoulder with the hand placed near the middle of the woman's back and the fingers pointing down toward the floor.

Basic step (American Social style):

- Starting with the left foot, the man takes two walking steps forward on two beats each, slow-slow.

- The next step is another step forward followed by a side step to the right. Both of these are to a single beat of music, quick, quick.

- The final step in this pattern is to bring the left foot beside the right and that is done slowly over two beats or one slow beat. The weight stays on the right foot during the closing of feet so that the left is ready to start the next step. The basic step can curve to the left, and that makes it ideal to get around the entire dance floor knowing only one step, although the woman may get bored.

- The woman takes three steps backwards starting with the right foot, then a step to the side, and finally closes the feet together with no weight change. This keeps the right foot ready to go into the next pattern. The count is slow, slow, quick, quick, slow.

A number of teachers use a distinctive way to remember the step by spelling it to the beat of the music. In a group lesson, we all move around dancing the basic Tango step and saying "T-A-N-G-O," like children in kindergarten. The facial expression of the dance partners in Tango is supposed to be one of subtle sexual confidence. Heel leads are compulsory on forward steps, and toe leads are used when going sideways. It is danced with the knees flexed at all times without any exaggerated rise or fall. For beginners, the knees are flexed through all the dance steps as if there were a low ceiling and rising at any point would mean an imaginary hit to the top of the head.

Partners

I take a Salsa group lesson a short time before the next practice dance, so I am determined to try the new moves. One of my first dances is a Swing with a woman who is more advanced than I am. I stick to several basic moves and turns, but do them extremely well. When we are finished, she comments that she enjoyed dancing with me. This is especially rewarding since this is the same woman who told me three months ago I was doing the Tango completely wrong and she started avoiding me as a dance partner. Some of the more advanced women ignore the newcomers until there is no other choice of partners and we are the only remaining option. By the time a Salsa is played at this party, the new steps are so deeply buried in my memory that I dance them only half right. I will get better. Slowly but surely, all the new dancers get better.

Dancing does not always feel good. During a Foxtrot, I step on the toes of a young woman who tells me that I am wearing a nice tie. Also, and this was not my fault, when moving backwards I accidentally bump into the dance studio manager. That is an accident but in my confused state I forget to apologize. One of the rules of dance etiquette is that any time a dancer bumps into another dancer, they are to apologize politely to each other.

There is a woman at the studio whose name I hear but am unable to remember the pronunciation. She is from China, has a limited vocabulary, and an undecipherable accent. Her ambition and determination are strong, evidenced by the fact that she participates in all the advanced group dance lessons and does not actually know many ballroom steps. She is not one of the women at the studio that I consider intimidating, so I am at ease talking to her; I doubt whether she understands any English. When we dance, I enjoy the conversation with her because as long as I smile after anything I say, she just smiles back. I say to her softly, "My boss looks exactly like an octopus," and smile. She smiles back at me. I say, "I just poured a cup of hot coffee down my pants," and she continues to smile. She nods slowly as if digesting this and keeps dancing. As this one-sided conversation ends, I recognize the need to dramatically improve my communication skills.

Sadly, my first dance instructor leaves the studio and moves to Alberta. My new dance teacher is Tania, a young woman originally from El Salvador in Central America, and she has a tattoo peeking out between her breasts. She is a perky brunette standing a touch under five feet tall and frequently wears slightly low-cut tops that often makes it difficult to avoid staring at her cleavage. The tattoo is a symbol that is complex and unfamiliar. How can I look at my feet when something so distracting is blocking the view? This becomes a challenge when dancing with her. A true gentleman knows that it is preferable to look your dance partner in the eyes for a Latin dance and over the woman's right shoulder for the smooth dances. Taking lessons with Tania becomes an adventure.

She gives a Salsa lesson to a young student who is uncertain of the dance steps and is determined to look at his feet. From an upright position, his head begins a slow descent until the top of his forehead touches her chin and his nose is pointing at the tattoo. She removes her right hand deftly from his grasp, casually takes her index finger and puts it under his chin lifting it back up, smiling and continuing to dance the whole time. This is effective for a few seconds before the chin slowly sinks down again as the steps become more difficult to remember. Her finger again lifts his chin up. By now he sees the finger coming. He keeps his head up and forgets the steps, lapsing into a mess of stepping on his own toes and twisting his ankles against each other. It is supposed to be an energetic Salsa, but he loses both his concentration and his balance.

Salsa is a lively Cuban dance in which the biggest challenge for beginners is to move the feet fast enough to stay on the beat. It is easy to learn the basic steps and is popular among people who are younger than I am. There are many variations of the basic step but the one I learned is as follows.

- The man takes a small step forward with his left foot, shifting all the weight to that foot.

- Then the weight shifts back to the right foot on the second beat.

- The left foot is brought back to the original position beside the right and is held there for two beats.

- Next, the man takes a step back with his right foot, shifting the weight to that foot for one beat then shifting his weight back to the left on the second beat.

- Finally, the man moves his right foot beside the left and holds it for two beats. It starts over again for another basic step. The count is quick, quick, slow, quick, quick, slow. It can also be counted as 1-2-3-pause. Some salseros count it as 1-2-3, 5-6-7 with pauses and no movement on the 4 and 8 counts. The feet are to be turned out as in most Latin dances, meaning the heels are close to touching when the feet come together, and the toes are apart.

- The woman's steps are the opposite of the man's. The woman takes a step back with her right foot, shifting all the weight to that foot for one beat.

- Then the weight shifts back to the left foot on the second beat.

- The right is brought beside the left and is held there for two beats.

- Next, the woman takes a step forward with her left foot, shifting the weight to that foot for one beat then shifting her weight back to the right foot on the second beat.

- Finally, the woman moves her left foot beside the right and holds it for two beats.

From this basic step, the dance gets far more complicated. There are crossover breaks, cross-body leads, underarm turns for the woman and man, swivels, dips, and more. The music is catchy and rhythmical. I listen for the distinctive bonk of a drumstick hitting a cowbell that is endemic to Salsa music. That bonk is the first beat in a bar, and I step on the first beat or cowbell bonk to start the Salsa.

Salsa is danced in ballroom studios with a regular Latin hold. However, in Latin clubs and outside a normal studio, the hold is often different. Both arms for both partners are extended at waist level, parallel to the floor. The man's palms are either facing the woman in a palm-to-palm hold or facing upward with fingers curved around the woman's hands. The woman's hands are placed in the man's with the palms being either down or facing the man.

CLASS NOTES AND COMPETITIONS

At the next Spot Dance event a few months later, my routine is a Triple Swing. It is a challenge and takes a longer time to learn than my previous Waltz routine. I dance all the steps correctly when I practise at home by myself, but when I try it at the studio with my instructor, Tania, I make numerous missteps, and it looks nothing like a Swing. "Of course it's tougher in the studio," she says; "you have to do it with a partner." Without thinking much, I find that funny and start to laugh. So far I have only twenty seconds memorized for the one-and-a-half-minute routine. Coming out of my introverted shell for the performance of a Swing, I dress in tight black jeans and a white T-shirt. One of the figure skating student dancers rolls the sleeves under my shoulders and on one arm draws a red heart with her lipstick. Apparently this is known as "getting in character." I am gaining confidence, and when it is time to perform my Swing routine, I do a decent job.

One man slightly older than I am is always polite to me, saying hello and smiling. He comments on my dance improvement and we talk. He is not good with names, and I realize that he does not know who I am and only remembers my face. We talk about being nervous doing show dances, and he tells me something that I will never forget: "You know," he says, "I never did particularly well in any spot dance or show routine, but the improvement I achieved during the preparation was priceless."

The most notable performance that night is by an attractive young blonde in a tight, black miniskirt. Her dance is a slow, suggestive Rumba. She and her teacher begin with Latin hip motion; their feet remain glued to the floor during this prologue to the routine. As the music and hip motion continues, they begin to move their feet and the hem of her miniskirt starts to rise up her shapely legs. Picking an unobtrusive place in the routine, she removes one hand from the dance hold, lowers it casually to the bottom of the skirt and with a tug, pulls it back down. They continue to dance, more Latin hip motion follows, and as each step is taken, the skirt moves up again. At the next opportune moment, she removes both hands from the dance hold and pulls the skirt down, this time with vigour. There is a group of single men in the audience who are suddenly extremely attentive. Spectators are normally encouraged to applaud in a dance show when a dance couple successfully completes a well-performed step. In this case, wild applause breaks out with each successive riveting movement. It is a captivating dance, and seems especially mesmerizing for the men. There are no rules of etiquette to cover this. I make a mental note to try a full costume rehearsal before dancing anything in public.

The single men at the studio discover some unorthodox moves in dance. During a behind-the-back pattern or waist roll in the Latin dances, men find out that they can "accidentally" rub a hand across the woman's backside. This is danced in a playful manner or pretending and feigning surprise that it happened and then being apologetic. Some also use this as a tactic to see if it elicits any reaction, often resulting in either a smiling flirt or a potential slap to the jaw. Only the bolder men try this. The other single-guy move is in the Merengue. The couple reverses position during a turn so that they hold their hands out to the side but their bodies are facing away from each other, as opposed to facing each other. If the knees are bent sufficiently, the man can lean slightly forward as the one-two count is playing and gently rub backside to backside with the woman. Once again, it is a playful move that can be attempted as a joke. When danced with certain women, it may force the man to duck quickly in order to avoid a fistful of repercussions when the couple is face to face again.

These shenanigans are not the sole domain of the men. Women have some playful moves, too. They wiggle their hips furiously in the Latin dances and seductively rub their hands up their thighs, which is very effective when wearing a shorter skirt. Some will pull their dance partner into a tight, closed position dance hold and rub everything they can up against the man's body, resulting in full-contact dancing. In some cases, it can be nice full-contact dancing; in many other cases, it may be intensely uncomfortable, so the dancer should politely extend the frame with solid arms in order to maintain a reasonable distance.

One of the awkward moments for me is in Triple Swing. The man's left hand is held in a waist-level position in the basic hold. As I perform a swing out or get back into basic hold from a woman's underarm turn, my left hand goes too low and our two hands sometimes accidentally rub against my groin area. It becomes a bad habit and tough to break because I concentrate heavily on performing the proper steps without allowing any other distractions. This is a very bad dance habit. Most women are either unaware or politely pretend that it did not happen. I improve the ability to hide my embarrassment whenever it happens and practise better arm control in my kitchen by keeping my hand at waist level for all the Swing steps.

Men also discover how to dance with a partner for a full three- or four-minute song while they are still unable to lead more than a few basic steps. It is frustrating dancing when the only steps learned so far are basic boxes. The solution is to make small talk while dancing. This has the effect of distracting the woman from the man's limitations. It also allows her to talk, and sometimes that consumes most of the dance. While the talking is happening, there is a good excuse not to initiate other steps such as turns or spins, which might seem like a rude interruption in a normal conversation, since the woman has to face away from the man in a turn.

First, I dance a few basic steps, and then make small talk, typically starting with, "Hey, there are a lot of people here tonight." I gauge the reaction, perhaps getting a faint smile, before moving on to ask her a question where I will be fascinated by the response. This eats up time and shows interest. In my early days of learning to dance, I had many dance partners and I had very limited ability. When dancing with a partner who is at the same level of ability, it normally works well because both partners are trying to perfect every step. There is a lot to think about—holding the head up, stepping to the beat of the music, keeping the dance hold, keeping the arms solid, and so on. When I am partnered with a better female dancer, I find dancing to be an even greater challenge because as a leader, the man thinks he has to do more to keep his partner interested in the dance. This can be a disaster if the man tries dance steps that are not completely comfortable, and this makes it worse for the woman when she knows the man is leading a step incorrectly.

One Saturday afternoon while waiting for a group lesson to start, Chris nudges me and gestures unobtrusively to the thin, shapely dance instructor in the middle of the floor teaching a student a new step. "Nice thong," he states dryly.

"Eh?" I reply verbosely, thinking he is referring to the music and was referring to the "song." I strain my ears to listen.

"It's pink," he replies, and now I am totally confused.

As sunshine screams in through the full-length windows along the long wall, the backlight clearly illuminates the brilliant pink thong underwear visible through the thin brown cloth skirt being worn by the dance instructor. She starts to wiggle her hips to Latin music. Chris is drooling. His mouth hangs open, and he is oblivious to his surroundings. This is my first thong sighting experience. Perplexed and slightly embarrassed, I look away—but only at first.

Pro-Am

My teacher convinces me that I should attend a Pro-Am event that will assess the progress of my dance skills. It is only for students of the dance studio as well as any nearby affiliated studios. I enter ten dances and I will be rated at a level of proficiency in each dance. The fee is $10 per dance, and at the end we will all get a nice plaque. The event is held at the Westin Hotel in downtown Ottawa, across from the Chateau Laurier. On Saturday morning I arrive and find a woman from the studio lost in the parking garage where all levels and all sections look alike. After some creative searching, we eventually find her minivan, and she retrieves her second load of clothes and shoes required for the event. Being a gentleman, I offer to carry the packages, and she leads me along to the competition hall. There are many packages, and I can barely see around them. In the dance hall, all the single men are sitting together nervously and waiting with a number pinned on the back of their vests. Doug and Jim have both arrived, and we exchange subdued welcomes, unsure how the day will unfold. We wear the appropriate dance clothes: black trousers, white shirt, black tie and black vest. We all look like fancy bartenders.

I line up a few minutes before my first event with my teacher on my right side. We walk onto the floor and do three consecutive standard dances for thirty seconds each. The judge looks thoughtful. I am not sure if this is a rating of my ability to dance, the success of my teacher at teaching me, or my stamina.

After two more sessions, completing the required ten dances, I head back to the table where all my fine-looking friends are in a state of hunger and thinking that the dance hall would be far more appealing if it had a bar and pizzeria. The next event is a best-in-class category for amateurs dancing with their teacher, and our friend Will is giving it a try. He has no hope of winning, even though he is better than all of us put together. Although he has great posture, he is competing against people who have far more experience than he does. Will gained the unkind nickname "Dancing Queen" by people where he works when they discovered his pastime, but his wife, Ruth, adores him, and all the men at the dance studio admire and respect him for all his hard work.

The hard work shows, and he looks more macho than any of us. We rally support and, in the tradition of dance competitions, start to call out his number as he is dancing. This will either motivate him or make him more nervous, who knows? There are four fully grown, divorced men in their forties yelling out a two-digit number that is pinned to the back of a dancer. After a first uncoordinated yell in which none of us is calling the same two digits, we stop and make sure we all remember his number. Then we try to synchronize our efforts with a whispered 1-2-3 to get started, and yell loudly together at the same time. It works about the same as trying to stay on the beat while dancing. As expected, our friend Will does not place first, but we are all certain that he had a good time.

At the end of the day, the organizers have arranged for professional dance partners to perform, and it is an incredible show. The outfits are no larger than a paper napkin, but very strategically placed for both of them. The man's chiselled muscle definition is jaw dropping, and after a long, tiring day, the women spectators are suddenly wide-eyed. Some of the more avid women spectators appear to have tiny droplets of saliva forming at the corners of their mouths. These dancers make a Tango look like an extreme sport. It has lifts, spins, and dramatic holds unlike what I normally do in a Tango. They perform a Samba that is riveting, fluid, and dynamic. The woman does the splits, both legs extended in the opposite direction in a straight line, and the man lifts her up from that position with a single finger and not a tremble in his posture. The dance continues, and now the man has shiny perspiration over his bare, hairless chest. Women in the audience are looking flushed and staring shamelessly as I quickly look about for a pitcher of water in case any of them faint. The female partner is no less mesmerizing. She moves her hips in ways that don't seem possible. Men's imaginations run wild. The dances are sultry, smouldering, and precise. It is a demonstration of what hard work, great technique, and sculpted bodies can look like.

I get my plaque at the end of the daylong event. There are tiny rectangular plates on a piece of wood for every dance that I entered, and a small metal button with a colour indicating how well I had performed: bronze, silver, or gold. I drive home satisfied and prop up my plaque on the kitchen counter. The following morning, I see that the glue has weakened and all the little rectangular plates have fallen off. Success must be fleeting, I think to myself. As much as I accomplish, there are always more challenges ahead.

It is nice to realize that compared to the average population I am now actually a decent social dancer. On a couple of occasions, women I dance with tell me, "Women think that men who can dance are hot." When I get home I have to stick my head in the freezer to keep the swelling down. Later I convince myself they must be thinking about that chiselled male professional dancer.

Two of my dance friends are convinced by our teacher to enter a larger dance Pro-Am competition in Montreal. While certainly an adventure, it seems way too strenuous for me to consider at this time.

A number of people from the dance studio are registered. For this type of competition, the costs are significant. As well as their own entry fees and room at the hotel, they have to cover their teacher's expenses. Women have the added expense and task of finding the perfect dance dress. I decide early on not to go and I have a good excuse with a previous commitment that weekend.

One Friday evening after a group lesson, I decide to go to an open dance night held at a different studio and ask Chris if he needs a drive. Since I am taking him, I also ask a nice Asian woman if she is interested. She is thrilled and starts thanking me in advance. For a while it is irritating, because she walks around the studio saying goodbye and thanking everyone while we are standing there with our coats on waiting to go. When she thanks me a second time, I accept it as a sign of hero worship. I am her dancing idol. She is a recent newcomer to Canada, and we are in the middle of another frigid Ottawa winter. She must not be used to the cold weather yet, because it takes her ten minutes to get dressed. This tiny woman puts on her big coat, wraps a huge fluffy scarf seven times around her head and adds an oversized Cossack hat. We can no longer see her face. Two peephole eyes are buried in there somewhere, so I cautiously take her arm and lead her to the car. It reminds me of the movie *Cool Runnings*, when the Jamaican bobsledder arrives at the airport in Calgary and walks outside for the first time in Canadian winter weather. He quickly runs back in and puts on every piece of clothing in his suitcase. She could have rolled down a flight of stairs and not been bruised!

In the car, we discover two interesting characteristics about her. Although it is difficult to comprehend a whole sentence, from what scraps of words we manage to understand, it becomes clear that she loves to dance and has performed cultural dancing in her home country. And second, through the layers of clothes wrapped around her, the words keep coming out—she loves to talk! We arrive at the dance party, pay the entry fee, and find a place to hang our winter coats. There are probably forty or fifty dancers here, and the dance floor is large and wooden. The music is loud with a strong beat, very helpful to a beginner such as myself, and the DJ announces the type of dance before each song so no one gets confused, with each partner doing a different dance at the same time. What a great party!

With infectious music and an atmosphere of fun, my ballroom dancing feels much better. The DJ includes a few ballroom line dances through the night. This is a sequence of repeated steps that both men and women perform at the same time, facing the same direction. They help people learn to move well to the beat of a specific ballroom or Latin dance, as well as being great practice for learning specific steps. They seem very difficult at the start, although many people are doing them flawlessly. I give one a try and halfway through the song, I manage to get all the steps without falling over. I am very proud of myself. In fact, as I become more comfortable, I add a few silly hip throws into it. Before it is over, my dance friends on the sidelines start cheering, since I am the only dancer from our studio doing the line dance. I get a couple of high fives from friends when it is over and I return to the group. Now I know how John Travolta's character felt in *Saturday Night Fever* after performing complicated steps in a competition.

Around eleven-thirty p.m., I decide to leave. Chris says he is staying longer and has arranged a ride home with someone who is heading downtown. I ask my new Asian dance friend where she lives and give her a ride home. When I drop her off at her house, her appreciative head nodding is prolific, and in my fatigued state I do not understand a word she says. I reply politely in eloquent Canadian, "Uh, like, you're welcome, eh?"

Thursday and Friday are dance practice nights for me, since I attend two parties, each at a different studio. I receive a very nice compliment Thursday night on my Waltz and another on Friday regarding my Swing. I am thrilled that other people think my dancing is improving. I put a lot of work into it, and there are so many dances to learn. On Friday, my sixteen-year-old daughter's friend cancels their plans at the last minute, so I invite my daughter to come with me to the Friday night dance practice, and, despite my fears that our worlds will collide, it goes rather well. A couple of my friends dance with her, not intimidated at all because they think she knows less than they do. Having taken years of ballet, jazz, modern, and tap dance lessons, she follows exceptionally well. She is also extremely supportive of my venture into ballroom dancing, which is unlike the family members of most of my male friends who like to dance.

Many people comment on my poor posture, but only two people do so in a positive way. My dance instructor, Tania, suggests a series of exercises in order to strengthen the muscles below my rib cage. These muscles are important for a man's ballroom dance frame. Another woman talked about her own problems with posture due to working at a computer all day and sympathetically told me that she paid a lot of money to go to a posture specialist. I decide to work on the exercises, and gradually, over time, my posture shows signs of improvement.

After one Friday evening group lesson, I suggest to four different women that they go to a Friday dance being held at another location. Not only do they all show up, but I think they are all expecting to keep me to themselves as a dance partner. Needless to say, I am constantly in demand for every dance. Several of my male dance friends also show up and they are kept busy, too. It is a good night for dancing, and having several people who already know each other adds to the fun. Being part of a group of people who all know each other reduces the social pressure to make small talk, and we switch partners every dance to try out the new steps that we are all learning together. My social life is changing, and I am meeting some great people.

Tania decides to leave the studio to pursue other activities, and I am asked to say a few parting words about her at one of the student dance parties. She is extremely well liked for her energy, dedication, and bright smile. Every private or group lesson starts with Tania's big smile and positive attitude. It is infectious. Somehow I recognize that I have changed from the shy beginner who never spoke to anyone at the dance studio to a respectable dance student and the person now being asked to speak in front of the other students at Tania's farewell event.

"I am saddened, as everyone is, by Tania's departure," I begin. "Tania, thank you for your bright smile and enthusiasm in every single class you teach. You make it very easy for us to learn. I am sure that everyone will remember their Spot Dance night with Tania. How can you forget? You walk nervously to the middle of the floor with Tania on your arm in her lovely dress. You separate and face each other, waiting for the music to begin. The male students standing there looking into Tania's eyes are probably all thinking the same thing: I wonder if Tania has any other tattoos?"

The men who have witnessed the low-cut dresses understand the joke and are raucous with their laughter. The women grudgingly chuckle beneath their breath. The studio owner was not paying attention to my farewell speech and, seeing the reaction, wonders if I said something inappropriate. When the dance music begins, I quickly turn to Tania and ask her to dance the Cha-Cha with me.

CHA-CHA (OR CHA-CHA-CHA)

The Cha-Cha is a fast-paced and sexy Latin dance that includes good hip movement, fancy footwork, and playful turns. It is an inviting, teasing, and happy dance. While there is a lot of Latin music to dance Cha-Cha, there are also plenty of modern songs, such as Pink's "Let's Get This Party Started," Shania Twain's "Up," and Michael Bublé's (among other artists who have recorded it) "Sway."

There is a common basic step for both International and American Social styles, but different studios and teachers tend to start the step in a different way. The most common style that I see is the American Social.

- The man starts by taking a side step to the left with the left foot on the one beat. This is actually a clever starter step used to get the dancers on the proper beat of the music.

- On the two beat, the right foot is moved to a position back and behind the left foot.

- The next beat, three, requires a weight shift from the right back to the left without moving the left foot.

- Next is the cha-cha step. The right foot moves on four to the side. The left foot closes to the right on the half beat and the right foot moves again to the side on the next beat.

- The count is 1-2-3, 4-and-1, with the "and" being in between the two beats. Another way to think of this is: 1-2-3-cha-cha-cha, 2-3, cha-cha-cha.

- The step is finished with the man taking a forward step with his left foot then shifting weight back to the right. Once this is complete, a cha-cha step is taken to the man's left.

- The woman starts by taking a side step to the right with the right foot on the one beat.

- On the two beat, the left foot is moved to a position forward and in front the right.

- The next beat, three, requires a weight shift from the left back to the right without moving the right foot.

- This is followed by the cha-cha step. The left foot moves on four to the side. The right foot closes to the left on the half beat and the left foot moves again to the side on the next beat.

- The step is finished with the woman taking a backward step with her right foot then shifting weight back to the left. Once this is complete, she takes a cha-cha step to her right.

Hip motion in the Cha-Cha, as in most Latin dances, comes from the bending and straightening of the legs at the appropriate times. This is different in Social and International. In Social style, I land on a bent leg and straighten it to move my hips. In International style, I land on a straight leg and sink into the other hip for style. Also very important to note in any style is that when the hip moves, the shoulders need to remain calm and do not move. I know it is tough, but it makes no sense when you see people moving their hips and shoulders in unison up and down like a seesaw. It looks like they are having fun, but it is not the sign of people who have benefited from good dance instruction and learned proper technique.

The other good technique in Cha-Cha is to emphasize the first beat in every bar. This can be accomplished by holding it slightly longer than the other beats and making that step far more deliberate and dramatic than the others.

A few days later, the studio owner is giving me a special lesson to improve my dancing. She starts with my posture, pulling up my rib cage and pushing down on the top of my shoulders. This continues until she is satisfied. We move into dance hold, and when I take the first step, my posture falls apart. This is a recurring theme throughout my dancing. I get discouraged and start to consider other locations to learn variations on dances such as street Swing and street Cha-Cha, where posture is less important, if at all.

Street Cha-Cha and street Swing vary from mainstream ballroom dancing, with the visible component being far less emphasis on perfect posture. In street Swing, I see people dancing bent over at the waist with their rear ends sticking out, although I doubt that it is taught this way. The side steps have no rhythm and look clunky. Often they use upper body movement to emphasize beats instead of a well-controlled hip motion. When the woman performs an underarm turn, the man has no idea where she will finish. To me, this looks sloppy. When dancing a pattern where the partners are frequently separated, such as Swing and Cha-Cha, perhaps perfect posture is less important. It looks a lot more attractive and cleaner with good posture, but it is not essential for social dancing. I talk to people who prefer learning steps rather than technique or posture because it gives them more to do and makes them feel like they know how to dance. For me, there has to be some semblance of technique and decent posture, or eventually dancing looks like a jumble of many steps and nothing close to what the dance is supposed to resemble.

There are many dances to learn and a lot of dance schools in the city. I feel the need for more than my Arthur Murray studio experience and what I consider to be high-cost packages, as well as the unfortunate rotating door of new teachers. My original teacher, Melanie, left for Alberta; my next teacher, Tania, left for personal reasons. My next two instructors are far less experienced but very enthusiastic. The group lesson schedule no longer appeals to me. I am grateful for my experiences but it is time to move on. I look to other dance studios, workshops, and clubs to expand my horizons. If it is a ballroom dance *adventure* that I crave, then I am about to find it!

4

STUDIOS, TEACHERS, AND COSTS

DANCE STUDIOS

Once the decision is made to learn ballroom and Latin dancing, there are several ways for someone to get started. I classify places to learn into three basic categories: franchised studios, independent studios, and non-profit organizations such as local school boards or dance groups for specific dances that are trying to encourage more participants.

The most name recognition belongs to the franchised studios such as the Arthur Murray or Fred Astaire studios. They follow a standard methodology for teaching and may offer a package of private lessons, group lessons, and practice parties for one specified price. In some cases, the single price might end up becoming a contract or an agreement for the student to take lessons for a period of time and for the set price. These types of studios are of course franchised, so they appear in numerous major cities. Arthur Murray will allow students from one city to participate in activities at another studio in another city with no additional fee. This can be helpful, for example, if the student is visiting another city for a period of time and wants to maintain his/her current level of skill. Franchised studios are the McDonald's of the dance studio world (but much more expensive than McDonald's). They serve up the lessons in a very structured and standard way. The group lessons focus on one dance and one or two patterns in that dance. The teachers undergo continuous training to keep them up to date and improve their teaching skill.

An independent studio would generally be started by a current or former competitive dancer or a dance couple that has decided to teach. Students can sign up for private lessons or group lessons in a somewhat less structured pay-as-you-go format. Group lessons can consist of six or eight weeks in a package deal, and payment is for the entire session. Private lessons are paid for as they are taken, although the studio might have a cancellation fee if a time is booked and the student either fails to show up or does not provide sufficient notice that she/he will not attend. Many studios offer additional practice time by way of scheduling practice parties. Some are open only to guests of current students; the ones that are open to all dancers might charge a small entrance fee. There are also independent teachers, some who teach in their homes and others who rent whatever space is available at a reasonable rate.

High school night courses are advertised as part of continuing education, and community centre courses may be offered as part of a city recreation program. An administrator finds a teacher and registers students. A curriculum is prepared with the intent to teach specific steps of certain dances in each level. This category normally has the lowest prices and can be a hit-and-miss way to learn. While some teachers will be excellent, others do not deserve a passing grade. When I talk to people who take these kinds of lessons, they seem far more indifferent than I would expect them to be. My assumption is that while the instruction may be competent, there is no atmosphere, passionate music, or excitement about dance.

Finding extra practice time as a student will be a challenge unless there is an empty room at home. There might be reasons such as financial, location, or convenience to select this option, or it may be the only alternative offered, depending on where a person lives.

There are also free lessons at a variety of places, if you can find them. Dance studios that have open practice parties may teach a lesson prior to the party and include it as part of the entrance fee. In this case, you learn one or two steps of a dance. There is also a variety of dance groups or social clubs in most large cities. Latin dance clubs and Swing dance groups frequently offer free lessons before the regular dancing begins. While this may allow a person to learn different steps in a dance, it is not the best way to become a better dancer. Learning steps without a good frame or posture creates problems for you and your dance partner. When a new step is learned, it should be accompanied by reinforcing all aspects of what it takes to be a good dancer and a good partner.

Once a person decides to take dance lessons, which option should he or she select? The answer is to find one that best suits one's goals—although that may sound way too cliché to be of any use. Are the lessons to be taken as a single person or as a couple? A single man would likely be in high demand and should easily find a partner for group lessons at a studio. A single woman will have more difficulty and may want to register for private lessons until a suitable partner becomes available. A couple may want to start off more slowly with night classes or more quickly with private lessons. A studio also provides more opportunities to meet people. Evening classes at a community centre may be a less intimidating way to get started. Another option is to get a group together and take lessons with a teacher at an independent studio. A teacher should be happy to have three or four couples at the same time for a lesson, and the rates would be more reasonable than for private lessons.

While dance studios are a viable business like any other business, some of them fail to realize that their strength is in the students who attend. For example, some studios try to monopolize their students, and the owner cringes whenever his/her students attend another studio for a dance workshop, practice, or a free lesson. Students create a social network, finding ways to talk to each other either before a class or when they see each other outside the studio. Student relationships start building a bond that forms the strength, character, and culture of a dance studio. When I started to attend another studio for practice dances, I realized how much more I needed to learn. I craved to learn those moves and styling from the variety of dancers I saw. It gave me the incentive to take *more* lessons from my own dance studio.

Dance studios are as different as restaurants. They come in many sizes, shapes, and flavours. My favourite studios have a large, rectangular wooden floor with mirrors on at least two walls. This might seem trivial, but many studios have supporting posts in the middle of the dance floor, which impose skillful choreography in order to avoid colliding with them.

All teachers will follow a syllabus or curriculum that is a list of figures from which they teach. Not all studios or teachers follow the same syllabus. If asked, teachers should be willing to show people an outline of steps at each level.

DANCE TEACHERS

Whether a person is a social dancer or has a burning desire to excel at a competitive level, the single most important criterion in learning ballroom dance is to find a teacher that suits the dancer's temperament and style of learning. The best teachers create enthusiastic students.

When I started lessons at an Arthur Murray studio, my teacher was well suited to my learning style. She was bright, mature, energetic, and possessed the uncanny ability to recognize my limitations. When I got frustrated, she moved to a less complicated step and made her instruction easy to understand. When I was overwhelmed with information, she looked at me and said, "Let's leave it there for now and move on to something different." If I mastered a step quickly, she would feed me more technique or styling or improve my ability to lead. Each teacher has his/her own particular strengths, and as my goals and needs evolved, I sought out other teachers. To master International style dances, I looked for the best International style instructor. For better club Salsa moves, I went to a Salsa expert. At other times I just wanted to have fun dancing. Deciding on goals for dancing helps determine what to look for in a teacher. Not all teaching styles will work well with a student's personality and personal learning style.

A ninety-minute group lesson or workshop can become depressing if you have to listen to someone who is having a bad day. On the other hand, an overly bubbly, giddy teacher might be enough to turn anyone away from dance lessons. It is a fine blend of enthusiasm, knowledge, and communication skills that makes an excellent teacher. When learning for fun, an energetic personality might be the best choice, while learning precise international steps may require a meticulous taskmaster.

Finding a good teacher is not an easy task. Dance teachers are an unregulated group, so there is no guarantee of even a minimum level of knowledge. As a result, almost anyone is eligible to be a dance teacher. Some teachers are certified, while others have a lot of experience dancing. Some have competed, and some are still competing and are still taking lessons. Others may have taken their last lesson twenty years ago and teach what they know or maybe what they remember. Some dance teachers take a couple of lessons and claim to be knowledgeable enough to teach. The results might not be the same as trusting your investments to someone who has no qualifications, but it is an investment in yourself, so it is wise to check a teacher's background.

One caution about teachers is that they can confuse students and often contradict themselves or each other as to how to dance a given pattern. Teachers are only human and some may not know if a step is a toe lead or a heel lead. They might teach it the way they learned it or what feels natural to them when they dance it. They can talk about different muscles and which ones work in which steps. Sometimes they don't pay attention to alignment or the line of dance, thinking they can correct that later, while other teachers will point it out right away. Arms are also a big area of difference. Some teachers believe that arms should be in constant motion—in Latin dances, for example—while others suggest minimal movement to help the dancer maintain concentration on the foot position and pattern. One teacher will insist that an arm be parallel to the floor; another one encourages a dramatic movement with elbows bending down.

Taking dance lessons can, at times, be frustrating when there seems to be variability or different interpretations of a single dance pattern. Regardless, I try to learn as much as I can from every lesson. Over the years, I have taken lessons at ten different dance studios, receiving lessons from twenty-three different dance teachers, talked to numerous other students, and read as much as I can about ballroom dance. There are definitely correct and incorrect ways to perform a series of steps in a dance. For example, toe and heel leads are well defined for steps in any style of ballroom dance. Yet other items, like arm movements, are more open to interpretation.

Ballroom dancing is a small world and in any city it is likely that teachers from different schools have crossed paths before. They may have taught at the same school at one time. They might have competed against each other or they may even have been dance partners at one time. Whatever the history or non-history, teachers in general tend to be competitive and prefer to retain their students. One dance studio I attended asked me if I was receiving instruction from any other dance teacher or attending any workshops held outside the studio.

The rationale given me for asking such questions was their need to understand any unfamiliar dance patterns or techniques for teaching purposes. I felt that the true reason was to identify the possibility of losing a student. Animosity between studios can exist and it is not always unwarranted. When students from one studio mix at a dance event with students from another studio, it is possible that some sort of dance communication contamination can occur. In other words, students may rethink their goals, preferred teaching style, or teachers and consider a different studio. On the other hand, I have witnessed outright recruiting or poaching of students by teachers who attend dance parties at locations other than where they normally teach. It is not very ethical, but it happens.

Founded in 1949, the association that promotes teaching standards in dance in Canada is the Canadian Dance Teachers Association (CDTA). Some instructors go through a process of learning syllabus and become certified with CDTA, while others follow a different certification process with a dance studio. There are teachers who teach American Social style of ballroom, others who teach International style, and some who teach both. There are teachers who participate in competitions and some who have never done so. There are very good teachers and very good dancers, and sometimes there are teachers who combine the best of both when giving instruction to their students. Of course there are poor teachers as well. They may not know the correct steps or they may not be able to communicate properly. For a serious student of dance, it is often wise to seek another perspective once in a while. This could be from a coach or another teacher at the same location. Learning to dance can take many years, and hearing a new point of view might accelerate that process. Even students who believe that they have the best teacher in the world find that listening to another point of view can be beneficial. It takes time for words and instruction to sink in.

Typical questions to ask a prospective dance teacher

- What is the cost of lessons?
- Is there a contract?
- What style is taught: American Social or International?

- Do you compete or have you ever competed in ballroom or Latin dance?
- Are you certified?
- Are you still taking lessons or advancing your learning?
- How long have you been teaching?

Finding a good teacher can be as much work as finding a good used car. As with a car, it might be that you need to settle for one that is basically very good while you keep looking for a better model. In addition to information gathered from course outlines, biographies, and a list of frequently asked questions, checking with other dance students may turn up a lot of valuable information.

THE COST

Purchasing dance lessons is similar in many ways to other purchases. It does not always follow that you get what you pay for. It is possible to find a very good price and receive excellent value. In other cases, the consumer has to remember the caveat of "buyer beware." One way for a couple to get started is to take lessons with a group at a community centre or night class. This option is likely to have the greatest variability of skills, good and bad, in the available dance teachers. It is unlikely that these teachers would be full-time dance instructors or competitors, or that they would be continuing to take lessons to improve or reinforce their knowledge and skills. Does this matter? Perhaps not. If one is more interested in the social aspects of dancing, then any choice is probably a good one.

Taking lessons at an independent studio is another option and probably in the mid-range of cost. Group lessons at a studio might actually be no more expensive than elsewhere, and the only factor to consider is the convenience of the location. The group lessons will typically be a set of four, six, or eight lessons, and there is usually no rebate for a missed lesson or for anyone who drops out halfway through. Group lessons are an excellent way to get started and offer good value for beginners. However, they are not ideal as a long-term learning strategy, for a number of reasons. I see people who take group lessons for a couple of years and pass through several levels or categories. They know a lot of steps but lack the style and technique that comes from a good teacher in private lessons. At some point, the distinguishing characteristic of a better dancer and more enjoyable dancing comes from knowing technique, not a greater variety of patterns.

The studio might also offer workshops that provide an opportunity to learn a new dance or challenge the student with new steps or techniques. For a typical workshop, there would be a single, one-time fee for anywhere from an hour to two hours of instruction on a dance.

The cost of an hourly private lesson varies, and prices change over time. To give some idea of the range, fees for typical private lessons can vary by as much as 70 percent. Private coaching lessons for dance competitors from a highly advanced dance coach can be more than double the rate for a regular private lesson. A private dance lesson normally lasts forty-five to sixty minutes. Lessons may consist of a teaching segment and an administrative portion, so in order to avoid any misunderstandings, it is wise to investigate this beforehand. The student also needs to check in advance regarding the cost and the teacher's qualifications and possibly talk to someone else who knows the teacher. As a wary consumer can expect, it is possible to find a teacher who charges lessons at the low end of the scale and be amazing, as well as the chance that a teacher with a much higher rate may deliver far poorer results. It is also wise to investigate cancellation policies. Policies usually exist for cancelling private lessons, the standard typically being within twenty-four or forty-eight hours. Last-minute cancellation of a lesson normally incurs a fee. One benefit of private lessons is that they can be scheduled at a time convenient to the student, assuming they also fit into the teacher's timetable. They can be at a regular weekly time or may be varied or changed by mutual agreement and with advance notice.

The franchise studios tend to offer package deals for a longer time frame. An example of a package deal might include one private lesson a week, two group lessons, and a free practice party, or some combination thereof, for a single price, running over a period of six months. The student pays an up-front fee and makes monthly payments. The studio might ask the student to sign a contract agreeing to the terms and prices. The good side of this is that the studio has a long-term commitment and knows what revenue to expect. For the student, it provides continuity of learning and a single sign-up rather than registering for each session separately. The negative aspect of this type of arrangement is the cost for those who feel it is too high and the committed contract for those who want to drop out or have a valid reason for wanting to stop the lessons. In that case it may depend on the generosity of the studio owner as to how to deal with the situation.

The frequency of dance lessons depends on a student's goals, lifestyle, and learning ability. Taking lessons once a week is a generally accepted standard for a serious dance student. Taking lessons less frequently than that dramatically increases losing knowledge and ability. There is a loss of continuity, and the improvement in skills will be less noticeable. In my experience, the retention of dance steps and technique can fade during a two-week vacation. Dancing truly is a sport where the skills need to be maintained through regular use. Taking lessons more than once a week is for someone seeking more than a social activity. It leaves little time for practice and can lead to the lessons themselves becoming a more expensive form of practice.

THE CURRICULUM

Dance teachers need to know what steps to teach in each dance and have a progression of steps that students can learn as they improve their skills and technique. This list of dances and progressively tougher patterns is known as the curriculum. Teachers may follow a different curriculum and each can have its own set of titles.

- Ballroom Level 1, Ballroom Level 2, Ballroom Level 3, etc.

- Introductory or Beginners' Ballroom, Intermediate Ballroom, Advanced Ballroom, etc.

- Introductory Bronze, Intermediate Bronze, Full Bronze, etc.

This is a method of organizing different steps and patterns into a teaching schedule. The levels taught at different locations may contain the same basic elements or different dance patterns and they may be taught in a different sequence. The franchised studios will all teach from the same curriculum so they will have consistency from studio to studio. It is unclear if any particular method or progression is better than any other. It is more likely that commitment and practice by the student have a far greater impact on acquiring dance skills than the process by which they are taught.

TEACHER, STUDENT, AND STUDIO ETHICS

In a world where strange behaviour grabs news headlines and lawyers scour the landscape for attractive lawsuits, a focus on basic ethical conduct needs to prevail. Ethics encompasses both proper conduct and morality. In the dance world, some actions can be guided by appropriate rules of etiquette, while other actions may unwittingly cross the line of acceptable behaviour.

The basic role of a teacher is to teach. The role of a studio owner or dance lesson organizer is to provide a reasonable site. The role of the student is to participate. All should exhibit good behaviour and a positive attitude. Both the student and teacher need to show up on time and both of them should accept the outcome of a cancelled lesson. On a more questionable foray into how inappropriate conduct develops, one can look at a range of student and teacher behaviours.

Association outside of lessons

When I attended university, some professors joined their students for a beer after class at the local pub. How friendly can this get before it interferes with the judgment of either participant? The same applies for teachers. I know a studio that has a strict policy and does not allow any association between students and teachers outside the studio or an organized competition with the exception of an annual barbecue. On the other hand, I had a teacher who held a luncheon for all her students at her house. We had a great time.

Unwanted touching

Placing hands on another person's body can result in a variable degree of acceptance, depending on the person. However, there is a point where it becomes inappropriate. It needs to be adjusted to the level of dance ability and to be within the comfort level of the other person. What is acceptable touching for a high-level competitor may not be acceptable to a woman starting her second lesson. Some women are uncomfortable when a male teacher introduces closed hold position or puts both hands on either side of the woman's hips to demonstrate Latin hip motion. Both dance partners need to communicate clearly to avoid awkwardness.

Hugging and kissing between teacher and students

A personal bond gets forged between students and teachers over time, so some degree of relationship will exist. For a couple that knows the teacher well and is comfortable with him or her, it might not be uncommon to share hugs after a good lesson or a great result at a competition. On the other hand, a teacher or student could make one another uncomfortable with excessive kissing or touching. Communication is the first step, and continued unwanted actions become unacceptable.

Intimate relations

Sometimes the student-teacher relationship goes beyond a passion for dancing. Teachers are in a position of trust, and it becomes difficult to draw the line for a student or teacher who starts a relationship. Once they start sleeping together and continue to take lessons where the student is paying, the situation clearly becomes a moral dilemma. The best scenario would be for the student to find another dance teacher, although people do not want to give up a good instructor. They could end up being partners for life, but a more frequent reality of a student-teacher relationship is a harsh breakup and uncertainty regarding the financial obligations around previous dance lessons. What constitutes a lesson and what is simply helping out a partner? Undoubtedly, people become attracted to each other. The uncertainty is about a teacher's moral obligations and how the position of trust may or may not have played a role in physical attraction.

Students' rights

New dance students are typically naive and unclear about their obligations and risks in registering for dance lessons. As with any other business, the purchaser or student should have some rights vis-à-vis the process and outcome and not simply adhere to the obligations that are placed on him or her by the seller. Registration for dance lessons normally requires students to sign a declaration absolving the studio from injuries or liability. Payment is requested for the lessons in advance. Some studios are exceptional at being fair, while at other studios it seems far too one-sided, with the studio having far too much control over the students.

Students deserve to have rights, and I have not found any references on Rights that address the dance world. Here are some basic guidelines that would make life a lot easier and avoid disputes.

- The student should be provided with all cost information prior to agreeing to a first lesson or signing any forms. This includes the cancellation policy.

- The student should understand the policy around a lesson cancelled by the studio or teacher. Will another teacher fill in? Will the student be able to use the lesson time for practice without charge? There should be mutual agreement as to whether lessons cancelled by the teacher would be rescheduled or dropped and reimbursed.

- Studio policies should be included in a pamphlet or listed clearly on a Web site. This should include any etiquette or behaviour guidelines or policies that the studio encourages or enforces.

- If relevant, the studio should explain the process of finding a dance partner and the options available to the student for learning to dance with or without a partner.

- Teachers should clearly explain why and ask permission before placing hands on any area of a student's body that could make the student feel uncomfortable. For example, aside from a closed dance hold, the teacher might want to demonstrate hip motion by placing hands on the student's hips or correct dance posture by placing hands on the chest.

- The studio should explain the policy on shoes or clothes to be worn during lessons. If shoes or other items are sold at the studio, through a catalogue, or on consignment, the process whereby this is to happen should be explained.

- It should be clear to a student who plans to participate in a Pro-Am dance event what the costs will be. Where the teacher is being funded by more than one of the participating students, the cost-sharing method should be identified as well as the names of the other students contributing or participating.

- Studio promotions should be identified as such. For example, an offer of a free lesson or dance assessment should not spend the majority of time on the promotion of other sales offers. In the consumer world this is referred to as bait and switch tactics.

- There should be no hidden policies or ad hoc decisions made based on information that is not shared. If a student does something that the studio disagrees with, there should be a private conversation to discuss it.

- Similarly, if a teacher or studio does something questionable, the student should have recourse to a process that allows a complaint to be reviewed fairly and without negative repercussions to the student.

5

MOVING ALONG DEVELOPING GOOD DANCE HABITS

SETTING GOALS

At regular intervals, it is wise to have a conversation with yourself or your partner and decide what the goals are for dance. Do you want to learn new dances? Do you want to learn more complex and interesting dance steps? Do you want to excel at a few dances and improve your technique? Maybe you just want to have fun, lose weight, or improve your fitness. Whatever is decided, the next step is to evaluate what has been achieved so far and what is planned. The goal and the plan should be in alignment. If you want to be a full-blown competitive Silver level dancer, then taking group lessons at night school is not going to work. If the objective is to have fun and meet a lot of people, then you may want to go to a busy studio. If the time available to take lessons is a problem, then maybe you should take private lessons and talk to a teacher who can schedule around your free time. You might also consider making a budget and identifying how much spending is planned for dance. Dancing is more than a great hobby, and costs have the potential to spiral upwards with lessons, coaching sessions, dance events, shoes and clothes, and competitions. Is dancing meant to be a long-term investment or a low-cost means to social outings?

Dancing is not like riding a bicycle. Once you know how to ride a bicycle, the work is over and the fun begins. Dancing is a lifelong learning activity, and the increase in fun correlates to the increase in skills. Dancers are only limited by how far they want to go, how good they want to look, how many different dances they want to learn, and how much time and money they want to spend. It is a hobby and a sport all in one, providing both entertainment and fitness.

At some point, the number of dance steps and patterns become useless without a corresponding improvement in technique. One critical technique improvement is the connection between the dancers. How to properly lead and follow dance steps adds greatly to the smoothness and look of a dance. Another opportunity to improve technique is learning good arm movements, which not only increases confidence but adds to the overall visual appeal.

The ideal model of a dance couple that exhibits good lead and follow is in the silent confidence of the partnership.

THE LEAD

Leading is a critical skill in dancing because social dancing is all leading and following, with the leader making decisions during the dance as to what pattern or series of steps will be used. These decisions might be based on the traffic flow of other dancers, an assessment of what skills both partners possess, what makes the leader feel most comfortable, or any of a number of other considerations. The skill of learning to lead needs to be learned along with the steps. This means, for example, that by understanding the man's body position and what foot his weight is over, the woman can prepare for the next step. She may not know what the step is—although having prepared properly which foot to move and feeling the position of the man's body as he moves, the woman will *look like* she knows exactly what to do. Leading well is a combination of technique, good habits, and empathy for the partner, especially in the standard dances. The leader's steps and movement have to be definite, and I quickly realize that I need a lot of improvement in this skill. The feet have to move with confidence. The posture is straight with a lifted rib cage, and steady arms with a great frame consisting of well-positioned and firm left and right elbows. Turns have to be gentle but firm. I discover that taking a private lesson with a good teacher solely to improve posture, frame, and leading is well worth it. A good lead makes the woman's ability to follow easy and fluid. I notice that as my lead improves, I receive more smiles from my dance partners.

A heavy lead is when a man forces the woman through every step, usually with his arms, regardless of the signals he sends with the rest of his body. The signs of too strong a lead can be a frightened look on the woman's face and a painful, forced smile after turns and spins. Men who use a heavy lead do it because their body is not in the right position, their frame is soft, or their movement is not definite. The pet peeve of a number of women is men who force women into a turn whether or not they are prepared. When the woman is not prepared, it can feel as if the man is trying to rip her arm off at the shoulder!

A lead that is too light conveys nothing to a follower. The movement may be uncertain or the frame might feel mushy. Women move around the floor with a confused look on their faces. They feel frustrated because they are good dancers but have no idea what to expect. They will often be in the wrong place or position to perform a step properly and feel guilty about it. With this type of lead, the dancers may frequently find difficulty dancing to the proper beat of the music.

Leading a dance becomes a complex task when dancing with different women but improves with practice. The man's posture should not change based on a woman's height. Tall men should not fall into the trap of leaning over into a smaller woman. Finally, a good leader does not try to show off all the steps learned to date in order to please the woman. (The section on Gaining Respect has more on this topic.)

Beginners tend to take large steps in Latin dances and smaller steps in standard, which is a common mistake. When I am having trouble staying on beat in the Cha-Cha or Triple Swing, I learn to take smaller steps. In Latin dances, a larger step will stifle any hip motion and reduces the opportunity to press the feet against the floor in order to develop hip motion. As a dancer advances in the smooth or standard dances, teachers will encourage bigger steps, but saying it does not explain how to do it. There are numerous suggestions that help me take a bigger step in the smooth dances. In a dance lesson, the instructor may give direction to bend at the hip, lower slightly at the knees, brush the floor with your foot, stretch out the legs, and keep the weight longer on the supporting foot.

THE FOLLOW

There are some good tips for women when they are dancing with men who have little semblance of a solid frame. In order to avoid getting stepped on, women are told to lift their feet early, before taking a step. This is not the same as actually taking the step. The secret in smooth or standard dances is to get the foot ready to move. It helps if the woman's left hand is firmly positioned on the man's upper shoulder muscle on the right arm and the left elbow is firm while resting on the man's arm. When the man starts to move into a dance step, his solid right arm will exert a corresponding amount of pressure, which encourages the woman to move. Similarly, when the man is going backward, the woman should feel a reduced amount of pressure. Maintaining good timing and understanding which foot has weight and which one is going to move is also critical for good following technique.

However, anticipating the lead often results in trouble on the dance floor. It is not an easy task knowing what the man is going to do next. (That applies in life as well!) On the dance floor, it is important to remain calm and feel the lead, however subtle it may be. In smooth dances, the size of the man's steps needs to be determined quickly. A good follower will adapt by making sure she is not the one leading the steps.

Women can become sensitive to the pressure provided by a solid frame and allow this to guide her in following the man. A good follower has a nice, solid frame, with elbows maintained in front of the body and never falling or being pushed behind the shoulder. If the arms are not locked at the elbows, it will feel to the man as if he is pushing on a rope. The man will be incapable of leading any step. In dance teacher language, this is referred to as "spaghetti arms," although a more appropriate expression would be "wet noodle."

If the man is dancing the steps to the correct beat of the music, then following should be easier. If the man's steps do not match the music, then the follower has two choices. She can dance to the actual beat or she can follow the off-beat steps being executed by the leader. A good follower lets the man lead however poorly the steps may be executed.

When a woman dances off the beat, anticipates the lead, or moves her head, looking around the room in a random fashion, it feels to the man as though she is dancing with someone else.

Even if the woman is more experienced at dancing than the man, she should follow nicely and not display any over-the-top styling that might intimidate the man. While it is important for the woman to look good, if it is overdone it might be a while before another dance partner is willing to endure the same fate. One woman I danced with lifted my hand to turn herself because she was bored and wanted one. That's not the trademark of a classy dancer.

The follower has another important role, as was previously mentioned. She also has to help in navigation when the man is moving backward and does not have a line of sight to obstacles. In the event of an impending collision, the woman gently squeezes the man's right arm to indicate trouble. Freezing and shouting, "Watch out!" is probably only going to increase everyone's stress level.

At one event, I dance with a woman who is renowned through the dance studio as the best follower. As we dance, I discover the accuracy of her reputation. She follows me flawlessly and easily in spite of any misstep or confusing signal that I send her. Curious, I ask her what her secret is: How is it that she follows so well? Her response is simple.

"I wait for the man before I take a step."

In reality, she is very well prepared and hesitates just slightly and unnoticeably before she takes every step. The entire dance slows down in her mind, and when the lead is given, she follows it.

THE CONNECTION

Connecting to a partner is critical to good movement in the dance. The dance frame consists of the upper body position, arm, and hand contact. The connection is maintained throughout the dance with all movement originating from the body. This means that the hands don't push to lead the steps. In standard dances, the lower joints bend to start a movement, and that should be enough for the follower to sense the step is coming. It is also important for the leader to be clearly on a supporting foot and for the follower to realize what foot that is. If a couple stops in the middle of a dance for whatever reason, the leader and follower have to non-verbally communicate what foot is the supporting one and where the next step is going.

DANCING WITH DIFFERENT WOMEN

Salsa is a high-energy dance that is enhanced with a lot of spins and turns. I dance with a very tall woman, lead her into a spin, and as she turns, my hand accidentally whacks her on the back of the head. Being gracious, she finds this funny, and we both laugh it off politely. It is less funny when I perform the next spin with identical results. Men have to adapt to taller women. While dancing, I have knocked off a woman's hair extensions, berets, and other assorted items from a woman's head by not understanding where I need to stand, how to hold my arm, and where to place my hand. Since a taller woman is likely to take larger steps, the man needs to stay closer to her. The arm leading a spin has to go straight up—perhaps with no bend at the elbow at all—and the hand needs to rise deliberately and be held above the woman's head. She should not have to bend over and duck under the hand, regardless of how tempting that is. When women dance with a shorter man, similar rules apply. The woman should try to take smaller steps, especially in turns and spins. Any time the man lifts his hand for a woman's underarm turn, there has to be a close proximity for it to work.

At another dance party, I dance a Swing with a long-haired young woman who arrived at the studio before her hair had dried from a shower. I give her an American spin and find myself standing too close to her. She whips around in the spin and the heavy, wet hair swings around and hits me in the face. It feels as it someone has slapped me with a hardcover book. I lose my balance then recover; she is oblivious to what has happened. We continue, and, because I know so few moves, I give her a second American spin. This time I duck below the hair as it swings past, and fortunately the song ends soon after.

"Are you all right?" she asks, recognizing that something has happened but not realizing the force of the wet hair.

"Sure," I reply shakily and wander away.

For tall men dancing with very short women, every effort has to be made to maintain good posture and to avoid leaning over. That gives a hunched look that is not appealing and makes it look like the man is dancing with a child. The same applies to women who dance with shorter men.

Women have to be careful with their arm extensions. If the timing is not correct, the potential exists to hit the man on the side of the head. I have come close to having an eye taken out and I have been scratched on the chin and cheek by long, beautiful, glossy fingernails. (In some cases, the man can prove it to the dance partner by showing her that marks from the scratch match the colour of her fingernail polish!)

Dancing with heavy-set women often requires a firm lead. Also, I don't make them change direction sharply, choosing instead to be gentle in every turn. Women with a slight frame may need a lighter but still a definite lead. In both cases, the lead has more to do with how heavy they are on their feet rather than body mass. Men need to be cautious with women who are light on their feet because a heavy lead in this case can make the woman look as though she is being thrown around like a rag doll. It is always important to be consistent and firm with the lead as well as to make an appropriate adjustment for the partner.

ARMS

Once the basic dance steps are mastered, and movement around the floor happens without much effort, the next progression is for both partners to do something expressive with their arms. In a woman's underarm turn in any dance, each partner will have an arm free, and the arms usually end up dangling down the side of the body. Dangling, uncoordinated arms do not look graceful. The visual effect is sloppy and far too casual. Depending on what type of dance is being performed, the arms can express themselves as dramatic, sexy, pretty, or graceful. I once saw a man lead a woman into an underarm turn while putting his hand in his pocket. That's what men do with their hands when they are feeling self-conscious. Being self-conscious about arms can be overcome with practice. At first, arms can look jerky and sloppy, but with practice they add enormously to the dance. Unfortunately, it also adds more to think about for both partners while dancing: What do I do with my arm when it flies free without any obvious destination?

Arm movement should flow naturally from the motion of the body in a manner similar to what happens when a Frisbee is thrown:

The torso moves first, then the upper arm, then the lower arm; then the wrist is snapped out with a flourish. In dance, the man's wrist is normally held straight and the elbow is always slightly bent, with the thumb pointing to the floor and the arm held parallel to the floor. Women maintain the same slightly bent elbow but can bend the wrist. The fingers have different styles: tucked together, splayed, or some combination of both. As dance skills progress, it will be useful to ask a dance teacher for different arm movements.

In Latin, a woman can use her free arm to put it straight up in the air or perform a hair curl, where the hand moves from one side of the head to the other just above the ear, then slides down the body. It looks incredibly sexy when done properly.

BALLROOM FOOT POSITIONS

Ballroom has five foot positions similar to ballet in number and in some aspects, but they are not really the same.

First position—The feet are together touching and facing the same direction. This is the stance for starting smooth dances and when the feet are closed.

Second position—The feet are still beside each other but are apart.

Third position—The feet are together but angled away. The heel of one foot is against the instep of the other foot.

Fourth position—The feet are apart with one foot in front of the other.

Fifth position—The feet are angled apart with the heel of one foot against the toe of the other foot. This is used in Latin for fifth-position breaks.

b

DANCE CHARACTERS

My dance world is filled with people who enjoy themselves immensely, and they tend to be the most polite and respectful people anyone could hope to meet. As with other groups, there are always some typical characters that stand out. In my experiences as a dancer, I meet several that leave an impression.

Age is no impediment to dancing, and every dance studio seems to have its role model senior citizen. At one gala dance event, we meet a woman who is still dancing at ninety years of age. There is also Jakki, a sweet, seventy-something woman who attends every regular Friday and Sunday dance party, as well as many others. Her goal is to become the oldest woman in Canada taking dance lessons. She has shoulder-length blondish-white hair and sincere blue eyes behind her thick glasses. Her body is thin and at times looks frail. Jakki is a cancer survivor and has a love of life that is uplifting. An aura of positive energy surrounds her. She takes lessons at least twice a week and graciously helps new dancers whenever she sees an opportunity. Although her husband passed away a number of years ago, as I get to know her, it is obvious that she still loves him dearly. Her children have grown up, left home, and are following their dreams in other cities. Jakki is a lovely woman, completely disarming, and everyone loves her. Those with good observation skills notice that she has bows on every pair of shoes she owns.

I ask Jakki to dance every week at practice parties. She may be a senior citizen, but she is a model dance partner. Every time someone asks her to dance, she is thrilled. There is a beaming smile on her face the entire time she is dancing. Sometimes she sings or hums along with the song, and it is so charming that it adds a special flavour to the dance. She is always supportive and never criticizes her partner, even though there are many times when she would be justified in doing so. If I make a misstep and accidentally bump her knees during the dance, she apologizes whether it is her fault or not and asks what she should have done to avoid the incident. At her age she is frail compared to other women that I dance with, so I take extra caution in navigating smooth dances to avoid contact with other dancers. In the Latin dances, I gently lead the turns.

One of my first teachers tells me about her experiences with a student that she refers to as a commander. This is a person who announces the next step out loud during the dance. A male commander acts like a ship captain. "Take in the jib! Change heading to starboard!"

In dance, this translates to forewarning the partner before every move: "Coming up will be a Natural Turn! Next move is a Hesitation! Get ready for an Underarm Turn!"

It indicates a lack of confidence in the partner and/or the lack of ability of the leader to effectively communicate the lead to the follower. In either case, it can be a distraction on the dance floor and takes away the spontaneity of moving around the floor to music.

Women also can be commanders. They try to help while dancing, but are actually in the helpless position of following instead of leading, and this might be frustrating. "Give me a stronger lead. Let's do a Spin Turn. That right arm has to be more firm. The side step needs to be bigger."

For some women, men don't live up to their expectations. I guess the same holds true on the dance floor.

I meet women all the time who try to anticipate my dance steps and I think of them as "guessers." The guesser gives up all effort at following a physical lead and looks for visual cues or thinks about previous steps as a way to predict what might be coming next. Normally the frame is weak by either or both partners. The resulting dance often has the partners moving in slightly different directions or at different times, as neither partner is sure what the other is doing. This takes a lot of effort and is mentally draining. On the other hand, this style may work well with the commander—although the dance will be far less spontaneous.

Sadly, some dancers develop a habit of finding fault with every dance step, whether it is their own step or their partner's. I refer to this type of person as "The Critic." They have two forms: Some criticize while dancing, while others remain polite while dancing and wait until it is over to give a complete analysis. "That Foxtrot was acceptable for American style, but the movement is too small. You did the same turn in every corner—you need to learn more steps."

Sometimes criticism is thinly disguised as a compliment. "Your frame was good, and I did not mind your head moving back and forth like a windshield wiper."

If you watch the movie *Shall We Dance* (the American version), they have a character that perspires profusely. It is understated compared to the reality of how people perspire in my dance world. As a beginner, I did not perspire very much. The steps I took were small, and I did not dance a lot on any given night. As my skill increased and the number of dances increased, so did my need for perspiration control. The first action I took was to stop wearing long-sleeved shirts with a tie. I dressed in good-quality short-sleeved golf shirts or dress shirts for practice parties and dropped the tie for group lessons. One man I knew always wore a long-sleeved shirt to practice parties. Before the evening was half over, his entire shirt was dripping wet. One summer evening, I danced with a woman who became so soaked in perspiration that at the end of the dance my right arm was completely covered in her perspiration. I spent several minutes in the washroom and washed it off. Excessive perspiration affects both men and women and, while it is not considered the norm, it is not uncommon.

I see some men and women who do not actually know any ballroom dance steps but pretend to. They move their feet to the music and dance around the floor with a totally perplexed partner who is wondering what dance they are doing. They have good musicality but need a few lessons to learn how to channel it. They might impress a few more dance partners after taking lessons to learn the proper way to dance.

Dancers are generally the nicest people on the planet. However, there are always a few times where people get frustrated or think they are king or queen of the dance floor. During a practice party in a gym, I ask a woman to dance a Tango. We are both beginners; I know this because she uses a very common expression, "I don't know much about how to dance." We move to the edge of the floor and are trying to find a respectable dance hold position to start the Tango. Just as we are ready to take the first step, I feel a double tap on my left elbow and turn to see a dance couple directly behind us. It is the man who had just flicked my arm, and he is now giving me a brush-off signal with his right hand as if to say, "Get out of my way or get moving." This is unusual, because most men realize that you need to navigate *around* people, not through them, especially at the start of the dance.

Some people are vigilant about the line of dance and feel that it must be strictly followed. It does make dancing safer, although it can result in conflict. I witness this on a dance night at a dance practice party held at a dance studio on Rideau Street near downtown Ottawa. It is held in the basement of a community centre, and, although the space is relatively small, it has a nice wooden floor. A Waltz is playing, and my dance partner and I are travelling the line of dance halfway along the long wall when I hear a commotion toward the middle of the floor.

"You are travelling against the line of dance," claims an obviously upset man. He is middle-aged with receding short brown hair and a round face.

The larger man is facing away from me, so I do not hear his exact words. Apparently, the reply is not satisfactory.

Again the upset man tries to make his point. "You are going the wrong direction in this dance and you bumped into me!"

I hear more muttering from the tall man, no older than his accuser but with a full head of white hair and a hunched-over upper body. I feel the tension rise in the room as more people stop to look. According to the upset dancer, the tall man reached the corner of the short wall, turned, and went back diagonally from the corner, not directly against the line of dance but enough to scatter most of the oncoming dancers.

"This is the second time you have done this tonight and you have to stop! You are bumping into people! You need to follow the proper line of dance."

As quickly as it began, the confrontation stops. The faces of the female partners of the quarrelling duo register shock. I understand this happens in competitive sporting events, but this is the first time I witness it at a social ballroom dance event. Dancing is a contact sport, and it is important to follow the rules of the game as well as rules of etiquette. If either of the two males had been a touch more polite, the situation would have been different. There is a lot of male testosterone flowing when trying to impress a date with your dance moves.

I met a very tall young man at one dance studio who dances like a professional and has an equally proficient partner. Rumours circulate that during a supposed practice session one afternoon, they were caught having sex in the men's washroom of the dance studio. The studio owner chastised them and asked them to leave the studio. On hearing the news, I am appalled by their lack of decorum, although I also wonder what dance they were doing before going into that washroom; probably a very, very good Rumba. My imagination wanders.

For some dancers, the activity is more about the social aspects and less about the learning. When I dance with a specific woman who enjoys talking, she frequently appears to be more engaged in having a good conversation than dancing. Normally, it is a fine balance. I dance with an older woman, and she rambles on through the whole dance, which is fine with me because I stick to basic movements and don't worry about trying to lead her into anything she will miss and possibly hurt herself.

Some women like to flirt. This can be either attractive or very disconcerting. The identifying characteristics are a woman dance partner who has a more than playful smile, suggestive dance moves, and grasping arms. In a Latin dance, she wiggles her hips and rubs her hand suggestively over her body whenever it is free. In smooth dances, she loves closed position. She is like a spark that just won't go out, trying to attract and dance with men so that her dance card is filled the entire night. Her actions are usually over the top for the setting. It can be a release of emotion more than a display of dance ability. For men, unwanted flirting can be more subtle. They touch more, hold a hand or arm slightly longer than is normally comfortable, and hug their partner after every dance until the woman manages to squirm free.

A show-off in the dance world is a person who knows dozens of steps in each dance but has no frame, posture, or lead and tries to impress a partner by outdoing him or her in steps. A man will lead all types of steps that he knows flawlessly—but he cannot lead the woman. A woman will pick an opportunity and lead herself into advanced steps, leaving the man wondering how to get back on the beat.

In addition to students who try to do too much on the dance floor with bad results, there are teachers who think the world is theirs and that everyone stops to watch every time they dance. At one lesson, I am working with my instructor in a corner of the dance floor. One of the young teachers starts a routine with her partner. It looks like a Samba and travels from one end of the floor to the other end, where I am working on a new step. At an unfortunate moment, my teacher turns to look at me, and the teacher performing the Samba crashes into her, putting a heel into my teacher's ankle. My teacher was visibly upset and shocked that the other teacher did not navigate around us. Some teachers have an arrogance that goes beyond poor attitude. At best, it is a cocky confidence, while at worst it is inconsiderate and disrespectful.

SAMBA

The Samba might be the most rhythmical of all the Latin dances. Practising the full hip motion without warming up first can cause sufficient muscular soreness to prevent a person from walking normally for several days. The basic step forward and side steps are similar to the Salsa, with an added syncopation twist. The syncopation step in Samba is when you dance a step in the middle or slightly off the beat to present a better effect. Samba is the equivalent of cool jazz in the dance world.

- The Samba side step starts with the man taking a step to the left with his left foot. That is on the first beat.

- At the middle of the beat, the man moves his right foot to the same side and slightly behind the left. This is counted 1-a, or 1-and. The right foot moves on the "a."

- With the weight now on the right foot, the weight is shifted back to the left foot on the 2 beat. The left foot does not move. It is just a weight change. The full count is usually 1-a-2. The movement of the right foot to the side is not actually at the middle of the beat but as late as he can afford to do it without missing the weight shift to the right foot for the 2 beat.

- On the next beat, the man moves his right foot to the side, followed by the left foot on the half beat, to the side and slightly behind the right. The weight shift back to the left foot happens on the final beat. This is counted as 3-a-4.

- The woman's steps are the mirror opposite of the man's. The side step starts with the woman taking a step to the right with her right foot. That is on the first beat.

- At the middle of the beat, the woman moves her left foot to the same side and slightly behind the right. This is counted 1-a, or 1-and. The left foot moves on the "a."

- With the weight now on the left foot, the weight is shifted back to the right foot on the 2 beat. The full count is usually 1-a-2. The movement of the left foot to the side is not actually at the middle of the beat but as late as she can afford to do it without missing the weight shift to the left foot for the 2 beat.

- On the next beat, the woman moves her left foot to the side, followed by the right foot on the half beat, to the side and slightly behind the left. The weight shift back to the right foot happens on the final beat. This is counted as 3-a-4.

This is only one version of the basic step. There is another version that goes forward and back, and teachers talk about lifting the feet like stepping over a small log. The Samba has many interesting steps and moves around the floor counterclockwise in the normal line of dance. It is a Latin dance, so the Latin dance hold is used, and foot turnout is essential.

7

SINGLE SOCIAL DANCE MAN

A love for Swing dancing suddenly seizes me, and I start to attend a few Swing dance society dances, including the free lesson at the start of each party. I learn a behind-the-back American spin that sounds and looks interesting but is quite useless and awkward to do. The instructors at these lessons sound like excited teenagers who cannot stop gushing with tips that overwhelm me. They are well-meaning, nice people, but somehow I begin to feel old.

It is good to be learning dance steps outside the strict regimen of a formal dance studio. At this location, I am also introduced to the Lindy Hop, which has forward and backward leg kicks that force me to make a mental note to stay off the dance floor when people are doing Lindy, or at least give them a lot of space. The upright ballroom posture is not a prerequisite here, and there are numerous new people to meet. Everyone is in a good mood, and the atmosphere is one of fun and informality. At this event, there are no standards for dress, and people show up in everything from ragged jeans to fine-looking "zoot suits."

The Swing dance crowd consists mainly of young people in their late twenties, and at one point I meet a young man who used to deliver the newspaper in my neighbourhood. He is doing well, looks like he is really enjoying himself, and once again I feel old. Some colleges and universities have Swing dance clubs, and these contribute to the crowd gathered here for the Swing dance nights. They teach another new step before the Swing dance starts, and I feel like I have only half-learned how to perform it. It will be useless to anyone outside this crowd because I don't lead it well enough, and only an exceptional woman would be able to follow. A lot of women work on the recognition principle of following a man's lead. They are totally confused until they recognize what the move is, then an auto-pilot is activated in their brain that takes them through it. Dancing is a fluid and easy movement—that is, as long as your partner is able to follow what you plan to do.

At the Swing dance party, I meet a red-haired woman who is much younger than I and we dance a Triple Swing. She proclaims, "You must be a ballroom dancer."

"Yes," I reply, "how did you know?"

"You do that shuffle thing with your feet that all ballroom dancers do in Swing." At this point in time, I am not aware of the varieties of Swing or the nuances of foot placement. Her steps are huge with big knee lifts. Apparently our two differing awkward styles did not mesh. She asks if I know any Argentine Tango, which I don't. She wants to learn the "real" Argentine Tango, not the ballroom version, and likewise with the Salsa. She wants to learn "real" Salsa, whatever that means. She phrases her words in such a non-judgmental way that it is enjoyable listening to her.

SWING

There are several versions of Swing. For simplicity, it is easier to teach new students the Single Swing and move along from there. Arguably the most popular Swing is Triple Swing. This is the dance of good, old-time Rock 'n' Roll. When you dance with feeling for the music, there is no other feeling like it. The music comes alive inside you.

Single Swing

- The man takes a step back with his left foot, moving all the weight to that foot.

- The next step is to shift the weight back to the right foot, which should not have moved.

- The left foot is then moved to the side without moving the right foot.

- The weight is shifted back to the right foot.

- The timing is quick, quick on the back break and slow, slow on the side steps.

- The woman takes a step back with her right foot, moving all the weight to that foot.

- The next step is to shift the weight back to the left foot, which should not have moved.

- The right foot is then moved to the side without moving the left foot.

- The weight is shifted back to the left foot.

The key is to make sure the weight changes happen for each foot, or the dance will not work, and the timing will definitely not be Rock 'n' Roll. As a couple becomes comfortable, this dance slowly rotates to the right. The dance hold is different for the man's left hand. It is held below the waist with palm facing to the left holding the woman's hand gently with the thumb on top and the fingers in the palm of the woman's hand. For a Triple Swing or East Coast Swing, the back steps are the same as Single Swing. The side steps include an extra step that makes the feet go side-together-side. A good teacher will add the proper technique and movement.

SOCIAL DANCING

On the social dance scene I meet Mike, a respectable-looking young man in his thirties and a good Latin dancer. He goes to practice parties at different dance studios, and, without his providing any encouragement, the women who dance with him offer their phone numbers. This confirms my suspicion that women are always looking for a good dance partner. Who knows if it leads to more than dancing? Mike has more phone numbers than he can handle. He enjoys dancing and does nothing to discourage the women. I see Mike at a dance party on Friday night, and he tells me that he has received two more phone numbers. In spite of his legacy in Ottawa, he decides to move to Toronto.

I meet a middle-aged man, Alan, who tells me about his experience at a local dance studio. He signed up for private lessons, but was looking for some additional classes or group lessons to accelerate his learning. The studio receptionist asks him if he wants to join a men-only group later that day. Thinking that this is a great opportunity to improve his posture, frame, and lead, he arrives and listens to the instructor. Men have some special challenges, such as learning to lead and navigate around the floor. All is going well in the class, until halfway through the lesson, one of the taller men places his arm gently on Alan's shoulder, looks into his eyes, and in a very suggestive voice says, "I hope you save a dance for me later."

Alan is concerned as the meaning of this all-male group suddenly becomes clear. It is a group lesson for same-sex male couples. As the lesson nears completion, he quickly runs away, never to return. Only a few enlightened studios offer group classes for same-sex partners.

My friend Doug says to me, "I wanted to take dance lessons and instead I got a soap opera." Like most social gatherings, there are hookups, breakups, flirting, gossiping, and crying.

There were two tightly knit groups at my previous dance studio. The more experienced dancers were a group who mostly associated with each other, and their dance ability was well beyond the basic and intermediate levels. They had gatherings of their own outside of the studio and tried to dance with each other often because they were all at a higher level. Then there was my group, the new but not novice dancers. We started at roughly the same time as each other and saw the same people in all our group lessons. I considered this to be the friendliest group. We did not know enough to be troublesome but we knew enough to be happy. Finally, there were the raw beginners. Who knows if they will form a group of their own? Beginners are unstable. Some stay to learn the basic dance steps, and some never return. The other social group is the teachers. There are teachers who don't like each other and teachers who develop personal relationships with each other.

There are dancers that date and then break up. You can usually tell what is happening by the expression on their faces. While they are in a relationship, they smile at each other and make engaging small talk. Once it's over, they avoid looking at each other as if they are trying to relegate the other person to another planet. There are pregnant women and pregnant teachers. Doug finally gets to dance in a closed hold position with his teacher. It is not that exciting, since it is only because she is pregnant and he cannot avoid her midsection. As dance lessons and the pregnancy progress, he gets kicked by the unborn child during the smooth dances.

In my quest to discover and assess new dance venues, I head downtown on a summer evening. I enter Caliente's, a Latin dance club in the Byward Market. I arrive at 9:30 to get a good seat, not realizing that for young people the evening doesn't start until after ten. The club is nearly empty except for employees. There is a long wooden bar along one wall, and all the bartenders, male and female, wear the same green, flowery, Caribbean short-sleeved shirt with black pants. The bouncer beside the door is dressed all in black, with trousers, black dress shirt, and an oversized jacket. He gets bored and wanders over to talk.

"Do you dance?" he asks.

"Yes."

"You must be a ballroom dancer."

"How did you know?" I reply, curious.

He reads people well, especially dancers, since he used to teach ballroom and Latin dancing at an Arthur Murray studio but left it in favour of specializing in Salsa. Perhaps he recognized me from my clothes. I wore the normal Latin outfit for a ballroom dancer, a plain black T-shirt with black pants. The bouncer also teaches Salsa dance steps at the club two nights a week, and I think to myself what a great combination of jobs he has.

Young people who look slightly older than the legal drinking age soon fill the place. The women wear hopeful smiles and bright clothes sparkling with colour. The men strut around with confidence and are ready to drink and dance. The music volume is turned up to an eardrum-shattering level, drowning out any other sounds, and so people begin to communicate visually. The club is now filled with smooth Salsa dancers, all too young, energetic, and intimidating for me. Couples pack the floor and perform double spins, hand flips, and waist rolls to perfection. They move effortlessly from one pattern to another as if they were all meant to be connected. There is no counting of the exact beat that I can see. They are all on the beat, yet moving smoothly as if there were no beat at all. Men's feet move or remain still, depending on the pattern, and when the feet move they are perfectly synchronized to the music and with their partner. I don't know nearly enough steps to keep up with this crowd, so I am soon on my way home.

One Sunday evening, I decide to attend another dance party that people talk about, the Dance Zone, near Rideau Street, past the Parliament buildings in the downtown area. I drive along the Ottawa River Parkway, admiring the picturesque view of the river. The road turns into Wellington Street, and I am able to drive past the Centennial Flame and Parliament Hill. Continuing past the elegant Chateau Laurier and along Rideau Street, I find the dance studio in the basement of a community centre. It turns out to be a very small crowd, mainly people much older than I am. It may actually be helpful to be older, since retired people should have much more time for practice. One of my favourite dance partners, Jakki, is here, and she hums or sings the Foxtrot lyrics quietly while we dance around the floor. It is a precious experience and a moment worth more than I can express.

I meet an attractive woman who is originally from the Philippines and works for the federal government. I had danced with her previously at a student practice party, but never talked to her, and now she is sitting nearby. After dancing a few fast dances with other men, she returns to the table and sits down beside me. She is perspiring profusely on her forehead and is trying to dab it with a Kleenex. I offer her my clean, white, folded handkerchief. She politely refuses at first and then graciously accepts. I never get to dance with her that night, and my hanky ends up covered in makeup.

While dancing with a woman that I had met previously, she tells me about an experience she had dancing with a man in closed position at a dance party and feeling a lump being pressed against her upper leg. It reminds me of when I used to go jogging in the middle of the Canadian winter and had to stuff a thick sock into the front of my underwear to keep everything warm. I have no idea what this dancing man was doing other than toying with a woman's imagination.

I meet a few male friends who have been in group lessons together, and we chat. I dance with some women that I recognize from other dance venues. They tell me their names and smile, which I interpret as either a sign of personal interest, or they are simply happy to dance with a man whom they are able to follow. I meet a woman named Sue who seems quite nice. She is just starting dance lessons, is an accountant, and is divorced. I help her through a few steps, and she gives me her phone number. Has my dancing miraculously crossed over to a higher level? Later in the evening, another woman offers me her phone number.

DATING

I am sitting at a table with my friend Jim on a Sunday night at a practice party held by a studio located downtown. A woman that I met a few weeks ago, May, walks up and asks me to dance. We do a wonderful Waltz around the floor, smiling at each other, and after the dance I walk back to the table and sit beside Jim.

Jim says to me, "Paul, you should ask that woman out!"

I reply, "May?"

Jim exclaims, "Well I don't think you should wait that long."

After several adventures going to dances alone and looking for dance partners, I decide to start asking women out. At least then I will have someone to dance with for most of the night, even if we switch partners occasionally and dance with other people we know. It seems like a low-risk approach and might not even be considered a date. I think of it as going somewhere with a buddy. Dancing is not a date. Dinner is a date.

On Sunday I attend a student practice party and take along Linda, a woman from my studio who wants to get in some extra practice. She is divorced with two children and has a high-income, high-stress job. Jim is already there when we arrive, so we sit at his table. He looks a bit surprised to see her, and I think it might be because he is interested in her and did not have a chance to ask her out before I did. She is wearing a lovely, flowing, black and white polka-dot skirt. Jim and I both dance with her at various times, and she looks happy. Taking a break, we all sit down at a small, round table, and Jim accidentally spills a full cup of Pepsi all over her skirt. We mop it up as best we can, and she takes it well. Sometimes women are simply grateful to be able to go out for a fun night of dancing.

On Friday I go to a group dance lesson. I meet Debbie there, someone I had danced with on a previous occasion, and ask if she wants to go to a dance party afterwards at another studio. If so, I would show her how to get there. I also ask Alison, a friendly figure skater, but she declines. Debbie follows me in her car and we show up together at the door. I sit on a nearby chair to change my shoes, and before I have my dance shoes on, Debbie has been asked to dance by someone else. I dance throughout the night, and as is normal for a man who is outnumbered by women, there is no time for a break to talk to anyone. The place is full of ballroom dancers, and I am busy dancing every song.

Another woman I know from dance, Julia, is here, and I dance with her once. I am not interested in her at all since she had a temper outbreak last month. I had messed up a step and she called me a "pea-brain," then apologized later. It was ten minutes after that episode that she came out of the washroom with several feet of unnoticed toilet paper being dragged along stuck to the bottom of one of her dance shoes. Was it karma, or just a bad day?

I dance with a woman who lives in Boston and is visiting relatives for the weekend. She found the location of the dance party by searching the Internet. We dance a Foxtrot, and she gives me a post-dance analysis like a movie critic.

"The start was fine. The steps are too small for International, if that is what it was supposed to be. Your turns are too weak, your sway is not correct, and your head is too far forward. In general, you did fairly well and if you work harder you should get better."

My sense of courtesy overrides any response and silence becomes the better part of valour.

I decide to ask a woman out dancing to a practice party on a Sunday night. She is a mildly decent dancer but has a personality that drives me crazy in only one night. Her house looks like it was rearranged by a tornado, she is bossy, and acts jumpy, as if she drank too much coffee. Maybe I am too fussy? I want to dance, relax, and enjoy myself. The next day she sends me a ten-page e-mail outlining everything she knows about dancing—mainly pages pasted from various Web sites.

I ask a woman out, and we head downtown to a bar. She is older than I am but an absolutely wonderful person. Since I look younger than my age the visual effect is noticeable. When my date goes to the washroom, a young female bartender slides up to me and asks how we met. I admit to being a ballroom dancer, and the conversation continues from there. I jokingly mention that ballroom dancing will be in the Olympics in 2004 as a demonstration sport, so that leaves me only two more years to get ready.

About forty-five minutes later, with my date in the washroom for a second time, a shapely young female bartender shuffles over to my barstool, looks at me, and says, "I could not help it, but I overheard that you are a ballroom dancer. Are you getting ready for the Olympics? You must be amazing."

Trying desperately to somehow stay on this ego high based on misinformation and not to disappoint her, I reply, "No, I will not be in the Olympics, but I have been in a couple of judged competitions where I got really high marks." I am thinking of the plaque and what colour the buttons were before they fell off.

We continue talking, mainly with her saying how impressed she is with me, with dancing, or the Olympics. My head is too dizzy to remember which. She is still gushing when my date returns from the washroom. It is flattering, but I don't consider dating women who are young enough to sound exactly like a teenager.

Freda is a tiny, brilliantly intelligent woman who appears to have had no experience with men. She seems very nervous and very talkative. We have danced a number of times at different practice parties, and tonight she agrees to let me drive her to a dance since she has no car. We do a Tango, and she gets me to move very close to her. I know that this is how they dance it in advanced classes, but I am not quite comfortable rubbing the inside of my thighs against the inside of hers as we move slowly and sharply around the floor. After dancing with each other for a while, then with other people we know from previous dance events, I ask her to dance again and casually add something silly like, "You know how to Salsa, right?"

This is fairly innocent, yet friendly, I think to myself.

She agrees to dance but responds, "Don't you patronize me, or I'll get angry."

That's not very endearing. I don't think she means it to be harsh, but hey, who knows? Although she was initially very reluctant to attend, she seems to thoroughly enjoy herself and is dancing constantly. I struggle to get her to leave near the end of the evening. In fact, she dances the final three dances with the same man and is only ready to leave when the music stops at midnight. I think about going to the guy and telling him, "Get her phone number, you dummy," but I don't. It is an interesting experience and definitely not a date. I drive her home and do not walk her to her door.

Doug, Jim, and a third dance man that we know all meet at a dance party. We are slowly building up the "Single Guys Dance Club." We all have a great time. I meet a new woman who is roughly my age and very quiet. She is a pretty brunette, a beginning dancer, and is taking lessons at local high schools. We dance, talk, and there are no signs of interest. I also get a chance to talk to one of the other single women, Molly, a redhead. It is helpful that I get a chance to know people a bit before considering anything further. Molly is a nice person and attractive, but she seems to have a negative attitude. During a break I sit next to her and try to chat casually. She says little or nothing, never looks at me, and has a "looking into space" stance. When I was much younger, this meant either "get lost" or "I'm very shy." In my case, it was always the first one. I dance with someone else, and it is a good contrast in personalities. This woman is trying very hard to follow my lead and learn, yet smiles through it all. Why not? She is dancing with a charming, polite, and good-looking man. I look in the mirror to make sure it is me.

I notice an older woman across the room who is sitting by herself and ask her to dance. She turns out to be an excellent dance partner. She is from Saskatoon and is only visiting Ottawa for ten days. She loves dancing so much that she was determined to find a place to dance on her visit to Ottawa. When I ask how she managed to find this party, she replies that she looked in the Yellow Pages. Older women can be pretty smart. Next, I dance twice with a new woman who is a good dancer and very attractive. Then a man who is a better dancer monopolizes her for the rest of the night. That hardly seems fair and is poor dance etiquette with so many single men around. I also dance with another single woman who is tall and Asian. I don't know her name. During the evening, I dance with a lot of women and all the names get mixed up in my head. There are three Heathers, two Wendys, and several Moniques.

Being inexperienced with the singles scene, I learn a lot about women while learning to dance. I try to improve my social skills by complimenting them when I think they deserve it. When a man compliments a woman, the expected response is a smile and a thank you. Perhaps women are too nervous or too conscientious,

I don't know. A comedian tells a story where a thick book is shown to the audience and claims it is the complete rule book on women containing what they want, how they react, and why they do everything that they do. She opens the pages to show the audience, and every page is completely blank.

Man (me): "You look very nice tonight."

Woman (response): "Well, I guess I could lose a couple more pounds and I do work out as much as possible, but the place I used to go to closed down so now I go to another place which is not as good although they have a good aerobics class and the instructor is very energetic so the class tends to be tough to keep up with most of the time and there are a lot of people that don't keep up so maybe they should think about that."

Man (to different woman): "That is a lovely dress you are wearing tonight. I like it."

Woman (response): "I got it when I went shopping with my daughter and she picked it out but we went to a few different stores first and I thought that I should get something that would be good for dancing in, although I'm not too sure about the colour, but it is loose and I can move around well in it, which my daughter did not really consider because she just liked the colour and we were running out of time so I bought it."

On a Saturday night, I take a woman out dancing, which goes quite well with some Swing dancing, Cha-Cha, and Rumba. After dancing, we go for a drink and munchies at Kelsey's in the south of Ottawa. When we are finished, I walk her back to her car. We each drove our own car there, probably her safety mechanism in case I turned out to be a serial killer or possibly a very bad dancer. We stand in the parking lot beside her car and make small talk about how much we enjoy dancing. I give her a little good night hug and after that she still stands there. I think to myself, *Okay, what now? Why is she still standing here?* I also know that this is going to be the end of the evening because when I gave her the goodnight hug, she did "the dodge." This is a tactic used when the woman suspects that the man might actually try to kiss her, so she turns her head during the hug in order to be sure to end up dry. I had no intention of planting a kiss but I noticed the pre-emptive dodge. We are still standing there after the hug and saying nothing. So, being oblivious, I just give her another small hug and say good night again. She opens the car door and gets in her very small sporty car. When I try to bend over to bid a final goodbye, I hit my forehead on the top of the doorframe. What I realize the next day is that all evening I was a perfect gentleman, opening doors, fetching water, and paying for items. I did not realize that as we were walking across the parking lot, she pressed her remote control to unlock her car doors. She was waiting for me to open the car door for her, something that went right over my head because I always use a key to open my car door.

Most of my dating experiences have been limited to taking women to dances, and I decide to take the next step. I have not taken a woman out for dinner in several years. Tonight I find myself with a date at a small Japanese restaurant on a Saturday night. We make small talk, eat the appetizers, and wait for the main courses to arrive. I do not realize that my elbow has slowly nudged my unused wooden chop-sticks into a tea candle at the side of the table to my left. I look down casually and see the ends of my chopsticks on fire, and the flames are three or four inches high. They did not serve any water, so I can't use that to douse the playful flames. There is red wine in my glass but that would be a colossal waste. So, I quickly chug down a half glass of wine, and then use the bottom of the wine glass to stamp out and smother the flames. My date takes it all very calmly. Several minutes go by, and I overhear the maître d' asking people at the next table if they smell smoke. It is an interesting dinner.

A woman I know is excited about a new dance. I receive an e-mail from her saying she saw it on a television show. It is a Spanish dance where the person stamps her feet and clicks little castanets. I know this one is called the Flamenco, but she refers to it in the e-mail as the "flamingo" dance. Obviously she must be confusing it with that other dance normally done in Florida where you stand on one leg for an eternity then flap your arms and fly off when someone approaches.

One woman that I see at various dance locations and dance with a few times a night sends me a strange e-mail. I never felt any connec-tion other than the dance hold, so I am surprised when she writes that she is sad and feels rejected when I leave a dance without saying goodbye to her. This will undoubtedly lead me to a new experience with a woman because I now have to break up with someone that I never actually went out with. When I see her again, she insults me while we are dancing. She tells me that I do not smile enough and that my posture is terrible. She turns me sideways and tells me to look in the mirror. I reply that I'm glad she did that because I notice my shirt looks like it has a tail and needs to be tucked in at the back. How do people become so negative? It must consume a lot of their energy. My life needs to be on a positive track, and I have no patience for negative thought, negative expression, or immaturity.

After several dates and realizing that taking women out to dinner might not be my strong point, I stick to dance parties and continue to dance with a variety of women. Dancing a Waltz with a woman that I have no interest in beyond a dance, I mistakenly think that it would be nice to compliment her dress.

"That is a nice dress you are wearing."

Her response is sarcastic: "Oh, so you like dresses, but not me."

Shocked, I realize that she is reading more into my asking her for a dance than I intend. I am speechless, have no reply, and think about how her bitterness is more than a comment but is buried deep inside her. I hope she finds her way out of it, and my list of dance partners shrinks by one.

During one dance, a woman tells me that something looks wrong with my moustache. "I cannot explain it," she says directly. "Something is different. Your moustache looks odd."

Moustaches are not something to tamper with in men, because it is well known that a man's moustache is sacred. There is no food in it and it is neatly trimmed as usual. There may be a couple more grey hairs than normal. A different woman tells me that she does not really like it and suggests that I shave it off.

ADULT SINGLES DANCE

I attend a singles dance for people thirty-five years of age and older. None of the men know how to dance other than shuffling around and moving their bodies uncomfortably on the dance floor. They get louder after a couple of drinks and stop caring how they look. The women seem to increase the amount of hip gyration in proportion to how attracted they are to their dance partner. Some women get tired of waiting to be asked and go dance by themselves. The men line up along the wall beside the dance floor to get a good view of what is going on, looking the women up and down as they pass by. If they would only learn a few basic Rumba steps, they would have the confidence and ability to impress a partner. With a decent lead, any woman would be pleasantly surprised. It certainly is a good start.

I see a couple of other dance students that I know from various lessons and approach them. It is good to have someone to talk to. My friend Jim dances with a woman who tells him her life story during a four and a half minute song. She spills it all out, a pending divorce, two bitter children who need to grow up, a husband that recently moved in with another woman who is not divorced yet either. She includes the story of her job, where she is from and how life has treated her. At the end of the dance, she gives him a polite smile. Jim walks over to where I am standing and tells me that he suddenly feels exhausted.

It is obvious that most of the people here are well over forty. They give out tickets for a door prize, one of those rectangular beer coupons with numbers along the short side. When they read the winning number, everyone in the room squints at their ticket, scrambling to be under a stronger light and holding the ticket at the end of a fully outstretched arm. They have to make four or five draws before finding a winner, because no one that age can read numbers so small, and they are all too self-conscious to put on reading glasses.

They have a Merengue mixer, and I am partnered with a woman who looks to be over seventy. She is frail and sad that her husband has passed. I dance slowly and take small steps. She holds me at both elbows as if I were her son and talks about the decisions she made along the timeline of her life. There is regret and despair in her small grey eyes. We return to the mixer after the dance, and my next partner is a blue-eyed country gal who drove over forty highway minutes to get to the dance. She is brimming with energy, talks in a loud voice, and implies that she is looking for a husband. Her hair is a perfectly dyed blonde. She wears a nice white blouse and a pretty skirt with tiny polka dots. It sounds like she is in a hurry to get what she wants, and I am thankful the dance lasts only a few minutes. The next woman I dance with has a vacant look in her eyes and is dressed in black. My impression is that she is either totally disinterested, wanting to make that crystal clear, or totally depressed and this is the best she can do. I wonder why she joined the mixer. For the last mixer dance, I meet a woman who speaks in a slow monotone voice, saying she has two troublesome children from a recent divorce and this is her only night out every second weekend. There are dark circles under her eyes that the minimal makeup job doesn't conceal. She reeks of cigarette smoke and looks horribly unhappy; I try to maintain extra distance from her during the dance in order to avoid having an asthma attack.

My social life and my dance life have become a mixer of unsuitable partners and drama. Although learning to dance renewed my confidence and brought me a good dose of satisfaction, it may be time to move on to something new. There are other joys in life to experience and other paths to travel.

It is a difficult time for me, and I struggle to stay positive in the dance lessons. My face is smiling when I dance, although my heart is not in it. I keep dancing because I think it helps me endure life's little tests of my spirit. There are several stressful situations: my mother survives an encounter with bowel cancer; my father, in his eighties, develops skin cancer. After a growth is removed from my father's cheek, the doctor discovers that some cancer cells still remain. Dad goes back for more day surgery and more skin is removed. His face looks awful, but I reassure him that it looks fine. It heals well, though not quickly at his age. I think of my mortality and ponder my future. How important is dancing? Is this what I want to do? How long will I continue?

PART TWO

HAVING FUN

8

JUST DANCING

THE DANCE PARTNER

It is a dreary Friday night as I leave home. On this cool and overcast March evening, I drive alone to the weekly dance party at a studio for nine o'clock, uncertain how much longer my dance activities will continue. As a light drizzle begins to fall, the windshield wipers wave rhythmically back and forth, prompting my brain to connect the song on the radio to the beat of the wipers. My left foot uncontrollably begins to tap. There is plenty of free parking at the dance studio, and I try for a space near the entrance. I pay the entry fee to Daniella, a woman sitting at a table by the door; she is also a part-time dance instructor at the studio. I took a few lessons with her earlier in the year to learn the basics of Quickstep and improve my Cha-Cha. She asks if I am accompanied by anyone tonight, and I reply that I am not. As I start to move away, she mentions that two new female students are at the party near the other end of the studio and would I mind asking them for a dance or two so they will feel welcome. "No problem," I respond, without looking up.

I trudge along to a chair to change into my dance shoes as I survey the room to see if any women are sitting alone. They will be my main dance partners for the night. It is still early and the room has not yet filled with dancers. Then I spot her across the room sitting with her friend. She is a petite blonde beauty with an attractive, slender figure and an indescribable appeal in the way she wears her clothes. I am excited. I check my clothes to make sure I look halfway decent, pick some lint off my pants, and glance down to make sure that I remembered to put both socks on that morning.

It takes thirty minutes for me to get the courage to ask her to dance. "Would you like to dance?" I ask politely, extending my hand.

"Yes," she replies quietly, "but I am a beginner."

We manage our way through a Cha-Cha, despite my nervousness. She is wearing a strapless red dress, revealing clear, smooth skin and that delightful figure. We introduce ourselves and the dance continues without much more conversation. She has the most engaging brown eyes that I have ever seen. When the dance is over, I escort her courteously off the dance floor and to be polite I ask her friend to dance next. These are the two new female students. Before the night is over, I ask for a second dance from the charming brown-eyed beauty. Her smile lights up the entire room, and I am smitten. I silently thank all my dance teachers and make a promise to myself to work harder if only I can maintain balance on these wobbly legs just this one time.

The evening ends, and I lose track of her. In my honourable single-man tradition of making sure the single women all have an opportunity to dance, I get distracted—and now I realize that she is gone. Although I return every week, she does not appear again and I become despondent. Finally, it is two months later, and I notice her sitting patiently waiting for someone to ask her to dance. This time I cannot afford to be so shy and I ask her quickly for a dance. When we dance a Rumba, fireworks go off in my head every time I look in her eyes. She looks incredible, is polite, and is an enjoyable dance partner. We move gently in unison to the romantic Latin rhythm. She is wearing a lovely sequined silver top and black skirt.

"Your eyes sparkle," I offer sincerely.

"That must be my contact lenses," she replies innocently. "They are very dry tonight."

I ask her out for dinner.

Dinner at the Mediterranean restaurant goes well, even though in my excitement I stab a piece of lettuce too vigorously and splash salad dressing on my shirt, exactly where my heart is. We feel an immediate connection and attend dance practice parties together and dance with each other frequently. Every time I touch her, a warm feeling races up my arm and, judging from her smile, I have to guess that she might be feeling something too. There is an undeniable chemistry. On the dance floor, we experience more than just a connection of two dancers; there is a special feeling between us. We start taking lessons together and go to every dance event that has a reasonable dance floor and sounds like a good place to dance. Jill has less dance experience than I do but makes up ground quickly with incredible energy and determination combined with a fierce passion for the music. She learns quickly.

Jill was born in the Azores, and her parents moved from the poverty of the rural island of Pico to Montreal when she was three years old. She grew up in the Chateauguay area of Montreal and learned to speak three languages, English, French, and Portuguese. She is a slim, five-foot-tall, vivacious individual with class and energy. She loves dancing. Her shapely figure and blonde hair attract a lot of interest and, like all fashionable Montreal women, she has a knack for knowing how to dress well. On the inside is a tender and caring woman. When we meet new people or see old friends, she expresses a genuine camaraderie that is far too rare in the world. When we dance, she takes pride in exhibiting both proper technique and overall enjoyment.

TAKING LESSONS TOGETHER

We register for group lessons at an independent studio. During one group lesson, we are told that there will be a different dance instructor because, as the owner of the studio explains it, our male instructor went to day surgery for the "snip-snip" operation, and did not realize that he would not be able to dance or even walk well afterwards. Most of us recognize the reference to a vasectomy. It is about five or ten minutes into the class when a man with a thick European accent shuffles next to me and touches my shoulder.

"Excuse me, but my English is not so good. What is the 'snip-snip'? What does that mean?"

I struggle to explain in a low voice, trying to decide how to communicate the after-effects of this delicate operation and can only come up with such epic lines as, "He can no longer make babies," and "It stops working in a certain way."

In the end, I think the man concludes that our precious instructor had the whole sausage chopped off or at least seriously damaged. He winces in empathetic pain several times during the dance lesson.

We start a group dance lesson and during warm-up I give Jill an underarm turn left during a Waltz. It is an awkward lead and she struggles.

The instructor walks by and says, "Did you really think she was going to be able to follow that lead?"

I consider his tone a touch on the rude side and am surprised that a teacher would talk like that. He starts the ninety-minute class by talking for thirty minutes, telling us every nuance of the hold position, feet, and movement, and reviewing most of the steps we should have learned by now. People shuffle their feet, losing interest and getting impatient to do more than listen. This is a dance lesson—why is there no dancing? Not everyone learns by standing around, and not every instructor is the right one for us. We are not discouraged but decide to drop the group class with that instructor and go somewhere else for lessons.

We find an energetic and enthusiastic teacher for weekly private lessons and improve our Salsa, Swing, and Rumba. We also look around the city and find workshops at different studios for Salsa, Cha-Cha, and Swing. We go to practice parties twice a week, dancing for a minimum of three to four times during most weeks. There is a monthly Salsa workshop at a local studio. We register for it and try to learn the complex intermediate-level pattern. Teachers have told me that a student rarely learns a new pattern with only a one-time introduction, and yet here we are with the belief that somehow we will retain it after several attempts during the forty-five-minute workshop. Learning a pattern after seeing it only once is a big challenge. However, we hope for success, since we have a solid understanding of the basics of Salsa as well as the ability to practise in the next few days. There is a Salsa party after the workshop, and people demonstrate a multitude of patterns. There are spins, fancy foot patterns, hand flips, and dips. We pause and reflect on how learning a dance can be accelerated with a focus on only one or two dances. We work on about twelve different dances and try to improve them all.

We are now moving into what I consider to be intermediate-level social dancing. We start to feel good about ourselves; we are able to dance around the room looking as if we really know what we are doing. There are still dances such as the Viennese Waltz that are commonly played at dances, and perhaps we should start to learn a basic step or two.

At this point, we discover that there are a lot more dances than expected, and a lot more to discover. In Latin, there is the sexy

Bachata, the dramatic Paso Doble, and the smooth Bolero. In California, there is a West Coast Swing that is very different from the basic Triple Swing or East Coast Swing. There is the Argentine Tango, which is different than the normal Tango. And new information surfaces—for instance, one can dance a Hustle to the same music as the Cha-Cha! Where does it end? How much more is there to learn? Dancing is a lifelong learning activity. The Swing dance genre also has Lindy Hop and Balboa, not to mention older versions like the Charleston. If a person's taste is more toward country music, there is the Two-step. If that's not enough why not do some Polka? Rather than getting discouraged at all the potential dances, it is easier to simply set goals. These are all good dances. With a good customized plan of action, a dancer develops skills according to his or her preferences. The ultimate goal is the same for everyone. Go have fun!

On Saturday night, I take Jill to a West Coast Swing dance in a community centre. It has a beautiful sprung hardwood floor with less impressive painted concrete walls and a tall ceiling like a school gymnasium. Jill does not know West Coast Swing but is eager to give it a try. We have been taking dance lessons together for six months, and this is developing into an excellent dance partnership as well as a deep romantic relationship. We dance some East Coast Swing, Cha-Cha, a couple of Rumbas, and a Waltz. There is a short group workshop, and we try the country Two-step. The dancers grab their partners and form a big circle around the outer edge of the dance floor. After a bit of instruction on footwork, timing, and dance hold, the music starts, and we are all moving counter-clockwise doing the Two-step. It is great fun with these basic steps, although we are wary of the next progression. The steps get more challenging, the foot positions are tricky, and my arms go everywhere except the right place to lead the steps properly. This will require more practice.

As is usual when out dancing, we meet a few other dancers that we know. We laugh at our common problems and quickly become acquainted with a few more people who love to dance.

On Sunday, a dance instructor we know has a potluck lunch at her house in a small town called Carleton Place, a short drive outside Ottawa. Around eighteen or twenty people attend, which is considered a very good turnout. The buffet is laid out along the kitchen counter, and people have an opportunity to make small talk. At the start of the lunch, the only item that we know we have in common is that we are all dance students. By the end of the lunch, we have new friends and have learned more about the people we already knew. The food is great, and afterwards we even do a bit of dancing in a small room with a wooden floor. One of the women attending tells us that her car had stalled a couple of blocks from the house and asks people to help her. So, after most of the food is gone, a group of us go out to look at it and possibly give it a push to get it started again. It must have been funny to see an eclectic mix of twelve adults walking through the small town looking like they want trouble, whereas in reality they are all ballroom dancers. She gets in the car, turns the key in the ignition, and it starts right away. We are proud of having to do nothing at all and walk back to the house with our dance posture chests held a bit higher.

The new dance movie *Shall We Dance* is about to open in Ottawa. The movie was originally to have been filmed in Toronto, but due to the SARS health scare at the time, filming was moved to Winnipeg. The producers put out a casting call to high-level Canadian dancers to help fill in the competition scenes. One of the competition scene dancers selected is a local teacher and studio owner that we know, Josée Lepine. The studio arranges a special preview showing at the theatre, and most people decide to treat this as a semi-formal attire event. The theatre in the west end of Ottawa is packed, and everyone is waiting for the moment when Josée and her partner will appear. It is over halfway through the film when we finally catch a glimpse of the instructor as she and her partner dance by in the background. Nevertheless, it is a great time; everyone is dressed up and in good spirits.

As I watched the movie, I thought of the similarities of all the dance characters to real people I know at the dance studio. The characters are exaggerated, but not that far from reality. I empathized with the plot and the main character, although I look nothing like Richard Gere. His character's desire to keep dance lessons secret from other people is often close to the truth. For men, there is still a bit of stigma in learning to do ballroom dancing. A key message for all of us who view the movie is the intense love for dancing that develops from learning how to move well on the dance floor. When the movie is over, we all pour out of the theatre and travel to Josée's studio for some free dancing.

Unlike previous women I have danced with, Jill thoroughly enjoys every moment. She floats with the music and does her best to follow a dance pattern when I destroy a step. During a lovely Waltz, Jill says, "Every time I dance with you my heart beats just a little faster."

She talks about how much she loves to dance and how much fun she has when we dance together. Our romance is growing. We feel a special chemistry between us and finally know what it means to have that. We enjoy being with each other and enjoy doing everything together. It also becomes a relationship where we support and help each other through good times and the more difficult times.

After taking group lessons and some private lessons with different teachers, we go to see my former teacher, from whom I first started taking lessons at the Arthur Murray studio. Melanie has returned to Ottawa after spending time in Alberta and is now teaching at an independent studio. It is great to see her again.

Taking regular lessons together, Jill and I notice a dramatic improvement in our dancing. We work on American Social style. Our worst dance is the Waltz, so that is what we pick to improve first. Our dance teacher immediately senses the close personal relationship between Jill and myself and says, "It's time for you to dance in closed hold."

DANCE HOLD: CLOSED POSITION

As dance skills become more advanced, dancers move to a closed hold in the standard or smooth dances. A closed hold is fairly similar to the open hold, except the dancers are much closer, usually touching, with the right side of the man's rib cage against the woman's right side. There is no rule saying the couple must be constantly touching during the dance, although it is important to be close to each other, have synchronized movement, and maintain a good shape and flow as the couple moves along the floor. In many ways it makes dancing easier, since the turns are tighter and the couple tends not to lose track of each other. On the other hand, there has to be a very good lead and follow to avoid looking like a lurching bus or catching the accordion syndrome. There are occasions when we glide across the floor, dancing as if there were wheels on our feet. To make it a more Canadian analogy, we glide as if we were on skates, and the hard, clear ice surface is unmarked by any scratch or bump. I now realize why so many figure skaters choose to improve their skills by taking ballroom dance lessons.

Dance posture continues to be an important aspect to achieve better dancing. One instructor tells Jill to extend herself upward as if she is wearing a necklace with a beautiful medallion on her chest and wants to show it off. I am told to think of the front of my chest as headlights and to shine them on the ceiling. My head also needs to move back and up with an extended neck instead of tilting forward. This all reminds me of when my daughter took ballet lessons. A good part of every ballet class was used to teach proper posture.

One of the visual illusions in ballroom dancing is the smoothness a dance couple shows as their upper bodies move around the floor. It looks like the whole dance is effortless because the top half generally does not move. Although it requires a strong and firm upper body, in reality, the lower half does all the work. The legs, ankles, hip joints, and feet are working intensely to preserve the illusion, and above the waist, the torso, arms, and muscles behind the shoulder blades have to be both solid and relaxed to be effective. I am reminded of the analogy of a duck gliding along the surface of the water, yet no one sees the legs paddling furiously to keep it moving.

Here are some good suggestions I receive as an intermediate-level dancer:

- Maintain a firm frame.
- Work your lower body to make the smooth dances glide and the Latin dances sizzle.
- Dance with feeling for the music.

The frame consists of both posture and dance hold. At this level, a dancer should be comfortable lifting up the rib cage, holding the head up, and keeping the arms solid with elbows to the side and slightly in front of the shoulders for the smooth dances. Most dancers have a good frame at the start of the dance, but the trick is to maintain it all the way through a four-minute song. The muscles will be more toned in time, and when maintaining a solid frame becomes a constant habit, it will be more noticeable when it falters.

In standard dances, the hips, legs, and ankles are used to create the smooth, grand movement around the floor. The legs need to move deliberately and purposefully. There should be nothing tentative about the movement now (unless you are trying to avoid being hit by a speed demon doing the Viennese Waltz through oncoming traffic).

Latin dances require hip movement. We practise in front of a mirror on a regular basis, and I recall being told that a man can impress women with even a small amount of proper hip movement. My hips are stiff, and I struggle to get them to move in the proper directions. On the other hand, women's hips look like they are naturally built to swivel. For women, it is important to learn the proper hip motion for each dance, because they are not all the same. Many women new to Latin dancing see dancers' hips moving and try to emulate the motion. They gyrate furiously because it looks like so much fun, but it looks much better if performed with control and discipline.

There is an immediate intimacy with ballroom dancing. The partners touch each other, and in closed position this is exacerbated by the closeness of the whole body, including the hips. Dancing in closed position for smooth dances during a lesson presents another challenge. When Jill needs help with a step that I am not doing properly, our instructor takes the man's lead part and dances Jill through it. On many occasions this is hilarious as the two women unsuccessfully attempt to keep from brushing breasts while dancing together in closed position; inevitably they get in the way. It is a consequence of teaching, and both of them burst into laughter as they make their way down the line of dance for a couple of closed-position steps until their breasts bump together.

DANCE MUSIC

For me, dancing is all about feeling the music. By the time a person is comfortable with a few steps in several dances, the next level is to gain a greater appreciation for the music that goes with each type of dance. A dancer who has feeling for the music may extend the length of the second beat in Waltz a fraction longer; or step firmly on the two-count in Mambo. In Cha-Cha, a dancer will hold the first count for a fraction longer than normal and make it a firm step with weight over that foot. In Jive, our steps are no longer an equal distance apart in the side step as the feet do a short side step then a longer side step, counted as 1-a-2. Bouncy Jive music enters my ears, moves through my spine, and produces energy that results in the appropriate body and foot movement for the dance. I love live music played by good musicians. Alternately, a good DJ with a reasonably good sound system works well for dancers. Dance venues that have only a small CD player and weak music create the biggest challenge for me in getting a sense of rhythm and style. If there is no passion for the music, it is only half a dance.

Most of the music we listen to in North America or Europe is based on four beats to a bar. The Waltz has three beats or is set in 3/4 time. The first clue to determine what dance is appropriate is the speed of the music. For a normal dance venue, we can keep it simple and assume these are the dances that will be involved:

Smooth: Foxtrot (Slowfox), Waltz (Slow Waltz), Tango

Latin: Rumba, Cha-Cha, Salsa/Mambo, Samba, Merengue, Jive/Swing

The first step is to quickly decide some characteristics of the song that is being played.

1. Is it slow or fast?

2. Does it sound like Latin music?

3. What is the timing of the beat, 4/4 or 3/4?

In general, slower music is for dancing Rumba, Waltz, and sometimes Foxtrot. Faster music will be used to dance Merengue, Salsa, or Jive/Swing. If the music is slow and you can count the beats as 1-2-3, 1-2-3, then obviously it is a Waltz. If it has a slow, sexy rhythm and is 4/4 time, then it is probably a Rumba. Foxtrot is a bit faster than Rumba but has a distinctive feel like you want to swing your arms, snap your fingers, and walk somewhere.

Tango has a unique sound punctuated with drama and abrupt pauses. Once you hear a few Tangos, it is easy to recognize the music. What is referred to as Rock 'n' Roll music is normally danced as a

Swing or Cha-Cha. If you hear heavy thumping beats on the 1 and 3 it is probably Swing. With slower Rock 'n' Roll music, a Triple Swing is appropriate or, to a faster beat, Jive. Cha-Cha music can be very distinctive Latin music, although Cha-Cha is also danced to many pop or pop/rock songs. A Latin Cha-Cha usually has a distinctive sound made by an instrument called a *guiro*, or scraper, which looks like a stick brush rubbed over a tiny cheese grater. Listen to some music by Santana and it should be noticeable.

If you are listening to Latin music and it is very fast with lots of instruments all over the place, including whistles, then that is probably a Merengue. People dance a simple 1-2 step to it—it is so fast you don't have time to do anything else. To stay on the beat, dancers keep the steps small. Beginners usually look like they are marching in order to stay on the beat. It is important not to swing the upper body unless you are in the Dominican Republic and have had a few drinks.

There are more clues when trying to decipher Latin music. Relatively fast music with a stick hitting a cowbell is Salsa. Medium-speed music with a playful feeling is usually Cha-Cha. Latin music with clearly accentuated heavy beats is usually Samba, although a popular modern Samba is "I'm Alive," by Celine Dion.

Once the basics are mastered, the next step is to move on to music that is a little more difficult to decipher. If you hear a Rumba that is far too slow for Rumba, then it is probably a Bolero. Think of a song like "Unchained Melody." The same holds true for Swing. If a Swing tune is very slow, it is probably better to dance West Coast Swing. The ultimate West Coast swing song is "Mustang Sally." A very slow Tango that sounds a little different is an Argentine Tango.

Deciphering the music

Beats per bar

2			Merengue
3	slow		Slow Waltz
	fast		Viennese Waltz
4	slow	Latin-like	Rumba
	very slow		Bolero

4	slow	Big Band sound	Foxtrot
	fast	links 4 and 1	Cha-Cha
		heavy 1-a-2	Samba
	fast	Rock 'n' Roll	Triple Swing
	very fast	Rock 'n' Roll	Jive or Quickstep
4	sharp	dramatic	Tango

Current pop music is also danceable as long as it has a consistent beat. Pink and Shania Twain have some great Cha-Chas. Rock or alternative bands heard on the radio play Swing tunes and their ballads are usually a Rumba. Rap music and reggae are probably the toughest to dance. Some reggae music works with a Swing or Samba. If the rap music is fast enough, it could be a Merengue, but that is simply turning the beats into foot movement with little feeling for the music.

The problem with some music is not about the beat but about the *feeling* of the song. Words and music that express fighting, death, and poverty might not be upbeat enough to encourage anyone to stand up and dance. Anything with a positive message is easily danceable.

Now that I have learned ballroom and Latin dancing, the music sounds different. The songs are the same but the interpretation or how to listen to them changes. I start thinking about what the count is and how to follow the beat. Where is the first beat in a bar? Hey, that song is a Cha-Cha! When I crave a good Foxtrot, I tune in to an appropriate radio station or pull out some old CDs that were previously considered boring. Singers that were dull are now interesting. For practising Swing and Cha Cha, I gain a renewed interest in '50s and '60s music. For a great Waltz, Jill and I rediscover Perry Como, Johnny Mathis, and Nat King Cole. Suddenly, Latin music has meaning. When energetic rock bands perform a slow, quiet ballad, it turns into a sensitive Rumba or Bolero. This is not overwhelming. We feel like our minds have been opened and we gain a greater appreciation for all music. I feel enlightened. From the Big Band era, Rock 'n' Roll, Disco, Latin, and country music, there are songs for dancing in all styles and genres. Not all songs in every genre are good, and yes, I can only swallow a small dose of Disco tunes at a time. The point is that one's taste and music appreciation can change and one can become open to enjoying a wider variety of melodic sounds.

9

USEFUL TERMS AND MIXERS

The world of dance has its own terminology, and there are many new and unfamiliar words. It is a unique vocabulary spoken by ballroom dancers and dance teachers. Below is a small sample of some of the more commonly used terms. The Internet is a good reference tool, and Wikipedia pages are helpful.

USEFUL TERMS

Back leading: I always understood this to be when the follower of a dance couple initiates the next step in such a determined manner that the leader has no other choice of steps to take. After researching it further, I find that this is officially known as "hijacking." However, I don't know of anyone who uses that term. The true meaning of back leading is when the follower anticipates the lead before the leader commits to taking a step. There is a subtle difference between the two terms: hijacking is deliberate and back leading is more or less unintentional.

Contrary (Contra) body movement (CBM): Officially, this is the small movement of the opposite side of the body during a step. When a forward step is taken, for example with the left foot down the line of dance, the body has three possible positions: The upper body could turn to the diagonal wall; continue to face the line of dance; or, in the contrary position, turn slightly to diagonal centre. In American style Foxtrot, every forward and back step could have a small amount of CBM in the basic pattern. The term "contrary" is used because opposites are involved. When walking naturally, the left hand swings forward when the right foot takes a step, and vice versa. It needs to be small and should not be a break in posture.

Contrary body movement position (CBMP): This refers more specifically to the foot position when the foot is placed on the same line or across the line of the supporting foot.

Cuban motion: This is a Latin hip motion created by bending and straightening the legs.

Develop: This involves the time it takes for the Latin hip motion created by bending and straightening the legs. When a teacher says to *take time to develop*, it usually means that the student is: (a) moving to the step too quickly or (b) finishing the step and just standing there like a frozen statue instead of continuing the motion with the hips.

Dip: A dip is where the man holds the woman with one or both arms under her back for support, allowing her to lower her body into a position more horizontal to the floor. There are side dips, where the dancers are facing ninety degrees from each other, and front dips, where the woman is lowered away from the man. Dips are frequently seen in shows and taught in American Social style dancing to add flair and to show off. The man needs to be very steady on the supporting leg and not let the woman fall on the floor. The man's supporting leg can bend, and the non-supporting leg can slowly slide to the side for dramatic effect. The woman's role in the dip is to look very good, comfortable and confident in the man's arms, while radiating sex appeal. In theory, a dip can be performed without the man's support. Women should think about bending over backwards, bent knees out forward for balance, and the back extended. With the right balance, a lot of the dip—if not all of it—can be done without the man; the man's arm merely acts as a backup safety net in case the woman gets carried away with the moment.

Fake step: The fake step (also known as "eating a step") is when the feet don't move to the beat in the expected timing. It generally refers to any action that changes foot movement—either one less step or one more than your partner. In other words, one partner has a step that continues on the beat of the music, and the other partner has to make a foot movement that does not match. A good example is in Cha-Cha when the partners go from a position facing each other to a shadow position where they are side by side. It was in learning American Social style dancing that I first heard the term "fake step" being used.

Footwork: Footwork is the official term used when describing what part of the foot touches the floor first. Teachers refer to "heel leads" and "toe leads" in the various steps. It may also include landing on the ball of the foot first then lowering the heel, known as "ball flat," using outside edges of the foot; or other aspects pertaining to the feet landing on the floor.

Foot position: Foot position usually refers to the position of the feet in relation to the body. Alignment of the feet helps understand a dancer's position on the floor such as "facing line of dance" or "diagonal wall." A normal dance floor is a rectangle with two longer walls referred to as the "long wall" in dance terminology, and the short walls are called the "short wall." The orientation or direction that a man faces in a dance is technically called the man's foot position, or where his toes are supposed to be pointing. The line of dance or the direction that dancers move around the floor is counterclockwise. Alignment can include foot position by making the distinction between the direction the dancer is travelling and where the feet are pointing.

When the man is standing in the corner with his back to a short wall and facing down the line of dance to the opposite short wall and with a long wall immediately to his right, he is said to be facing line of dance. When the man makes a one-quarter turn to the right, he is facing diagonal wall. When the man makes a one-quarter turn from the line of dance to the left, he is facing diagonal centre. When he turns halfway around from the line of dance, he is considered to be "backing line of dance." Less-used terms are "backing diagonal wall" and "backing diagonal centre." It all gets a little more complicated when the couple finishes the first long wall and turns in the corner for the short wall. You may think the man is diagonal centre, but he is actually diagonal wall facing the short wall because the references begin again at the start of each wall. The terms help dancers understand alignment of steps and where they need to be in a routine, which is especially important for me in International Standard dance routines.

Hand flip: There is a Salsa move where the man flips the woman's arm from one position to the next. The woman keeps her elbow and wrist stiff. The man takes her palm with his palm and gives it a quick flip. For example, if the woman's hand is resting in the man's palm in front of him at the waist, he gives it a flick with his wrist, and the arm moves up and barely over his head to land in the man's palm, which is moved and placed behind his back. It is usually done at least two times and has an interesting effect in the middle of a Salsa.

Hand slide: In Latin dances, the man takes one or both of the woman's hands, typically after a spin, and places them behind his head at the moment he releases them. The woman then slides her hand from his shoulder down his arm to be connected again when it gets to his hand.

Heel lead: When taking a step in dance, the heel lands first before the weight is moved to the foot. It should not be exaggerated with the toe of the shoe high in the air. In some cases, landing on a flat foot is also considered a heel lead.

Jack and Jill: This is a competition where the dance partners are randomly matched prior to starting so that no one has the advantage of dancing with his or her normal partner. See more in the section on Mixers.

Heel turn: Heel turns are when the heels of both feet come together, then the dancer rotates to face a new direction. There are heel turns for both the man and woman in a number of dances. In International Foxtrot, a Reverse Turn involves a heel turn for the woman and the Impetus Turn involves a heel turn for the man.

Line of dance (LOD): The line of dance is the direction dancers should move around the floor in order to have some semblance of order from what could otherwise be total chaos. This applies to all ballroom-style dances that move such as Foxtrot, Waltz, and Tango. The line of dance is counterclockwise. When you learn to move around the floor, start along one wall then turn left at the corner. If you cannot turn left, you are going the wrong way. Everyone goes in the same direction so that there are fewer collisions. There will be *some* collisions, but not with the force of people going the wrong way on a one-way street and suddenly meeting someone coming in the opposite direction. The line of dance imperative also includes the

Samba, once you get to know it. For on-the-spot dances such as Salsa and Jive, the best course of action is to stake out your space and stay there.

There are some cases where two different dances could be done to the same music, such as Jive and Quickstep. In that case, the on-the-spot dancers go to the middle of the floor, and the line-of-dance dancers move around the perimeter.

Outside partner: When the man's steps are to the woman's side instead of being in line, he is said to be dancing "outside partner." The man simply steps slightly more to the diagonal left in a forward step with the left foot and maintains a frame that keeps the woman to his right. The tendency is to exaggerate the frame twist or the diagonal step. The woman has nothing to do. It is the man that makes it work.

Promenade position: This is a position where the dancers seem to be dancing sideways. The position is to the leader's left, while the partners nearly face each other, with the leader's right side of the body and the follower's left side of the body being closer than the respective opposite sides. Steps of both partners are basically sidewise or diagonally forward with respect to their bodies. Normally the dancers look in the direction of the intended movement.

Shadow position: In this position, both dance partners' bodies are aligned and face the same direction.

Slot dance: This is a dance that moves back and forth along a straight line. Some teachers put a piece of tape in a straight line on the floor and encourage dancers to remain on or as close to the tape as possible during the movements. A typical slot dance is West Coast Swing.

Spotting: This is a well-known technique for spins used in ballet, figure skating, and dancing. The person doing the spin "spots" an object and holds his/her head in place as long as possible at the start of the spin. At some point the head turns around faster than the body and re-spots the same object. It is used to prevent spinners from getting dizzy when doing multiple spins.

Starter step: A step that is used at the start of a dance to ensure that the couple begins on the correct foot and dances on the proper beat is known as a starter step. It is intended to allow a nice takeoff into the first pattern and might be compared to cranking an engine to get started, then driving around. You need only crank it once. In smooth dances, it can be seen at the start of a dance to make sure the couple is synchronized with the music and on the same foot. It can also be a forward or side step; for example, with the man's left foot in order to begin the dance on his right foot. In the Cha-Cha and Mambo, it may be used in American Social style to start the basic pattern. Some varieties of Hustle and West Coast also have a starter step.

Strict tempo music: This term refers to the beats per minute or bars per minute of the music being played for a specific dance. It might help to think of it as the speed of the music—how fast it is. The slow Waltz tempo is twenty-eight to thirty bars per minute, which is much stricter than if the range were as much as ten bars per minute wider. For modern competitions, the tempo is within a narrow range to allow consistency in the dances. Ballroom dance CDs frequently advertise themselves as strict tempo music, meaning that they are within the specified range for that dance. That does not guarantee they are good songs for dancing or whether the beat is clear.

Supporting foot: A frequent expression used by teachers, it means the leg and foot that bears the full weight during a step.

Sway: Sway is a styling "look" that the couple has during the smooth dances. The upper body tilts slightly one way or the other, but there is no bending at the waist to create it. Sway should occur naturally from the movement of the legs. It is a difficult concept to perform well and extremely easy to do poorly. It should be very smooth and not look like a big windshield wiper going back and forth. Sway is a gentle tilt of the body away from the moving foot and toward the inside of a turn. There are exceptions, and this is a very simplistic explanation.

Syncopation: The easiest way to describe this in dancing is stepping on an unstressed beat. It is used for a more dramatic effect. It also refers to taking more than one step in one beat as in the Cha-Cha or Triple Swing.

MIXERS

Mixers are dance patterns performed by a group of people to music in order to select and change dance partners, adding some variety and a social aspect to the event. The desired outcome is to allow people to dance with several different partners so as to improve dance skills or meet new people.

Merengue mixer

The men stand in a large circle facing inward and the women form a circle inside facing outward. This can be reversed if it works better—usually the smaller group forms the inside circle. The Merengue music starts and everyone takes short Merengue steps sideways to the left. In this example, the men's circle will be moving clockwise, and the women's circle will be moving counterclockwise. The music plays for fifteen or twenty seconds. When the music stops, the man takes the woman directly in front of him, or as close as possible to being in front of him, as his dance partner. A variation on this mixer is to use a count of eight. Eight steps are taken on the spot; during the next eight beats, the dancers go into an open break leading into a woman's underarm turn left; after the woman completes the turn, she takes a large step that puts her in front of the next male partner. This type of mixer works well when there is an unequal number of men and women.

Basic ballroom mixer

For this mixer, the men form a line in single file along a long wall and face the short wall. The women line up single file along the opposite long wall and face the same short wall. Both groups walk forward, turning at the corner and meeting at the middle of the short wall. As each man and woman meet, they pair off for a dance. The next man and woman in their respective lines meet at the middle, and so on. Once a dance is completed, the partners go back to the end of their respective lines and walk in line to get a different partner. This also works well when there is an unequal number of dancers in each line.

Paul Jones mixer

This is a dance mixer that was popular in the early 1900s. A caller or master of ceremonies is selected. The dancers join their hands to form a circle, with women to the right of their partners. At a second signal, the dancers repeatedly do a right and left switching move known as the Grand Right and Left, a popular square-dance pattern. The man turns to face the woman on his right, taking her right hand with his right hand, and the woman moves to the man's right, getting passed clockwise around the circle. For the next woman in line, the man takes her left hand in his left hand and passes her to his left. On the next signal, the partners holding hands become dance partners. The circle forms again and the process is repeated.

10

DANCING AND SOCIAL SKILLS: RESPECT

Is there a special factor or undeniable charisma that catches the eye when a dance couple moves across the floor in what seems like pure pleasure? The outward presentation may represent great dance chemistry, a solid partnership, and positive energy. Unseen characteristics of the couple may also have an impact on the overall presentation. What level of respect does the couple receive from other dancers? Beyond the outward appearance, becoming a respected dancer should be a goal and it requires adherence to basic rules of etiquette and more. For an experienced social dancer, poise and courtesy need to be part of the overall image. Contributing factors are good interpersonal skills, impeccable social habits, and humble behaviour. When positive feelings surround a dance couple, it strengthens them and promotes an atmosphere of respect among all the other dancers.

Great chemistry is more than the connection between partners. It is a factor that makes the partnership greater than the sum of the two partners separately. Two reasons why some couples look so comfortable with each other is their ability to empathize with their partner's feelings and their combined desire to make every dance an enjoyable event. They understand each other's frustration instead of complaining about results, they take responsibility to work harder and perform better, and they share in successes because they have achieved them together. A good sense of humour is also essential. When something goes wrong we try to smile or laugh and move on. If it is a huge disaster, it will make a great story to tell. After a bad moment or series of poorly executed dance patterns, I like to wait for a Latin dance, and as we dance, I look into Jill's eyes and give her a mischievous smile. After a misstep or a disagreement, a little playful flirting is healthy.

On or off the dance floor, dancers build a reputation that follows them in the dance community. We feel an obligation, as more experienced dancers, to welcome new people. This not only makes them feel accepted but can lead to new friendships, and frequently we are surprised to discover experiences in common. The dance community is like a big family. Many friendships will be formed and many acquaintances made; we find that it enriches our life. We try to be a good family member, are open to new people, avoid creating a clique or demeaning others, and practise good etiquette as an example to encourage other dancers.

WITHOUT A PARTNER

The popularity of any individual depends on a number of factors, and being a good dancer is a good way to meet other people who have no dance partner. Good dancers are always in demand, and the key to becoming a good dancer is to learn the steps well and practise. Being a polite and respectful person increases the odds of finding a good dance partner and certainly increases the possibility of creating close friendships and relationships. The ability to lead or follow intricate or complex new steps is not the most important criterion for attracting a dance partner. Doing several basic steps extremely well with a smile can leave a far better impression.

Due to the nature of dance, there is the opportunity to meet many people of the opposite gender. A man who finds a woman attractive should not badger her, harass her, or stalk her in order to win her over. A more gentle approach will probably be more effective and will also garner good will with others who may be aware of what is happening. It is not acceptable for a man to ignore a woman's existing relationship or that ring on her finger and decide to insinuate himself into her life. Similarly, a woman may be infatuated with a truly divine dancer. That does not give her the right to monopolize or flirt excessively with him. There is a natural playfulness in the Latin dances, so all dancers need to be wary of the difference between simply having fun and an invitation for more.

Physical attraction is a more obvious factor in getting asked to dance. Good grooming and an appealing look are part of our culture of attractiveness. It is important to look good, but remember that as well as one's "look," a great personality, smile, and ability to dance will keep people coming back for more. When you feel you are not participating in enough dances, it may be time to try the line dances, if they are offered; or walk over to someone, introduce yourself, and make small talk. Sitting in a chair looking sullen is not inviting. Before meeting Jill, when I looked for a partner for a dance, my eyes would zoom in on women who seemed to be really enjoying the music, tapping their feet to the beat, and ready to go. When asked to dance, they would jump up and start moving before you could catch up to them.

A dance couple, married or simply regular dance partners, may decide to dance with many other dancers during a social evening. This is a great opportunity to share their skills. However, the smoothness of the regular dance couple might not easily translate to other pairings, and dancing might be awkward based on unrealistic expectations. The same rules of etiquette apply in this case. Dancers who are unfamiliar with each other need to dance within their ability and not try to show off every new step they have recently learned.

ROMANCE

Dancing is an intimate activity. There is one person in the arms of another with background music playing and the two people are moving around the floor in unison. That in itself is romantic. However, each dance is only a small conversation, not a lifelong commitment. Continued conversations and more dances may lead to more conversations away from the dance floor and eventually to more than just conversations. Dancing is a fabulous way to meet people. It requires good manners, discretion, and picking up on signals. Is he or she truly interested in you or was that just a good dance? The fortunate aspect to partner dancing is that it allows people to meet and get to know each other better before seeking a personal relationship. Dancers need to be realistic in reading signs, especially for men, since we are notoriously bad at it.

If a woman is already in a relationship, if there is a huge age difference, or if the two people have totally opposite interests, then it might be safe to assume this may not be a good match. Dancing is fun, and women can get carried away in a Latin dance by flirting and being playful, but it may not be a sign of interest. Good communication with a dance partner will clarify any misunderstandings. It would be good to find a common interest outside of dance, or see if there is interest in attending a dance party together. Also remember that a broken relationship can create tension if the two people involved continue to cross paths in group dance lessons or practice parties. It might be a good idea to be careful and honest all along the way.

The ultimate key to looking and dancing well is entirely up to you. If you feel good and are determined to enjoy yourself, you probably will. Others will see your attitude and want to be around you. There is a way that people dance together that reveals how they feel about each other. When I met Jill, we danced a slow Rumba, and she gave me a sizzling hot look right into my eyes that penetrated down to the tips of my toes. After cooling off, it prompted me to check out some of the other couples and how they looked at each other. A romantic couple has a lively presence on the dance floor. They are comfortable with each other, relaxed, and have an unmistakably confident look in their eyes when they look at each other.

INTERRUPTING DANCE LESSONS

Considering the hourly fee paid to dance instructors, it is not polite to interrupt someone else's private dance lesson. Unless it is urgent news, it should be held until later. If the news is for the teacher, it can be relayed between classes. If the news is for the student, it can be given after the lesson. In the case where an interruption is unavoidable, it is important to keep it short, thirty seconds to a minute, and pick a moment when it is likely to cause the least disruption.

Similarly, in group lessons, it might be tempting to relay a recently heard joke or engage in social conversation, but remember that other people may not find the conversation as enlightening. The teacher will generally keep the lesson on track, and there might be time in a long lesson to take a small break for socializing. When the teacher is speaking to the whole class, it is essential to cease any side conversations and listen. This also allows others to focus on the teacher and not be distracted by any annoying, whispered side-conversations.

INTERMEDIATE FLOOR CRAFT ETIQUETTE

Moving beyond being a raw beginner and developing into an intermediate-level dancer brings with it some new responsibilities. Dancing around the floor as a beginner, I would merely flinch when my poor navigating skills resulted in an expectation of getting hit by another dancer. An intermediate or advanced dancer has the responsibility to avoid hitting beginners. Certainly these pesky beginners should dance closer to the centre of the floor for standard dances that follow the line of dance. This is especially true if they are not moving enough, don't have confidence in the steps, or have to stop frequently to sort out the missteps. Sometimes beginners just dance anywhere, and everyone zips around them as though the couple were a stalled car on the freeway. Although the perimeter area of the floor is considered the fast lane, responsibility still falls to the more experienced dancers not to collide with beginners.

Dancing navigation is similar to the boating rules for the right of way. Under the boating navigation rules, certain vessels must keep out of the way of other vessels due to their inability to manoeuvre. A power vessel must chart a course to stay clear of a sailing vessel. The same is true for ballroom dance couples: a more experienced or powerful couple should give way to couples less capable of moving as well (although there is no requirement for one or two horn blasts depending on what side you are passing!). In dancing, the more experienced dancers are the powerboats and have full responsibility not to bump into and sink the less experienced dancers.

Dancing is a contact sport

The inadvertent physical side of dancing is when you get accidentally hit, kicked, or spiked. Most of the hits happen with the arms, and a lot of times the victim is the other dance partner. In a turn or cuddle, if the woman does not raise her arm straight enough or fast enough above her head, her elbow has a great potential to hit the man in the face. If a man is too close to his partner in an Alemana turn in Cha-Cha, the woman's elbow can smack him around chin level. Swing and Jive are other good dances to be cautious with the arms. The dances are fast with spins and turns that become dangerous. When I get hit in the chin with a woman's elbow, I realize that I have not lifted her arm high enough to straighten the elbow and get it out of the way. On the other hand, most men are not professional dancers, and a lot of women have arms that resemble limp noodles, requiring extra effort to lift the seemingly lifeless arm. There is also the danger of getting hit by someone else. Arms extended parallel to the floor on a crowded dance floor become weapons threatening those around them. A woman wearing a large ring who hits someone in the face is likely to inflict a cut, or at least a bruise, on her victim.

On a crowded floor, the arm movements are kept tight, since throwing out a wide arm is dangerous unless there is certainty that no one is there. Often it makes more sense for the woman to perform straight up arm movements and hair curls instead of side movements. For the man, the free hand can be placed solidly on the hip, fingers down. The placement needs to be deliberate and aggressive or it will look like someone holding an aching tummy or sore muscles.

One can get kicked when a dancer's foot leaves the ground and hits another person, usually in the calf or ankle. A prime example of this can occur when dancing too close to another couple in Swing. When a big, heavy man does a back break in Swing, taking a large step lifted off the floor, his heel can do a lot of damage. Jill got kicked in this manner once, and we had to leave because her bruised ankle swelled up to the extent that she had trouble walking. As the man, it was clearly my fault for leading her into a spin that ended up too close to the unseen, upcoming back break.

There are also some unusual ways to get kicked. In the Quickstep, some people perform a back heel flick with their feet. It looks like running on the spot with legs bent at the knees and the feet kicking up behind the dancer. I have no idea who came up with this crazy step. At one dance evening, I am doing Quickstep with Jill along the short wall and there is another couple moving in front of us when they unexpectedly stop in the corner. I plan to get past them on the inside of the floor—since, after all, they are stopped. As I go past the couple, with Jill's back to them, they start doing these back heel kicks, and the man's foot comes up high enough to kick Jill on her backside. At first she registers shock, but we quickly move down the floor, and then she starts laughing. "That man just kicked me in the bum!" she exclaims.

Getting spiked is that unfortunate event when the tapered heel from a woman's dance shoe tries to bury itself in another dancer's leg. Women's dance shoes have a narrow heel so when it hits the back of an ankle or a calf muscle, it feels similar to a dull spike, and the outcome ranges from bruising to bleeding.

Dancing on a crowded floor is particularly challenging, and the first change we make is to take smaller steps. For navigation on a crowded floor, the man has to keep a sharp eye on other dancers, forecasting movement and moving into open spaces. Good floor craft includes having a good sense for where the crowd is moving and keeping an adequate distance from other dancers. Regardless, in a small space on a crowded floor, contact can be expected. Accepting this and being polite are the best responses. On the other hand, when another couple is dancing aggressively around the floor, the leader may offer more protection to his partner by keeping his right elbow up and out and holding the left arm wider and more solid. This acts as a bumper for possible collisions and should only be used as a defensive move.

Another dangerous aspect of dancing is falling, and, based on my unscientific assessment, the most dangerous dance for falls is the Viennese Waltz, most likely due to the speed. The Quickstep is also fast, but the Viennese Waltz combines speed and turning. When a couple gets overly enthusiastic without a good technical knowledge of the movement, then falling is a near certainty. On the other hand, very experienced couples also have a potential to fall that can be instigated by any step that feels off-balance. At one of the dance parties, I witness a dance couple lose their balance and fall while turning the corner at the long wall during the Viennese Waltz with the gentleman landing on top of his partner. Thankfully, they are all right, although there will be bruises. During one of our dance lessons, another couple is working on the Viennese Waltz. They are about the same level of dance proficiency as we are, and I glance over at them at the same time as hearing a thud. They hit the floor, and the woman not only lands on her hip but rolls, hitting her head on the floor. She gets up looking slightly dizzy and goes to sit down. For many reasons, the Viennese Waltz is not taught until dancers are proficient at the regular Waltz. The turns in Viennese Waltz have to be taught and danced properly not only for technique but for safety. If the weight shift and steps are too rushed, the couple increases the risk of a fall.

Even at the professional level there are accidents. I recall the story of one of my dance instructors at a serious competition where she told of how bad she felt when she almost knocked a woman out during a competition. Wanting more details and verification, I managed to find a dancer who had witnessed that event.

"Oh, that other couple deserved it," she said. My dance instructor and her partner had moved into a corner of the floor to perform a series of steps during a Foxtrot. Another couple moved to the same corner and began a series of steps that blocked them in and left no room to get out of the corner to perform any other figures. It is a strategy that can be used to frustrate an opponent when there are several dance couples competing on the floor at the same time. In this case, my dance instructor's partner gave her a spin and her hand accidentally smacked the other woman. Before the woman could recover, they found an opening and managed to move back to the middle of the floor. The blocking couple did not use any similar tactics for the rest of the dances, keeping their distance from my instructor. This is serious full-contact DanceSport.

On an evening out, Jill and I are dancing on a small dance floor after a great dinner that includes a couple of glasses of nice wine. Why don't we ever learn? Don't drink and dance! It is a Salsa, and we are spinning and turning to the lively music. I do a cross body lead into swivels for Jill. At the end of the three swivels there is a right-side leg hook and dip. Jill forgets the third swivel step and, as I bring her close to me, she gives me a formidable forearm to the chin better than a lot of mixed martial arts fighters might achieve. I wobble. We look at each other and laugh. It takes a few more seconds and we are back on the beat, and I stick to simple moves. I try to think that any mistakes made in a dance are my fault. There is a theory that with proper frame and lead, a man can lead any woman through any series of steps. The challenge for the man is to be confident in alignment, manoeuvring around the room, seeking out space, and choosing steps. However, the woman also has a responsibility to make the dance successful. She needs to maintain posture, control, balance, movement, and styling, among other things. Both partners have to be alert mentally and physically to dance well.

11

THE DANCE STUDIO

MEMORABLE DANCE STUDIOS

One of the magnificent ballroom dance studios in Canada is the Grand Ballroom in Vancouver. While visiting Jill's sister in Delta one summer, Jill and I eagerly jump at the opportunity to attend a dance party. On arrival, we note that there is a large area near the entrance to change from street shoes to dance shoes, there are two dance floors adjacent to each other, both impeccable, and a well positioned DJ booth, elevated and halfway along one of the long walls. The main dance floor is the largest I have ever seen. After walking around searching for an unoccupied chair, we return to the entrance looking lost. The first person we meet is the studio owner, who graciously escorts us inside again and assigns us a couple of places at a table with plush chairs. The dance floor is busy, although there is certainly room for one more couple. We dance and soak up the surroundings, noting the polite movement of couples around each other. In some cases we notice people struggling with a step and, when that happens, they move to the adjacent floor that people use to practise correcting the step before returning to the main floor. The music selection, volume, and beat are all excellent. We stay for two hours, and halfway through the evening, a plate of raw vegetable sticks and chips is delivered to each table. Everything about the studio suggests it is well organized and well run.

While in Vancouver, we also visit the Crystal Ballroom for an open practice party that is publicized as an afternoon tea dance. In the promotional material, it claims to be the most elegant ballroom dance hall in Vancouver and it lives up to the claim, exuding classiness and good taste. This may be the most beautifully decorated dance studio in all of Canada. There is a rectangular dance floor of a generous size, totalling five thousand square feet of maple wood flooring. The striking decor starts with two incredible sparkling crystal chandeliers that hang from the ceiling and continues with matching crystal light fixtures along the walls. Taupe-painted walls with white trim are accented by burgundy velvet draperies for the large Palladian-style windows at one end of the room.

We pay at the entrance and settle in with the lightly attended Sunday afternoon tea dancers. There is indeed tea, as well as some cookies. We find an empty table and change into our dance shoes, then jump up and test the floor to the pre-recorded music selections. The dance floor feels excellent under my dance shoes, and the people are friendly, albeit skeptical of the newcomers. We are the only non-Asian people in the studio, something that Jill loves, since she is no longer the shortest person on the dance floor. After doing toe-heel swivels to a bouncy Triple Swing, we sit and notice that a number of other patrons have cornered what looks to be a teacher and points at us. Not sure what to expect, we simply sit there and soak up the dazzling decor. The teacher responds by showing the students a facsimile of our swivels, a step that looks good but is probably not familiar to those that saw it. We nod our heads as we leave and we receive warm smiles in return.

In Montreal, we visit Studio 2720, a dance studio that is built inside an old bank building, and meet the owners, who are often referred to as Canadian ballroom dance legends: the charismatic Pierre Allaire and the charming Mireille Veilleux. Dance students change shoes and hang up their coats in a steel-walled vault. In fact, there are two vaults, doors intact but always open, and there are three dance floors on two levels. The main floor is at street level, with windows facing the street and mirrors filling one wall on the side. This dance studio is steeped with character and nestled in a residential area of Montreal East.

A BALLROOM DANCE STUDIO

What constitutes a good ballroom dance studio? There are numerous dance studios across the country, some very successful and some that go out of business in less than a year after opening their doors. Starting and running a dance studio is a challenge, as it is for any other type of business. There are numerous aspects to consider, especially the costs of getting everything set up. From a dance student's perspective there are a great many items that make a studio comfortable. Below is a review of the components that need to be incorporated into a good ballroom dance studio.

It all starts with the facility considerations. Similar to other real estate, the three main criteria are, "location, location, and location." Although we regularly drove twenty-one kilometres to a studio because we liked the teacher, most students want to be within a reasonable distance from the studio. It needs to have good access roads, especially because of the Canadian winters. The location needs to be in a safe area and well lighted at night. My concept of an ideal studio would be in a small commercial or industrial area surrounded by a large population with a majority of retired residents and families—those most likely to take lessons. A small commercial office or industrial area normally provides good parking because of the offset of times when each of the two groups will be busy. A dance studio will be busier at night and on weekends. Parking along residential streets can be frustrating for the clientele, although I know of three studios where this situation exists, and they are still doing well.

The type of neighbourhood is another consideration. Along with the location is the importance of the population characteristics of the area, including density, range of ages, and level of income. This helps identify the potential student base to build from. There are times when a teacher brings along an existing clientele, but it always helps to have a local walk-in contingent nearby.

For any studio, the size and type of dance floor is critical. The best floor I have seen so far was at the above-mentioned Grand Ballroom in Vancouver. The floor needs to be wooden, of course, and has to be rectangular in shape. Laminate floors look good, with their nice lustre finish, but in my experience they can be slippery and don't stand up well over time unless they have been installed properly and have a good finish. I understand that the newer materials offer improvement, and since there are a lot of options for flooring, it is wise to obtain professional advice, whether installing a studio floor or a dance floor at home. The floor has to have the right feel for the dance shoes—not too slippery and not too sticky. I like the idea of having two floors, a competition-sized floor and a practice floor either on the same level or in a different area of the studio. The competition-sized floor is ideal for competitors to practise a routine in a setting that can simulate a competition. Also, a big floor allows several lessons or a combination of private lessons and a group lesson to occur at the same time. A smaller practice floor can be used for dances that don't travel—such as Salsa and Rumba—or in the case where dancers want to practise technique in the mirror.

The ideal dance floor has no posts, but that is not always an option. Posts are not only aesthetically unpleasant; they also create a hazard. A studio needs windows for natural light, and large windows are essential. At least two adjoining walls should have mirrors. They are an absolute must-have for a teacher to be successful. The student can see all the critical elements performed well or poorly in the reflection, the good posture, good frame, good turns, and good feet. It is helpful to have the belief that your dance is being executed correctly, but it is more beneficial to actually observe yourself.

Seating will be available on three sides: two sides with chairs and one with chairs around small tables. When a studio has seating only along one side of the dance floor, it creates a funny situation at parties and dance practices. When people stand up to dance a standard or smooth dance, they all start on the same area of the dance floor and travel around in unison as if they were all attached with an invisible piece of rope.

The inside of the studio can be designed to look spectacular, as was the case in the Crystal Ballroom with walls painted taupe with burgundy accents and with crystal light fixtures. The ceiling may also have a mirror ball or special lights to liven up a practice party. Where there is space, the walls will be covered with eloquent art, probably Bill Brauer or Jack Vettriano. This gives the atmosphere of a true ballroom. There has to be an inviting reception area and an office that can be either out in the open or sequestered behind a wall. The reception area should include a few chairs to allow people to change from street shoes into dance shoes. Of course, dirty street shoes cannot be allowed on the dance floor.

Access to drinking water is important, since dancing is a physical activity. The washrooms should be clean and maintained that way. Washrooms will be used frequently by those students who drink a lot of water during lessons. The washrooms should also be larger than normal, to be used as a change room, with hooks or hangers for street clothes. This is important for students who arrive at the studio directly from work or simply need to change into more danceable clothes; competitors who might want to try on competition outfits for a short practice; or competitors who will need to change out of perspiration-soaked clothing at the end of a practice. The studio needs a regular cleaning and maintenance schedule so that there are never dust bunnies on the floor and the place always looks professionally maintained. These details are a reflection of the care taken in the rest of the business.

My preference in a sound system is to have speakers hanging from the corners of the ceiling and a central volume control to allow music from all speakers at once or individually so that designated areas of the dance floor can be used without disturbing others. The system needs to have pitch control to allow easy changes for a slower or faster tempo to any song. This is a great teacher's aid, as well as being good for competitors who are looking for strict tempo music.

The studio also needs good temperature control. It should be kept at slightly lower than normal room temperature most of the time; as the studio fills up with active dancers, it will heat up. A good air conditioner is essential for the summer months, and in the winter, a good heating system provides warmth.

Of greatest importance, a good studio is dependent on good teachers and staff. A variety of teachers with different levels of proficiency in different dances can be beneficial. It is nice to see teachers enter competitions, because it encourages them to stay abreast of any changes in dance technique or training and allows them to represent the studio. It is always good to have teachers willing and able to dance in Pro-Am events with students. Some studios hire teachers directly while others consider them as contractors who teach their own students and pay a fee to the studio owner.

Ongoing staff training is important, and many teachers follow the CDTA certification process. Staff can publicize the studio by dancing in local competitions or performing shows when requested. Students will look for a consistency of instruction, teaching methods, and general quality. The studio will also need a policy on cancellation of lessons. In addition, since there are always more women than men, the studio can try and find a way to match up people looking for dance partners. As a studio becomes more popular, there will be a need to review the scheduling of lessons to avoid floor congestion.

Marketing is crucial for studio success. A good wireless handset telephone system is ideal and an answering machine with a warm greeting is essential for taking calls from potential students. In the dance world the best form of advertising is word of mouth, and if dance students are pleased, they will tell their friends. Other means to advertise include radio; flyers; local newspaper or Internet ads; ads in a program sold at competitions, offering discount deals or promotions; being the sponsor of events or charities; and performing demonstrations at New Year's Eve or other events.

Studios are similar to other businesses, and there are failures. If they are managed properly, they will succeed; if not, they can fail. Also, like any new business, it takes time to build up customers. I knew about one new studio that lasted only six months. The focus was on Salsa. The floor was shiny, slippery, laminate wood, and there was a post in the middle of the dance floor. The location was in a rather rundown section of the city, evidenced by abandoned storefronts along the street, although the area was in the process of being revitalized. Perhaps the owner received a number of months' free rent as part of the agreement. There was no parking other than along side streets. It was not in an area of the city that would be conducive to any kind of walk-in traffic, and advertising did not seem to change the level of people signing up for lessons.

I know of a second studio that went out of business quickly and quietly. It appeared as if the owners did not know what they wanted. They were advanced competitive dancers and they encouraged competitive dancers to join the studio. Dance parties were advertised as open to local dancers of all levels, but it was difficult to find any other information about the dance parties. Also, no one was attracted to the isolated location. The studio was in a desolate commercial district. However, the lack of a clear strategy or customer focus seemed to be the main cause of failure.

Components of a typical dance studio budget

Potential revenue

- Private dance lessons
- Group dance lessons
- Practice parties entrance fee
- Holding a studio competition
- General studio rental
- Holding regular off-site galas, parties, or barbecues
- Sale of shoes and/or accessories

Potential costs

- Rent (and/or property taxes)
- Heat
- Hydro
- Water
- Maintenance
- Insurance
- Accounting and banking fees
- Marketing and advertising: brochures, Web site, ad placement
- Training and certification
- Staff costs
- Alarm system
- Computer system and printer
- Telephones
- Internet access
- Dance music CDs
- SOCAN (music copyright fees)
- Dance Association fees

Most dance studios incorporate only some, not all, aspects of what it takes to be a great studio. In reality, any such dance studio would probably cost too much and take too long to get a sufficient number of students to earn the level of revenue required to be successful. The studios that I know are content to stay within their niche and have enough students to keep their business alive.

Dance Floors

Some dance studios have support beams or posts in the floor. Some have awkwardly shaped dance floors. Why are floors so important? Floors are the grounding needed for the dancer's feet. Not only do dancers need to work their feet into the floor, they also need to feel it, push it, slide and spin. While doing that, it is important that a dancer does not stress or damage the feet, ankles, knees, hips, calf muscles, and thighs. There are many types of floors and some have interesting characteristics.

Sprung hardwood. This is supposedly the best for dancing, easy on the legs and provides great traction.

Parquet wood. I dance on a parquet floor regularly and like it. On the negative side, the edges of the squares warp if they get wet, which creates a hazard.

Laminate wood. This can be problematic if not installed properly, and it needs to have a good subfloor. Old types were very shiny and slippery.

Tiles over concrete. As expected, this is painful for the ankle, knee, and hip joints unless taken in small doses.

Indoor/outdoor deck. We went to a dance party with a live band that was held on a large outdoor deck and had to be wary of the cracks between planks and warped boards. The surface was not level, and the heels of the women's dance shoes tended to get stuck between the boards.

Rugs at the edge of a dance floor. Some wooden dance floors end with a rug around all sides, so if you go past the edge of the floor, watch out! It is like stepping in a hole and coming to a sudden stop. I remember as a child running in the winter then sliding across a clean patch of ice only to hit a bare spot of grass or concrete and falling over abruptly.

A wooden floor placed over a rug. This is common in hotels that want to create a temporary dance floor. The wood part is good, but if the floor is not laid properly and has metal frames, a heel can easily catch the metal seam and cause trouble in spins and turns. It is more suited to freestyle than a dance where the feet slide across the floor.

Posts. Posts are mostly just a nuisance, unless the floor is being used for a competition. In that case, they may interfere with the line of dance and provide a challenge for movement around the floor with a routine. Some posts are in the middle and some are off to one side. However, they are very good for holding up the roof!

Bevelled edges. Some dance floors have an angled edge that connects the dance floor to a regular floor at a slightly lower level. If people are not aware of it, there is a possibility of sliding off and twisting an ankle or generally being surprised.

Floors installed without a subfloor. If the floor has not been installed properly, leaving a gap underneath the dance floor may cause it to bounce or dip in the middle with the weight of several dancers. This has a surprisingly entertaining trampoline effect—until it turns nauseating.

Cruise ships. The floor on a ship might seem to move until you have your sea legs. That is nothing to worry about. After all, it **is** a cruise.

Bare concrete. Dancing on concrete requires running shoes or sandals, as it will wreck the soles of normal dance shoes—not to mention the knees and ankles if one dances too long on it.

Sticky floors. Sometimes the finish on a floor is not maintained well, or is washed with the wrong solution. A sticky floor makes turns and spins challenging. In standard dances, once the foot is placed, it stays there, and a simple reverse pivot becomes very tricky. Apparently, Latin dancers like this because it facilitates hip development. Regardless, spins and turns are still difficult.

Slippery floors. A shiny, slippery floor makes it easy to slide, which may be acceptable for most dancers. However, it requires more control of the feet and precise shifting of weight over the feet. On the other hand, if there is trouble with balance, it is possible to fall.

Wet floors. Floors get wet from spilled drinks, leaking air conditioners, wearing outdoor shoes on the dance floor after it rains, or even perspiration from active dancers. It usually makes the floor sticky in isolated places, or very slippery over a laminate floor.

Shape and size. A standard dance floor is a rectangle, while some are square. Occasionally we dance on an octagon-shaped floor. It is a challenge to determine where the corners are! The standard size for a competition floor is fifty feet by thirty-five feet (15.5 metres by 11 metres).

12

BECOMING A BALLROOM DANCE INSTRUCTOR

TEACHER CANDIDACY

For anyone who is considering becoming a ballroom dance instructor, either full time or part time, there is a number of resources available. Interested people should contact a local dance studio or a dance teacher for more information. Two organizations in Canada are the Canadian Dance Teachers Association (CDTA) and the Canada DanceSport Federation (CDF).

Here are some excerpts from the CDTA *Student Teacher Syllabus*.

Practical Demonstration

Candidates must demonstrate with music the required dances dancing as their own gender. The required dances are: Waltz; Tango; Foxtrot; Quickstep and Slow Rhythm. The demonstration is restricted to the Student Teacher figures.

Candidates must also dance as the opposite gender, with or without a partner, to music, the required dances.

Theory (Oral Examination)

Candidates will be expected to explain the terms and definitions used in the technique charts and must be able to give a simple description of: 1. Feet Positions; 2. Alignment/ Direction; 3. Amount of Turn; 4. Rise and Fall; 5. Footwork; 6. CBM and CBMP; 7. Sway.

The student should also be able to give a simple description of:

1. Forward and Backward Walks.
2. Hold.
3. Time and Tempo of each dance.
4. One Precede and Follow to each specified figure.

The technical analysis and solo demonstration as man or lady is confined to:

1. Feet Position.
2. Alignment/Direction.
3. Amount of Turn.
4. Rise and Fall.
5. Footwork.
6. Timing.
7. Counting in Beats.

MEMORABLE SAYINGS FROM DANCE TEACHERS

Every dance teacher has his or her own method of teaching and they all have their own set of expressions that they rely on during dance lessons. Sometimes when we hear one, it makes us laugh instead of paying attention. Some help us focus.

"I can see China between your legs." While doing a New York (Crossover Break) in the Cha-Cha, our Russian-born Latin dance teacher tries to emphasize that the legs need to be closer together and makes this comment on the space between the legs. We have to work on squeezing the thighs together in the turns.

"When you do that step, it hurts my eyes." While doing Rumba, our lazy feet and sloppy hip movements detract from the essence of a well-performed Latin dance. We have to dance like we mean it and work to emphasize every step, making every step serious and deliberate. There is no coasting for serious dance students.

"That's orgasmic!" After a beautifully executed Natural Spin Turn, our instructor gives us high praise with this exaggerated comment. We know what she means because we feel the perfection and emotion in the figure, with all its subtle pauses and movement at the right moments.

"Let's stop there—I think I see smoke coming out your ears." After introducing a series of new steps during a lesson, my teacher looks at my face and recognizes a strained look. I am perplexed but not defeated.

Regardless, she thankfully moves on to something else to finish the lesson and allow time for the previous instruction to sink in.

"Today we build Rome." After a particularly stressful and difficult lesson, Jill tells her teacher, "Rome was not built in a day!" She is struggling to remember all that she is told and tries to get every single aspect of the dance posture, frame, and steps perfect. It will develop, but not all at once. At the start of the next lesson, a week later, the young male instructor remembers her comment from the previous week and replies with the quote above.

"Dancing is a vertical expression of a horizontal desire." This is the frequently used explanation of how people are supposed to feel when dancing a Latin dance. It certainly is true for the playfulness in Rumba, Bachata, and Cha-Cha, when each partner of the dance couple looks lustfully into the other's eyes. In the standard dances, the man's leg rubs the inside of the woman's thigh while they each look over the other's right shoulder to monitor traffic. I guess it's a more subtle expression in standard dances.

"I love you guys!" In most cases, taking lessons as a couple with a good instructor leads to building a strong rapport. There are many teachers that we love dearly and some of them love us, too—especially when we do something right.

"Life may not be the party we hoped for, but while we are here, we might as well dance." (Anonymous) This is not something we heard exactly as stated but have seen it posted on dance studio walls and in dance apparel stores. We all need to find a passion in life, and we have certainly found ours.

13

A DANCE PARTY LIFESTYLE

There is never a shortage of places to dance in a big city. We dance at charity fundraiser events, dance studio banquets, New Year's Eve parties, Viennese Waltz balls, weddings, any live music show that has a good dance floor. There are Latin clubs, Western bars, dinner and dance restaurants, and dance studio parties.

WEDDINGS

Jill's friend and next-door neighbour invites us to her daughter's wedding, which is being held in a scenic country setting south of Ottawa. When the ceremony is over and the party begins, music fills the room with recognizable pop songs. We dance a few Swings and Cha-Chas on the small tiled dance floor in front of the DJ. There is no room for any smooth dances that move around the floor. One guest's child of about eight or nine years of age does a cartwheel across the dance floor, and we move away to avoid getting hit with an upside-down foot. He runs back to his parents' table, chugs down half a glass of cola then returns to the dance floor with a grin on his face. As the music plays and dancers shuffle their feet to the next tune, he starts doing back flips across the floor, proudly displaying his talent. The location is picturesque, the wedding ceremony was touching, but our dancing is cautious.

We are invited to the wedding of two dear friends who met while at a dance event one New Year's Eve. The reception is held in a beautiful room at the National Arts Centre overlooking the Rideau Canal, and the wooden dance floor is a reasonable size. The DJ plays some great music, and the many skilled ballroom and Latin dancers fill the floor with fancy steps. At one end of the short wall, there is a door to the kitchen that the serving staff use as they go back and forth to clean tables and bring out dessert. The door has a wall a few feet in front of it with an opening out either side, turning it into a tiny alcove. As the dancers move around in a smooth dance, one couple enters the alcove on one side, dances behind it, and exits from the other side. As they continue dancing in a perfect flow to the music, people are either surprised or doubled over in laughter to see them re-emerge, not understanding how they could disappear then reappear.

PUNTA CANA

For a winter vacation, we go to the Dominican Republic and stay at a resort in Punta Cana. There are only a few English-speaking people here. Mainly there are East Europeans, and several of the women regardless of body type or size go sunbathing in "European" mode, otherwise known as topless. While some views are exceptional, we agree that some things are better left to the imagination. We hope to hear Latin music at the resort and perhaps learn more about the culture and origins of the music. Merengue is the official dance of the Dominican Republic. I don't think too many other people at the resort recognize the music or understand its status in the country. When we hear it, we let it soak in, enjoying one small bit of culture. The younger people are not all open to accepting the different sound and many go into withdrawal, craving pop, rap, or techno music.

On the first day at the bar beside the pool, I pick up a drink for Jill that has a fancy title: Banana Mama. She likes it and continues to order them all week, although she claims they are very weak in alcohol. I am drinking beer and guess that the bartenders are simply being stingy with the alcohol portions. On the day before we are scheduled to return to Ottawa, we meet another Canadian couple and Jill relays her criticism regarding the weakness of her favourite drink only to find out that you have to *ask* at this resort to have rum put in the drinks! Jill is not amused.

While in Punta Cana, we read an article at the hotel about the origins of the Merengue. According to the article, many years ago the inhabitants had no source of meat, but the island was overrun with parrots, so they captured and killed parrots for food. A big bonfire would be lit, and the people would grab a parrot, dance around the fire plucking the feathers furiously, in their joy at soon being able to eat. This simple dance became the basic 1-2, 1-2 steps of the Merengue. (The story is not given serious consideration from any historians.) The Merengue music we hear played in Ottawa sounds noisy and cluttered, although on the island the modern CDs have lovely, very listenable Merengue music.

It was a few days after reading the story about the origins of Merengue when Jill and I were walking along a sidewalk at the perimeter of our resort. Two men drove past on a motorcycle with a cage tied to the back containing two huge, colourful parrots and stopped in a parking lot that was beside a restaurant. Jill thought the parrots were beautiful and in her basic Spanish started a conversation with the men. They were very friendly and gradually she brought the topic of conversation to the parrots and the concern she had from the Merengue story.

"Are these parrots for eating?" she asked with a worried look on her face.

The men laughed heartily, "No!"

They were delivering the birds to a tourist booth nearby where parrots are placed on a tourist's shoulder and a photo is taken for a fee. The men placed a calm parrot on Jill's shoulder, and we took a photo. Unfortunately, we were both in swimwear and had no money to give the men. However, I think Jill gave the men a good story to tell their families. These parrots are far more valuable alive.

While strolling around the hotel pool in Punta Cana, we notice the hotel is offering massages on the beach. There is no one waiting in line, and Jill is excited by the prospect of a relaxing massage in the warm air with the sound of real ocean waves in the background. She hops on the table in her bathing suit, and I take a mellow stroll back to a lounge chair by the pool after picking up a cup of beer from the bar. The women doing the massage don't appear to have much training and are not certified to any recognizable level. As the massage proceeds, wind gusts pick up along the beach, and Jill realizes that sand particles are mixing in the massage oil. This feels more like an exfoliation than a relaxing rub, with the sand turning the woman's hands into sandpaper. How do you stop an oblivious service provider in the middle of a vigorous massage? As the woman moves toward Jill's face, the massage creates even more anxiety.

Before we left for the trip to the Dominican Republic, Jill waxed her eyebrows to make them a perfectly shaped arch. It started out well. She squinted into the mirror because her near vision was blurred due to laser eye surgery, which improved only her distance vision. She ripped off the wax strip attached to the right eyebrow, revealing a nice, clean, eyebrow line. Next was the left. It looked good, but as she prepared to yank it, there was a moment of doubt—a well-justified moment, because the strip pulled off more hair than intended, leaving Jill with only half an eyebrow! She shrieked, dove into her makeup bag, and lined the missing eyebrow so the damage was completely unnoticeable, especially to someone who also has poor near vision. Jill had carefully pencilled in the missing piece of eyebrow so well that I didn't even notice it until she told me the next day.

On this day at the beach, Jill's massage is nearly finished when the oil and sand are scrubbed over her forehead. Fearing the worst, Jill finds me after the massage and asks me to look at her.

"How is the eyebrow? Is it still there or do I need to get my makeup to pencil it back on?"

By this time, I am ensconced deeply in a lounge chair by the pool with a beer in one hand and warm, wonderful air moving slowly over me. Our room with the makeup bag is a ten-minute walk from the pool. Jill sinks into the chair beside me, unwittingly sipping an alcohol-free Banana Mama, and I wonder how long I can soak up the warm air before feeling guilty. My thoughts linger for a moment on the belief that the weather at this hour in Ottawa is probably around twenty degrees below freezing.

"Hey, you look great," I reply.

She is brushing off the oily, wet sand forcefully from her skin. "But is the eyebrow still there?"

"Everything is fine," I skirt the truth carefully. She is standing there looking strange with less than half a brow over one eye.

Later that evening, she utters a dismayed yelp when she sees herself in the mirror. After an eyebrow touch-up, some laughter, and dinner, we dance Merengue and Bachata outdoors to a live band, and my small deception is forgiven.

This is the trip where we become enthusiastic about dancing Bachata. At this resort, Bachata music is played constantly in the covered outdoor bar, at the beach, and inside the foyer. Each morning when we wake up, we turn on the radio and listen to a local station that plays a mix of Bachata, Merengue, and a touch of American pop music. Bachata is basic street music with simple instrumentation, guitar, and bongos, although the modern songs are played with electric strings. It is a relatively new public dance, with recordings first becoming public in the 1960s. Staff members at the resort teach a few basic Bachata steps beside the pool in a haphazard way to tourists wearing swimsuits.

At the nightly disco, we notice that the testosterone-fuelled local men always dance Merengue and Bachata in closed hold, except for spins. Also, they move their shoulders as well as their hips, whereas the formal ballroom studio mantra is that the shoulders should never move. The closed-position, hip-gyrating Bachata that we witness is more like making love in an upright position than it is a dance. In fact, both partners have big smiles as they walk off the dance floor. It must be the relaxed atmosphere and the warm, sweet air.

During a hot, sunny afternoon at the beach on our final day, an American couple teaches me how to body surf in the big waves. I catch a great wave, finally mastering the technique of taking a deep breath, holding my arms straight in front of me with my fingers pointing upwards and legs straight back, so that my body acts as a surfboard. The big wave carries me for a while then throws me vigorously up the pure white sands of the Punta Cana beach from the edge of the water, leaving a red skin burn on my chest. I tell everyone it is only mild sunburn. We return home after a solid week of rest in a far warmer climate than the February chill of Ottawa.

CUBA

The following year, we head to Cuba for a one-week winter break. The resort in Varadero has a disco that used to be a renowned popular place for local dancing, with both tourists and residents lined up at the door in hopes of being allowed to enter. We walk into the nearly empty disco at around eleven p.m. to find the bartender watching a baseball game on television, and no music. A few people trickle in, and the bartender turns the volume down on the television and presses the "on" button attached to a box that starts to generate some heavy beat, high-volume techno-rap/hip-hop music. After thirty minutes, we leave, disappointed, before our eardrums shatter. Apparently, the popularity of a place can be short-lived.

The warm air and sandy beach are a pleasant relief, although we encounter more surprises. Lunch is served in a high-ceilinged buffet area, where birds are seen flying around. Halfway through lunch one day, a bird nest falls from the ceiling directly onto Jill's plate of food. Fortunately, lunch was finished, and the nest was only half-built, so it was only debris that fell.

Although we realize that this is a tourist area—not downtown Havana—we are desperate to visit a Salsa club and, close to the final day of our stay, we take a taxi to the Mambo Club in Varadero. We are not disappointed. Here is a full live band with a band leader, and the band is composed of mainly older men wearing identical red jackets; they are playing energetic, driving Salsa music, filling the room with Cuban culture. There is a good-sized wooden dance floor in front of the band. A second-floor balcony surrounds the room in a horseshoe shape, with good sight lines to the band. Most people simply watch the band, while two lively entertainers try to show people how to do basic Merengue, Salsa, and Cha-Cha steps and encourage them to get onto the dance floor.

Jill and I know several basic Salsa steps, which is probably more than all of the tourists put together. At least we manage to stay on the beat and do it with the proper foot movement. Tonya is a young female Cuban who bounces around trying to make sure the patrons are having a fun time. She is an energetic, slender, dark-haired young woman who could probably pass for nineteen. Her male partner is somewhat older and might be wearing a hairpiece. As much as they overflow with enthusiasm, there is only reluctance in the crowd. We think this will probably change once the night moves along and the drinks take effect.

Only a few people are on the dance floor. Most of them simply wiggle their bodies or shift their weight from foot to foot. Tonya sees us dance a proper Salsa and Cha-Cha and a short time later she comes to our table and strikes up a conversation. Once again, Jill's Spanish language skills come in handy. Tonya asks me for a dance and we do whatever version of Salsa I happen to have learned. Later I find out there is a Miami version and a New York style. I do the "Here's-what-I-learned-around-Ottawa" style. Tonya has amazing rhythm and movement. I am dancing a Salsa with an authentic Cuban in a Cuban nightclub! I overcome the intimidation and start to enjoy it.

Tonya dances well, but is probably more familiar with choreographed routines, because she struggles slightly in following what I am trying to lead. On the other hand, the problem could be my lead.

We return to our table, and Tonya asks Jill about her dance shoes. Jill is wearing an old pair of black Latin dance shoes with a two and a half-inch heel. Tonya shows us the calf-high black boots she is wearing and says that it is impossible to find dance shoes in Cuba; she asks Jill how much she paid for her shoes. Jill replies that in Canada they cost her about one hundred dollars. Tonya continues to look at the shoes longingly and asks Jill if she can try them on, and the two women discover that they have the same size feet. When Tonya tries the shoes on, the look on her face is a combination of pure pleasure and *I always knew good dance shoes would feel like this*. Tonya asks Jill if she would consider selling the shoes to her. With sincere empathy in her heart, Jill tells a surprised Tonya that she plans to give the shoes to her as a gift before we leave. Tonya is excited but apprehensive.

"You will give them to me when you leave Cuba?" she asks.

"No," Jill replies, "I will give them to you tonight before we leave the club."

Tonya is beside herself with joy and thanks us profusely. We receive big heartfelt hugs at the end of the evening when the shoes are handed to her. Jill walks out barefoot, to the chagrin of the security staff, who are baffled because they had checked to make sure everyone who entered the club was properly dressed, including footwear.

Back in our room at the resort, Jill sees a tiny gecko, one of the many small lizards that are everywhere outside along the walking paths. Finding it very cute and sedate, she picks it up, cradling the creature gently in her hand, until it suddenly springs to life, jumps toward her cleavage, and disappears down the front of her dress. Jill dances a dance that I have never seen before.

GIVING SOMETHING BACK

Carl was a tall, elderly, retired gentleman who was very active on the dance floor as well as in life. He looked fit and moved well around the floor, so it was with surprise and sadness that the dance community learned that he had passed away. He had suffered a massive heart attack during a tennis match.

Jill and I decide to organize a dance event and donate the proceeds to the Heart and Stroke Foundation. The studio owner volunteers the use of the studio, and my daughter agrees to collect money at the door. Jill sets up a small, square table with a tablecloth and sets it in a corner of the studio. On it she places articles that she receives from Carl's family members: a photograph, some personal belongings, and his dance shoes. I copy some danceable music onto a few CDs and play them. At one point, my daughter asks all the people to stand behind her at the centre of the dance floor and she teaches them the Electric Slide line dance. Everyone has a good time for a good cause, and people we never saw before come out to support the event. It allows us to reflect and remember how lucky we are to be living a good life with the physical ability to dance. It also allows a few of us to grow a bit closer. People who had previously only seen each other in passing on the dance floor now stop to say hello and talk to each other.

On another occasion, we organize a dance practice for beginners. These are students at the studio who are too intimidated to attend a regular dance party. I copy songs more appropriate to this level, with no Viennese Waltzes or Quicksteps. A couple of teachers attend and give free advice and encouragement to the new dancers. Who knows how life will unfold, and how an event might change a person's life? One man tells us a year later that he was about to quit dancing until he attended the student party. Jill danced with him, provided some positive feedback, and he started to feel better about his dancing skills and decided to keep going. Another young man met a nice young woman, and they eventually got married.

We attend the regular dance party nights every Friday and enjoy them immensely. Dancers from other studios also attend, and it is an interesting challenge to navigate the floor when different styles are involved. We dance, catch up with friends, and make an effort to welcome new people when we see them. Saturdays offer a variety of opportunities to dance at different locations. On Sunday, we attend the open dance party sponsored by another studio, held in a community centre. With our one private lesson a week and many social activities, we find ourselves dancing three or four times a week.

DANCE SHOES

Perhaps the most important equipment for dancers is proper shoes. There are different shoes for different types of dancing, and undoubtedly, to dance properly, good dance shoes are required. Skates are needed to play hockey, and players on a soccer team wear soccer shoes. When you go bowling, it is necessary to rent a pair of worn-out, odd-coloured bowling shoes if you don't have your own. When you dance, you need to wear shoes that have been specifically designed for that purpose.

Men's shoes for standard or smooth dances have a low heel, soft leather uppers, and a soft suede sole. The reason for a softer, more flexible shoe is that it allows the foot to be more manoeuvrable. Regular dress shoes are too stiff and prevent the dancer's smooth foot action in a dance like Foxtrot, where the man lands on the heel of the foot, rolls forward, and then pushes off into the next step using the ball of the foot. With a hard-soled dress shoe, the rolling action becomes impossible. For Latin dances, a men's dance shoe has a higher than normal, 1 3/4-inch heel. This encourages a posture that is straight and leaning slightly forward. It also supports dancing more on the balls of the feet. The soft shoe acts the same as in standard, with more emphasis on the side of the foot. The side of the foot is used to push away into the next step, which would be very difficult to do with a stiff dress shoe.

At dance parties, rather than changing shoes based on the dance being played, it is best for a man to wear standard shoes and dance the Latin dances wearing a standard dance shoe. Doing the reverse of that is not as easy. It is difficult to dance standard dances while wearing a Latin shoe with a higher heel, since the heel movement is different, and a Latin heel does not provide the support needed for standard dances. In spite of this, I see men dancing all evening in Latin shoes, and I have to guess that they are sensitive about their height, wanting to appear taller, or perhaps they have only one pair of shoes. Wearing Latin shoes to dance standard or smooth dances is not something that I recommend.

A woman's standard or smooth dance shoe has a closed-toe area and also allows more flexibility for the long strides and heel turns required in the standard dances. They have either a slim or flared heel and look like pumps. There are accessory clear support straps available to help secure the foot. The woman's Latin shoe has an open-toe area, presumably to allow the toes to spread and give better balance and movement for the woman in Latin dances where there are a lot of spins and turns. Also, the support from splayed toes promotes greater hip motion. Latin shoes come in different heel sizes. Jill struggled with a 2 1/2-inch heel for a while, and she was unable to land good toe leads in many steps. She went to a two-inch heel and found that it made a difference. It may depend on the ability to bend the foot like a ballet dancer when pointing the toe, because normally a Latin shoe promotes the forward position required for Latin dances.

Paul's dance shoes

Men's Standard and Latin heels

Jill's dance shoes

Women's Standard and Latin shoes

Another accessory, plastic heel protectors, are becoming more common for women's shoes. A heel protector is a snug-fitting, clear plastic cap that is the same style as the heel of the shoe, slim or flared, and is placed on each shoe to protect the heel tip from wear. The protectors wear out and can be replaced at a lower cost than the heel tip. Beyond this initial intent, there are other benefits. They give better stability to the dancer, and the heel tip is less abrasive on the dance floor. Some studios, and recently some competition organizers, are making them compulsory in order to reduce deterioration of the dance floor.

When the soles of a dance shoe become very shiny and smooth, people rub a stiff metal brush on the bottoms of their dance shoes in order to get more traction. Since the debris and dirt cause problems with traction on the dance floor, it makes sense to do this away from the dance floor and into a trash can. Care needs to be taken to brush in a direction away from the shoe, with fingers out of the way or the fingers may accidentally receive a few nasty scratches from the sharp metal wire bristles. The rationale for brushing the shoes is to avoid sliding on the floor. However, one of my teachers told me that she never brushes her shoes. She explained that if the weight on the foot is always in the right place, then the shoe should not slide. I think about this, agree with her, and stop brushing my shoes (or perhaps it is because I get tired of brushing). The effects from brushing only last for the first few minutes of dancing anyway. I work harder on making sure my weight is in the right place over the supporting foot.

CLOTHING

For Latin lessons and practices, I normally wear black dress pants or black jeans and a classy black T-shirt, which is a common uniform for Latin dancing. I bring a loose sweater to warm up in and remove it when I get too hot. Jill wears breathable clothing, a dress or skirt to lessons and on occasion pants to a practice. It might take time to determine if clothes are going to cause problems during a dance. A dress that is too tight will restrict the length of steps in a smooth dance, and a long skirt can create problems as well. We dance a Jive in practice while Jill is wearing a loose skirt and on a high back leg kick with her toes pointing to the floor, she gets her heel caught in the skirt and nearly falls over. I am careful with the length of my pants; normal dress pants leave the cuffs hanging around the shoes. Usually the back of the cuffs drag on the floor, wearing out the cloth. In any case, that might result in stepping on them when dancing, so I have my pant cuffs taken up an extra inch for pants that I plan to wear for dancing on a regular basis.

There are times when we dance that items of clothing somehow get in the way. If Jill wears a fashionable belt with a large buckle, it creates problems during a closed position dance. One day at practice, I wore a belt that had metal protrusions. As we moved into dance hold, it connected with the snap above the zipper on her slacks. After a few steps, her snap came undone. As we tried to move further, the zipper went down. I tell everyone that during that practice I danced her pants off! Another time, our shirt buttons got caught with each other and we stuck together, fumbling to see how we could extract ourselves. It made closed position easier, although when we were finished it took some work by nimble fingers to disengage.

For one lesson, Jill wears a woollen turtleneck sweater, begins to perspire a few minutes into the class, and is exhausted before the class is half over. Another time, she does not want to get too hot at a lesson so she goes to the washroom and slides off her pantyhose under her skirt only to realize that she is wearing thong underwear beneath the pantyhose instead of well-covering dance underpants. "No big spins today, okay?" She whispers in my ear as she returns for the lesson. She has no reason to be embarrassed, and we stick to standard dances for this session. Now and then at the studio we see women coming out of the washroom with the back of a skirt tucked into pantyhose. Jill now packs an extra sleeveless top and underwear in her shoe bag.

DANCE PARTNERS

Ballroom dancing is not a solo activity, and as such, the dance partner relationship is critical to any objective. It takes two to tangle. Having a regular dance partner is a great blessing that sometimes may be taken for granted, while not having a regular partner requires at least the same level of effort to ensure harmonious dancing. There are factors that help a dancer be a good partner, and there are ways to find and keep a partner, if that is a goal. Two basic elements to being a good dance partner are to practise good etiquette and work to earn a partner's respect.

How to be a good dance partner

There is always something that a dancer can do to make the dance better. Dancers need to work continuously to improve their ability, dance at a comparable level that does not embarrass a partner, and have a positive attitude regardless of the situation.

Improving one's dance ability starts with listening carefully to instructors and to your dance partner. Instructors repeat themselves, which often tends to be helpful because it takes time to learn and properly perform any new dance figure. Either partner or both may be having difficulty absorbing the onslaught of information in a lesson. It can help to take notes after the lesson, recording any changes or improvements that both partners should practise. This normally achieves two results. The act of writing something down helps a person remember it, and the notes can be used during a practice to jog the memory, ensure the steps are done properly, or verify that nothing is forgotten. If one partner gets stuck, it might be more helpful to move on and return to the step later; or mention it during a lesson. It is always important to remember that dance is for fun, and there are times when perfect steps don't matter.

If a dancer does not have a regular dance partner, the chances are that dances will be performed with partners who are at different levels of ability. In this case, the more experienced dancer should accommodate the level of the less experienced dancer. For a man leading, it is important to start with the basics of the dance and to gradually try more complicated moves. Once the partner's limits are known, it is considerate to remain at that level of comfort and perhaps try one or two figures that may challenge the partner without making him or her feel inadequate or lost; this way, both partners will feel comfortable and enjoy the challenge. For followers at a more experienced level, the rule is to enjoy and know that this experience is improving the leader's ability. Do not try to hijack the lead or show off. During my first year of lessons, I danced with a woman who would do double or triple spins whenever I led a simple spin. One woman looked fed up with my limited ability, lifted my arm and turned herself.

"I was getting bored!" she exclaimed.

Another time, during a pattern where the dance partners separate from each other, such as the chase in the Cha-Cha, one woman did so many advanced moves, I had to stop and almost walked off the floor. Eventually we got back together, and I found the beat to finish the dance. I danced with that woman again, but never again let go of her hand during the dance.

Whether it is a lesson, a practice, or a dance party, there is always something that can be improved. There are times when it is appropriate to work on correction and times when this should be deferred. In all cases, the dancer needs to be constructive and positive. Do dance partners argue? Of course they do, often driven by the desire to be better and because dance steps can be very complex and confusing until they are learned. When a partner is stuck and cannot properly perform a certain figure, or is confused by the pattern, it may be time to move to another section of the dance or even another dance. Standing in front of each other gesticulating and talking in a loud voice is not known as a good conflict resolution technique. It may be a good time to return to some basic figures and have fun. When dance partners are in a discussion around any problem, it is always a good idea to stick to facts. I ask myself what I could do to contribute to a solution. When we stay calm and focused, look for positive aspects in each other's dancing, and work together, whatever problems we encounter have a way of getting resolved. If not, we make a note of the problem and ask for help from our dance teacher at the next lesson.

How to find a dance partner

It is easier for men to find a partner than for women. The ratio of men to women taking lessons is estimated at 1:8. For every single man there are eight women looking for a partner or dancing with their male teacher. This can be noticeable at dance practice parties where the men are exhausted from dancing every dance, and the women are bored or frustrated at dancing only a few times during the evening. On the other hand, as soon as women get discouraged and don't attend, the opposite happens. Some nights there are many more single men than women looking for dance partners.

There are several ways for men to meet a good dance partner. One way is to register for group lessons, and usually the studio will attempt to match up dancers who need a partner. The most important action is, of course, to take some form of lessons. Be humble and join whatever level is suggested and don't be too arrogant to drop down a level or two if a partner is needed at that level. It is all a good refresher.

Attending practice parties is another great way to get started and find a partner. There are numerous women who are willing to help a man who has little dance experience learn the basic steps, providing the man can be patient enough to learn. There are coaching workshops and free dance lessons where single women will be looking for a partner, and these are less intimidating places to start. Once a dancer makes friends with a few people, soon a lot of people will know that the man is looking for a dance partner. Most studios have a registry of profiles for people looking for a dance partner. Some people look on-line, although there can be some sad results there, as with any on-line service if you are not careful.

Women can follow the same basic approach. They need to join group lessons and go to practice parties. It is vitally important to smile and enjoy dancing regardless of who the dance partner is or the frequency of getting to dance. If the man leading a dance has poor technique, he will improve. If the man is a very good dancer, a woman partner's great attitude might bring him back for more. Persistence is a virtue in dance. Most practice parties have more women than men, but there will always be a group lesson or party where far fewer women attend. That is the one women won't want to miss.

One of the dance instructors was searching for a dance partner to dance in professional competitions, and she found a man in Florida who seemed willing to travel to Ottawa for practice. However, he may have believed that Canada was cold all year round because he wore a shirt and sweater, danced all night without taking anything off, perspired profusely to the point that it was running out the cuffs of his sleeves—and declared that it did not bother him. Apparently something bothered him, and he went back to Florida. There are no guarantees with dance partners. Taking them for a test run is wise, and actually finding a good one requires patience and the ability to keep searching.

LEADING: MORE TIPS FOR MEN

Dancing holds another challenge when dancing with different partners. The partner's height, posture, and connection can be as different as his/her personality and looks. For a man, it requires a solid posture and frame regardless of who the partner is.

Dancing with a much taller woman means the spins in Latin require a higher hand to lead it in order to allow her to easily turn under it. Since the woman is taller, the arm needs to extend straight up to give her more room and helps to avoid hitting her on the side of the head in the turn. Staying close is another important point. Sometimes a tall woman takes bigger steps and moves away from her partner. The leader needs to be close to ensure a good arm extension or risk having the woman's bent elbow smack him across the head. The second half is getting the arm down again. It might be necessary for the leader to gently force his arm back down after the spin if the woman keeps holding hers up in the air. Women sometimes use the man's arm for support in a spin instead of doing it under their own balance. The arm has to be moved down in order to lead the next step. When dancing a smooth dance, the man needs to keep his steps consistent in size to help the woman understand early what to expect as they move around the floor. In spite of trying to extend the size of the steps, it is always paramount to maintain good balance.

Dancing with a much shorter woman presents other problems. Normally it is the man's posture that suffers, as there is a tendency to lean over the woman, which does not look good. Bending the knees slightly and maintaining an upright posture, letting the arms go lower to the woman's height, is a more reasonable approach. It may be necessary to take smaller steps, although some women who are adept at following will have no problem with any size step.

Dancing with a woman who exaggerates every movement is a challenge, especially in a Latin dance. When a woman moves all over the place in a dance, the man needs to keep the arms more firm than normal. The woman should be given sufficient space in a Latin dance to do hip motion and spins, but this should never result in her taking control of the lead or movement around the floor. This will not feel good for either partner. On the other hand, if the man maintains a good frame and solid connection, the woman might be convinced that this actually enhances her hip motion and she will be less determined to break the frame.

The biggest challenge is dancing with a partner who has no frame or cannot keep the beat to the music. Once again, it is important to stay focused on the frame and the beat of the music and not be led astray. After all, a leader must lead. A good philosophy is to dance, smile, and know that this is great practice for both partners.

SUCCESSFUL SPINS AND TURNS: TIPS FOR WOMEN

At an intermediate level, the woman needs to be proficient at spins or turns because when some men (like me) get tired in the middle of a Latin dance, they might simply stand still and give the woman several spins. If a woman becomes heavy by leaning forward or expecting the man to provide more physical support, the man can lead her through a lot of spins and turns to alleviate the pressure. Women might need to be aware that if their male partner is leading a lot of spins and turns, it could be an indication that they are being too heavy.

For successful spins:

- Maintain good posture.

- Spin on the proper foot and maintain balance without pushing or pulling on the man's hand.

- Squeeze the inside thighs for a balanced and tight spin.

During the spin, the free arm needs to be close to the front of the body, or at least not in a position to slap anyone. When the spin is over, make sure the arm that the man is holding is loose and ready to move down from above the head and into the next lead. Keeping the knees slightly bent will help with balance, acting like a shock absorber. For turns, the same rules apply. In a crossover break (American Social) or a New York (International), the forward foot needs to turn out to help maintain balance. The turn is done on the ball of the foot and the arm is relaxed. Once the step is learned, it takes practice to make it perfect, and every spin becomes an enjoyable adventure. As a man, I love leading spins because it is so little work for me, and the women always appear to enjoy them.

Same-sex dance couples

In this enlightened era, some studios offer same-sex couple dance lessons. There are also same-sex couple competitions. It can get complicated, but in some competitions the partners change the leader-follower roles a couple of times during the routine. On the other hand, there are some studios that refuse to allow a same-sex couple to dance together, and if they take group lessons, it must be for men as leaders and women as followers. I have seen men take lessons as followers and women take lessons as leaders, since they want to learn the other role in order to be able to teach it. In reality, all dance students seek the same goal. They are simply trying to learn a very enjoyable activity.

14

DANCE LESSONS AND INSTRUCTION

Teaching styles vary, and some dance instruction is difficult to follow because the teacher talks about an outcome, not a method. The best example I can think of to illustrate this is the common exhortation by teachers to "take bigger steps" in the standard dances. One of the most important techniques that needs to improve for anyone interested in dancing at a more advanced level in the standard or smooth dances is to take large steps in order to cover more distance on the floor. However, bigger steps are an outcome of something you do. They are the result of moving the legs and exercising muscles in a certain way. We need to know the "how to" part. To take a bigger step, a dancer needs to keep the weight longer on a supporting leg. There has to be a bending of the hip joint and ankle joint at a specific moment and a need to move the leg and shift weight a certain way with good timing. If all this is performed properly, then the steps will be larger. Trying to take bigger steps without any change in technique will probably result in the man's knocking his partner over, losing the frame, and straining some muscles.

I am at a Quickstep lesson with Jill, trying to improve our International steps, and the young male instructor is encouraging me to take bigger steps. As I begin a Natural Turn, he pushes on my left shoulder blade to give me more incentive for greater movement and a bigger step. It results only in uncertain balance. We lunge around the studio floor with increasingly sore calf, thigh, and back muscles, trying to move more distance with fewer steps, only to leave feeling exhausted and uncomfortable.

We discover that different teachers give the same instruction in different ways, and sometimes it helps enormously. Now and then the same teacher says something in a slightly different way, and suddenly it is clear what we have to do; other times, teachers say something different about the same step and we are confused. Dance is an evolving sport. When someone finds a better way to dance a certain step with better shaping or more movement, he/she passes it on. Teachers who continually take lessons also continue to find ways to explain technique in a new way.

There are times when a person or a dance couple needs to assess goals. Are we dancing for fun or do we want to compete some day? Are we taking lessons to learn new steps? What dances need the most improvement? What other dances do we want to learn? Do we prefer Latin or standard? How often do we find time to practise? Knowing what we want helps determine the type and frequency of lessons and makes sure we are on the right path. Talking to a teacher helps, and talking to other dancers provides a wealth of knowledge. We continue to set and reset our goals and make decisions based on where we want to be. We also keep in touch with competitive dancers and find out how much commitment it takes to follow that path. People tell us that we look great on the dance floor and that we should consider entering a competition. This increases our self-confidence and perhaps inflates our egos, although the people who suggest this have no better understanding than we do regarding the dedication and mindset required to be successful in a competition.

KEYS TO HAVING A SUCCESSFUL LESSON

The key to learning to dance is to practise. When we are taking a lesson we attempt to get the most out of it. It starts by being on time, getting warmed up, and understanding that we might be more confused until the new instruction sinks in. There is no need to get discouraged. If learning to dance were easy, then everyone would be doing it like a professional. When I coached children in soccer, I read a great book that explained that people learn differently. Some learn by watching, others learn by being told, and still others learn by doing. In reality it is probably some combination of all three methods.

For a group lesson or a private lesson, our time is spent on only a couple of dances to keep it simple. We are not shy and ask questions, especially questions to clarify a previous lesson. Taking notes is a good idea. My preference is to do it immediately after the class, while it is still fresh in my mind. Writing notes helps memory retention. Referring to them later helps me to remember the moment and the words spoken in explaining the technique. When I am unable to practise a step, I try to do it in my head. Of course, I dance it much better in my head than in real life! It is also much better when I practise without a partner. The easiest partner to lead is the imaginary partner. Some people like to video a lesson or part of a lesson, assuming the teacher agrees to be part of the video. It is a good reference but can be time-consuming. My suggestion is to decide what you desire from a video, such as seeing a pattern in order to remember it, then take notes from the video or practise the step. Personally, I find a video camera distracting and only helpful in remembering a brand-new step or a new routine.

Once we know a new pattern, repetition is the way to ingrain it. With sufficient practice, it will happen with little thought, and we wonder why we found it so difficult. In private lessons, it is good to focus more directly on the most troublesome dance or dance steps. That is a good way to improve quickly. Finally, it is important to remember that it takes time. One teacher told me it takes three reviews of a new step before most people can do it. I recall a couple that registered for a lesson from the Canadian standard champions and spent two hours on the most basic step. Patience is good.

Tips for a lesson:

- Be ready.
- Listen, practise, and relax.
- Take notes or practise a new step right away to remember it.

Most important, dancers should have fun, learn a variety of steps, move around the floor freely, do dips and turns, and feel really good about what they know.

We work on "fun" routines to extend our knowledge of the steps in each dance, while still allowing me to lead easily and insert different steps or change direction on the dance floor. We also work on different dances such as the Bachata and Bolero. We attend monthly Salsa workshops to acquire new steps.

KEYS TO HAVING A SUCCESSFUL PRACTICE

Every practice requires a warm-up, especially at my age. I do some mild stretching of my legs and arms and then make sure I move the rest of my muscles. Sometimes, if there is space on the floor, I walk through a sequence of dance steps. When I am not at the studio, I try to dance a routine in my head. We review any notes from previous lessons and work on specific patterns that we last worked on with an instructor. We do a routine then pick the worst sections and try to fix them. If that does not work, we take it back to the next dance lesson. There is no expectation of perfection on the first try. Each successive routine that feels good is done again, adding a little bit more improvement each time. For example, when repeating a good Waltz routine, we think about doing the weight shifts better or the spin turns with more feeling. The routines are assessed. What went well and what is not working? We do it again. The outcome of a practice should be to solidify and make consistent the good parts of each routine and to understand the weak areas that need improvement. It is important to recognize what is not working or feeling good and needs to be brought to the instructor.

Tips for practice:

- Set an agenda. For example, start with standard then work on Latin dances. Decide what dances to focus on. Consider which dances need work on technique and which ones need more practice of the routine.
- Practise the steps to make them comfortable. Bring notes from the previous lessons to review.
- Make note of troublesome areas in order to get help.

Obviously, the best practice location is the studio, due to the large floor and mirrors on the walls to help us check our posture. We try to squeeze in time before or after a lesson and make special trips to the studio as time permits. Outside the studio we practise at the various parties or other occasions. However, when we learn a new step, we have to work on it every possible chance we have or it will slip away. My favourite dance practice area for new steps is in the kitchen. I put on a dance music CD and in that tight space I cook up a Triple

Swing while preparing dinner. Salsa is another good dance for a small space. For a Waltz or Foxtrot, I navigate out the kitchen door to the dining room, through the living room and around the coffee table, then back into the kitchen through the second door. I always travel counterclockwise along the proper line of dance and I swear that the coffee table moves a few inches on its own as I pass by a second time, bruising my shins. Learning can be a painful experience.

One of Jill's practice locations is the bedroom. Today she is getting ready to go out for a dance and desperately tries to remember the forward and backward Lindy kicks that we learned a few days earlier. She is wearing her dance shoes, and her feet are flying to the beat of a song on the radio. Unfortunately, one of her heels flies solidly into the rattan footboard of the bed. Jill hops around on the other foot trying to get her jammed heel out of the footboard and cursing under her breath about how nice the footboard used to be before the Lindy hole arrived. Eventually, with a great pull and wildly flying hair, she extricates herself and covers over the hole as best she can.

"You will never guess what I did!" she exclaims when I enter the bedroom.

OTHER LEARNING METHODS

What about learning to dance from DVDs? Admittedly there are some good DVDs on dancing. The main problem for me is trying to watch and do it at the same time. The steps are basically right, and the timing is not a problem. It is simply easier to get instant feedback from a teacher as you make an effort to follow what is being taught. Instant correction, live instruction, and interactive feedback are really essential to a physical activity such as dancing. Nonetheless, once you have a good grounding in the basics, it might be possible to pick up some additional steps or tips. I borrowed a DVD on Salsa dancing from my good friend Doug and learned a couple of new patterns that I now perform on a regular basis.

As for music, there are some good CDs and a lot of bad CDs that claim to have ballroom and Latin dance music. If a CD is titled "Foxtrot for Dance Instruction," it does not necessarily mean it will be good or even the proper tempo. Some music has obscure beats that are difficult to follow, while other music is simply not at all what the title implies. If there is a chance to sample the music before buying, that is ideal. Otherwise, caution has to be exercised when buying any music to use for dance practice.

CHOREOGRAPHED ROUTINES

A routine is a sequence of steps in dance that form a beautiful pattern and allow the couple to move around the room as if it is completely natural to them. There are three main types of routines: for competitions, weddings, and shows.

Competition routines are designed to allow the couple to perform most or all of the mandatory steps in the syllabus for their level. The dance pattern is set up to flow easily from one movement to another and also has to adhere to the designated preceding and following figures from a limited list of choices.

Weddings or special occasions such as anniversaries and retirement functions are another choreographing opportunity. In fact, many people who perform a wedding dance routine end up enjoying the experience so much that they return for more lessons. Wedding routines can of course use any steps, but should be geared to the level and capability of the couple. It has to look really good but not be too difficult, since most couples take only about four lessons before the wedding. Some factors to consider in a wedding routine might be:

- Is there a favourite song?

- What dance works well and looks good?

- How long is the wedding gown—will it get stepped on?

- How large is the dance floor? A smaller floor will be more suitable for a Rumba than for a travelling Foxtrot.

Normally, a teacher or very high-calibre student couples will perform in shows. Dancers for a show routine target crowd-pleasing steps and may include lifts, body flips, and rolls. One of the key elements is to find exciting music—dramatic for slow, flowing dances and catchy or bouncy for Latin dances. A show dance should take into account the age and type of audience. Whether they are young or old, knowledgeable about dance or not, can all be taken into consideration for a good dance routine. Many dance studios offer a show dance night where students of all levels perform a routine in order to show others and themselves how far they have progressed in their ability to dance. Our instructor strongly suggests that Jill and I should participate in an upcoming show. Jill has never performed in front of people and does not believe that she can overcome her nervousness. We defer making a decision.

A possible fourth type of routine is one that some couples receive from their teacher in order to help learn a specific series of steps. It is not uncommon for an instructor to put together a series of moves in a pattern that includes getting around a corner and helping the couple know what sequences go before or after one another. For example, the couple may learn a Waltz routine that starts at one corner and moves around the four walls and starts over again. Some of the steps will be familiar and others not. Dancing the pattern helps the dancers to practise all the steps. The downside of a routine is whether or not the couple can continue dancing in the event of an interruption such as forgetting the next step or a wall of dance traffic. Dance floors usually contain other dancers, and at a social dance it is important to be able to navigate around the floor.

15

UNLIMITED DANCING,
UNLIMITED FUN

Most dance studios organize an annual grand ball, and our dance studio has two, one in June and another in December. It is a formal event with students from all over the city participating. The hall capacity is close to four hundred people, and it is not uncommon for it to be sold out. A DJ plays some fabulous ballroom and Latin dance music and leads people in a few ballroom line dances at times during the evening. Men in tuxedos and women in gowns glide across the crowded floor, taking small steps. The dance floor is good-quality hardwood, large and rectangular. We feel blessed to have so many good friends join us at these grand events. At our table of twelve, I propose the toast, "May your dancing always provide you great pleasure, and may the friends you meet along the way provide even more."

At a practice party, I dance with our pretend mother, Jakki. She enjoys watching Jill and me dance, More than that, I believe she sees the intense love and caring that we have for each other, and it reminds her of her departed husband and her own relationship of years gone by. Her children have all grown up, are well educated, and have left Ottawa to pursue their dreams. In their absence, she calls us her adopted children. She is still as sweet as ever, and I notice the usual bows on her shoes. My steps have improved dramatically since I first danced with her and knew only two basic patterns in every dance. Now we move around the floor gracefully. She is light and nimble. She closes her eyes and feels the music as she moves. I think I must be a good lead for her to put so much trust in me. She still takes dance lessons and is determined to be the oldest person in Canada to take dance lessons. No one knows if she holds that record yet, but it is a firm goal in her mind and I am not betting against it. She says that Jill and I are perfect for each other and dance well together. She loves to watch us dance, and we love Jakki. There is a down-to-earth goodness about her. She provides support, encouragement, and inspiration to many people, and we think maybe she provides a little bit more for us.

PARTIES

One of the fun aspects about knowing how to dance is the parties. There is a common saying that ballroom dancers are always looking for a good party. Charity events are especially fun. There are many balls and galas in Ottawa, and one of our favourites is called Rockin' for Risk. It raises money to help children and families deal with autism. It is a Rock 'n' Roll dance at a large venue with a huge wooden dance floor and live music. With '50s or '60s Rock 'n' Roll, we expect to dance a lot of Triple Swing, Jive, and Cha-Cha. Many people dress up for that era, intending to have a very good time.

For this event, Jill wears a pink poodle skirt with a black poodle figure sewn on it as well as the letters "J" and "P," representing our first names. She adds a bouncy fake ponytail and white socks, and I grease down my hair and wear tight black jeans and a tight white T-shirt. We dance Swing and Cha-Cha non-stop for a couple of hours, and I start to realize how old I am. Jill twirls in her pink poodle skirt, and I feel like a greaser (or is that geezer?). We get compliments for our outfits and our dancing. People stop us and ask if they may take a picture of us, especially impressed by Jill's outfit. The attention is great fun. We see numerous acquaintances from the different dance studios, group lessons, and practice parties. The next day my legs will be sore and swollen from the knees to the tips of my toes. Tonight we dance. At some point, Elvis makes an appearance, at least someone that looks and sounds like him. A woman rolls by on old-style roller skates. I bid on silent auction entries thinking I can push the price up and accidentally win. It is a free car wash along with other small items. More important, the event is well attended and a lot of money is raised for a good cause.

At another Rock 'n' Roll dance, Jill dresses as Olivia Newton–John, with her normally straight hair fashioned in a bushy, curly style. I go as John Travolta from *Grease*. We both wear black pants with black T-shirts. We get three compliments in the first fifteen minutes after we arrive. Most people do not dress up. The night is full of dancing, talking to friends, and laughter.

Black and White

We go to a Black and White dance party that is sponsored by a dance studio across the provincial border, in Quebec. Men are wearing black suits or tuxedos and black bow ties. Most women wear all-black dresses or gowns. The DJ is great and music fills the room. This place is packed with energy. The dance floor consists of tiles over concrete, and before the night is over, my ankles are swollen. We dance well, although it takes a while to get used to the unfamiliar setting. There are plenty of good dancers here. A Jack and Jill competition is held later in the evening and takes a lot of time away from general dancing. We choose not to participate and watch from the sidelines as dancers unfamiliar with each other dance through the predetermined set of patterns allowed in the Cha-Cha. The next morning, my ankles, knees and calf muscles ache and are slightly swollen from dancing on an unforgiving floor.

Chez Arlu

We drive across the Ottawa River on the Portage Bridge to Gatineau and travel east then north to Val Des Monts. There is a dance club here called Chez Arlu that looks like a dome converted from an airplane hangar. It has a nice parquet wooden dance floor and tables with seating all around the floor. There is a bar, and a live band is playing tonight. It is a popular place for weddings, and there is a white arch behind the band. Dancing is good, and we meet a few people we know and others that we recognize but have not formally met. We dance a nice Foxtrot and Waltz then do a Swing. It is a good evening, although a very long drive.

Swing dancing

There is a Swing dance party on a warm and sticky summer night at the picturesque New Edinborough boathouse overlooking the Ottawa River. We are east of Green Island where the Rideau and Ottawa rivers combine. The water is dark and murky. The sun begins to set perfectly like a bright, orange ball on top of the river to the west. The rustic brown floor is wooden and creaky. The building is old, and it feels like we could fall through the floorboards any minute despite the sturdy frame and thick support beams. Someone sets up a CD player at one end of the room to play pre-burned CDs. The volume is increased to fill the room. Sometimes they play very old Swing music that must have originated from vinyl records because the sound is scratchy and the words are undecipherable. We dance and soak up the tranquil setting, which is more suited to Waltz than Swing, although it is a wonderful experience. When we feel too hot, we walk out onto a balcony that

extends over the river's edge and enjoy a nice breeze coming off the water. We breathe in the sweet evening air and bat away the mosquitoes. After a short rest, we return to more dancing above the water.

On another warm summer Saturday night, we drive across the Quebec border to listen to a live band playing at a marina clubhouse. The band is good, not great, playing recognizable pop songs that are Swings and Cha-Chas. The dance floor is a wooden deck that tilts from the side closest to the band to the side away from the band. I dance well in my running shoes, but Jill risks a heel sinking between the boards and if she gets stuck in a turn there is a serious possibility of an injury. We dance where the boards are tightly joined, and I avoid leading spins. We relax in between dancing at a nearby table that fills up with dance people who know each other from various previous dance venues. Darkness moves in, and the lights from the stage shimmer in the rippling dark water of the Ottawa River.

We attend a dance club inside a hotel bar in the east end with a live band playing mainly country music. We dance a few great Triple Swings and some Cha-Chas. The wooden dance floor is square, has three-foot-high railings along the sides, and fills up quickly with free-style dancers. The place has a long bar off to the side of the dance floor, and soon people are dancing to the background music played when the band takes a break. Alcohol has a way of encouraging everyone to dance. For trained dancers, it has the opposite effect, and we forget what we know. There are a few couples performing actual Swing dances, and I am careful to pick a spot on the floor and stay there. Free-style dancers mainly dance in a confined space, whereas newly trained Swing dancers can fly into someone's back with little forewarning when doing a throw-out. It is the telltale sign of a new dancer when the steps are too large in Swing. As the night wears on, the music volume increases, and the dance floor becomes too crowded for us to perform any recognizable dance.

Salsa

We go to Caliente's, a Latin dance club in the Byward Market area, and dance with the younger crowd of Salsa dancers who have limitless energy, incredible rhythm, and smooth dance steps. The dance floor is huge and wooden. It becomes crowded after ten-thirty p.m.

Bartenders in colourful Caribbean shirts flip bottles and pour drinks. The Latin-looking males exude machismo, strutting around talking to their male buddies and smiling at the women. The women are dressed colourfully and know how to move their hips to the music. We dance as well as we can, but mainly sit at our table sipping a glass of wine and watching the great variety of steps, spins, and hand slides. The music is loud and pounding, far too much so for my throbbing old eardrums. The main dance is Salsa, although Merengue is thrown into the mix. Once the place is packed close to the fire rule limits, some rap, house, or hip hop will be played in a blatant attempt to remain as a place to go for the younger crowd. The atmosphere is buoyant, happy, and inspiring.

The opportunities and locations to dance seem limitless. This sleepy government town is not so sleepy for ballroom and Latin dancers. Every week there are different venues, more places to dance, and a lot of people enjoying themselves because they know how to dance.

Rueda

Rueda seems like a cross between a Merengue mixer and Salsa with some square-dance calling thrown in. The participants form a circle with the pattern of a man and then a woman in sequence. An equal number of partners is required to make it work well. In the Rueda that I learned, the couples face each other to start. When the music begins, a basic Cuban Salsa step is danced in time to the music. The caller yells out a move that is to be done after the end of the current pattern.

We are at a house party doing Rueda in a large basement with a wooden floor, and the Salsa music is inspiring. The caller says *"Dame* (Da-may)," and we switch partners with a cross-body lead step. Next comes *"Enchufa,"* and we give the women a turn, walk behind them and grab hold of the next woman in line. It looks like a wheel moving sometimes in one direction and sometimes in the other. The caller yells out *"Dame Dos,"* which means to perform that move twice, so we do the move then skip a partner. The women are moving inside the wheel. Getting quite enthusiastic about our success to this point, *"Enchufa Dos"* is called, and we end up getting totally confused. The circle turns to a blob, and everyone is laughing.

Birthday

Jill's birthday is on July 7, which translates this year as 07–07–07, and I use it as an excuse to organize a dinner at a local dinner and dance club called Villa Lucia in Ottawa's west end. Not only are we celebrating a birthday, but on that morning Jill and I make the down payment on a new house where we will move in together. I invite twenty of our closest dance friends with a reservation for 7:07 p.m. Everyone shows up, has a delicious meal, and listens to the live three-person band. They have a guitar player who sings, someone on keyboards, and a drummer who also fills in any desired remaining instrumentation with a pre-programmed electronic box. Jill is unaware that the evening out is really a birthday party for her and starts singing along when the band strikes up the Happy Birthday song.

"I wonder who else is celebrating a birthday?" she says excitedly. "It is the same day as mine!"

Everyone at the table chuckles and sings the line "Happy Birthday to Jill" and at that very moment the waiter sneaks from behind and places a small cake in front of her with a single lit candle. She smiles widely.

"Paul, this is the best birthday ever!" she confides.

We are on top of the world and feel like the luckiest couple alive. The band plays lively tunes and our massive contingent of trained dancers fills the small tiled floor doing Cha-Cha, Swing, and Rumba late into the evening. Dancing to live music is always special, and everyone is smiling.

Azores

In August, we take a trip to visit Jill's parents, who left Montreal many years ago to retire on their home island of Pico in the Azores. Pico is a small island known for having the tallest volcano among the nine islands that make up the Azores. The last known eruption was in 1720, and black lava rock is common throughout the island. Tourists travel here to climb the volcano and ride a zodiac into the Atlantic Ocean for whale and dolphin watching. In the middle of the island, we visit the tiny town of São João, enjoying the view, the local wine, and perfect weather. On the weekend, this rural town on a small island in the middle of the Atlantic Ocean is having a summer festival. We arrive at the town square in the evening and watch the live band on the stage. A glass of beer or wine costs the equivalent of around fifty cents in Canadian currency. The festival is a magnet drawing residents from surrounding areas. Couples are dancing cheerfully in front of the stage to the rhythmic local music. After a brief observation, the dance looks like a slower, simple Merengue with a lot of *rondes*, where the man and woman face each other while moving around in a circle. I don't observe any turns or spins for the woman. One of the local men leads his partner wildly across the concrete deck, moving his feet in simple one-two counts with the beat. Who would have thought that here on a tiny Portuguese island in the middle of the Atlantic Ocean, knowing how to Merengue would come in handy? Jill and I decide to dance. Thankfully I am wearing running shoes and she wears some tight-fitting sandals with a wedge heel. We start off easy on the rough cement, stepping to the beat, smiling and enjoying ourselves. Then I give her an underarm turn left. This is followed by more turns, a cuddle, and a spin out. People are watching us. A few minutes later, a local man gives his partner an underarm turn. People learn quickly.

Halloween

A Halloween dance is always fun, although it is difficult to find costumes to dance in without tripping or sweating profusely. Jill dresses me up as Zorro, who turns out to be both of our childhood heroes, and she becomes a harem girl. My head heats up quickly dancing with a black hat. I have to remove my plastic épée in order to stop hitting people. It is strapped to my belt, and every time I turn around it slaps someone on the leg.

"Sorry," I apologize as the stick touches someone again, "I did not mean to poke you," forgetting that the word "poke" has another connotation.

"Look at Zorro," someone whispers. "He is going around poking all the women. What a man."

Jill decides one year that I should dress as a Hawaiian woman. Being a good sport, I grudgingly agree, providing she dresses as a man. Of course Jill has a great time dressing me up, buys me a long, black wig, and shows me how to wear a grass skirt. I shave my face clean, and Jill does an amazing job with my makeup. On the other hand, Jill has a lot of trouble looking like an ugly man. She stuffs a belly pack in

her stomach, wears a short sombrero, and blackens her face to make it look dirty. Actually, I blacken her face and struggle to keep her away from her makeup, which she keeps trying to put on when I am not looking. She is horrified to look so unfeminine. That is only the beginning. Once at the dance party, after several double takes, people think I am hilarious and I get way more attention than I need. As for poor Jill, people do not know how to react. They avoid her, and no one strikes up a conversation with her. She wants to leave after fifteen minutes. We stay and learn a good lesson. Don't judge people on looks alone. That is reinforced for me. What Jill takes away is that she will never ever agree to dress as a man again.

For the next Halloween party, a year later, we go to a costume store and receive advice about applying makeup. We decide on Count Dracula and his Countess. Jill does a phenomenal job on the face makeup. We have pasty white faces with darkened eyes and black lipstick and look very serious. We each have a long, black cape. My hair is slicked back and glued down with Vaseline. I dress in a white tuxedo shirt, black bow tie, and black pants. Jill gets into character by wearing a strapless red and black dress, long black gloves, and a long black wig. We win first prize, and I remove the cape before dancing the night away in a tuxedo shirt that gets overwhelmingly hot.

The dance studio holds a Western night dance party. I borrow a black hat and wear a black shirt and black jeans with a studded belt. Jill wears tight blue jeans with a white belt and a white blouse with the front tied above the navel. She wears a white hat, a small kerchief tied around her neck, and a beaming smile. As we dance, I avoid giving her spins or turns or her hat will get knocked off. People call me Black Bart. I guess I am the bad guy. Many people dress up for this event. There are fancy shirts, boots, and holsters with fake guns, but no one has more fun than Jill.

People continue to tell us how good we look together on the dance floor. Some people say that we should try competing. There is much discussion, wavering, and uncertainty. Should we give it a try? We have no idea what we are considering, the commitment that it would take and how we compare to other competitors. There is a lot of confidence initially because we have a great teacher and we know how to move around the floor well. Dancing together feels good, and our dance technique shows improvement every week. Where is our next challenge? We watch our friends compete at the Kingston Dance-Sport event in September and think that we should fit into the entry level. Will our confidence be shattered if we do poorly, or will we shine? We put the decision on hold. However, our teacher convinces us to set aside any qualms due to nerves or lack of confidence and to participate in the upcoming show dance night.

The show

Jill is crouched over at the waist with her head between her knees, feeling like she is about to faint. We are standing in the corner of the room off the dance floor with other dance students who are preparing to perform individual dance routines for the dance studio. Non-performing dance students, relatives, guests, social dancers, and curious spectators fill the chairs at both ends of the short wall and a single row of chairs lining the long walls. All seats in the Community Centre are full. We are five minutes away from performing our first show dance together to a huge audience, and Jill is so nervous she is ready to pass out.

"I feel dizzy."

"You will be fine," I reply, with a weak attempt at encouragement.

"Say a prayer," adds someone next to us.

Our names are announced. We walk proudly onto the floor and take our positions ready for a flowing romantic Waltz routine. We start a few feet apart facing each other and as the instrumental opening of our music begins we slowly raise our arms. It is the "Dark Waltz," by Hayley Westenra, a dramatic and emotional piece of music that can make the hair on the back of your neck stand on end. Camera flashes pop from all directions. At least we are well dressed, I think to myself. Jill is wearing a long black dress with mesh sleeves and bodice with a row of tiny rhinestones along the front. This is also the first time she has worn fake eyelashes. I wear the standard male show dance outfit for a non-professional dancer, which consists of black dress pants with a white shirt, black necktie, and black vest. As nervousness sets in, the routine continues a little differently than planned, and my lovely partner raises her arms too quickly and is stuck there with both arms extended waiting for the next cue in the music. Since our teacher told us that it is important to have continuous movement Jill starts moving her wrists, which results in her hands flapping like the wings of a bird stuck in the mud and unable to take flight. I am not much better. Although my arms rise more slowly I am also now stuck in a rigid pose waiting for the next cue and I choose not to make any more movement, based on what I see from Jill. Luckily, the words of the song are about to start.

We are the lucky ones.
We shine like a thousand suns.

We step exactly on cue, and Jill performs a flawless leg lift and spinout, which earns a polite round of applause. We slide into a closed dance hold position for the next steps, and I realize her whole body is shaking. It is like holding a small jackhammer and thankfully for both of us it lasts only a few more seconds. That is a minor distraction, because as I step out to take hold position I lose the music in my head and am now off the beat in my steps. Composure and timing return by the end of the first long wall. We continue with left side by side spins. After a spiral and turn, Jill completes the high leg lift from a left side dip to enthusiastic applause, which buoys our spirits. More camera flashes engulf us. As choreographed, we tuck our heads lovingly into each other's neck for a couple of simple patterns then emerge to normal posture, heads up, with luminous smiles. We glide through the rest of the routine, and I give her a graceful dip at the end. We turn to both sides of the audience at the short walls and bow. The best part for me is always when it is over. We walk off the floor, and our teacher congratulates us. Then more people come over to congratulate us. Our dear friend Jakki is here with bows on her shoes and embraces us warmly, giving us profuse praise for our efforts. It is touching that so many people are so supportive. Now people that we barely know are telling us how much they enjoyed the performance. Jill is not entirely convinced that we danced well until we speak with one of the dance studio's Latin teachers.

"You did well," she says with her Russian accent. "The dancing and the music . . . it was so beautiful that you made my mother cry."

And that was the experience that ultimately provided the motivation for our decision to start competitive dancing.

"Dark Waltz" routine

PART THREE

BECOMING A BALLROOM DANCE COMPETITOR

16

OUR FIRST COMPETITIONS

It is the end of the world and God and the Devil somehow agree to hold a contest between Heaven and Hell to decide the fate of all the remaining souls in the world. After much haggling, it is decided that the contest will be a ballroom dance competition. Once the arrangements are complete, God says to the Devil, "I don't understand how you could ever agree to such a deal, for you will surely lose."

The Devil only laughs and shakes his head. God continues, "After all, in Heaven I am blessed with all the best ballroom dancers to ever dance. I have champions from Blackpool. I have Fred Astaire and Ginger Rogers."

The Devil shifts his weight from one foot to the other then back again. "I agree that you have all the best dancers, but my side will still win."

God grows impatient with such arrogance. "How can that be?" he demands.

"It is simple," replies the Devil with a grin. "I have all the judges."

We had been drifting along, haphazardly learning different dance steps instead of having a clear goal of what we want to do and what we want to accomplish. My competitive instincts surface, and I declare that we should train to start competing. Jill does not want to compete because she thinks it will be too stressful. The dance show was evidence of that. Reversing myself, I agree with her and decide that it is too much work—only to have her change her mind later and think that it would be good for us. My anxiety around competing stems from wanting to perform every figure correctly, with the added stress that when I make a small, probably unnoticeable mistake during a dance, it becomes difficult to recover mentally. The error stays in my mind, preventing me from focusing on the dance.

The decision to compete goes back and forth for a while until we finally agree that we should at least make an attempt and target

April, a few months away, for our first competition. We start working on International style steps but do not have a routine. Our current instructor is more familiar with American Social steps than International, but nonetheless works hard to get us ready after our successful show dance routine.

We join the Ontario Amateur Dance Association and decide to ease ourselves into competing by starting in the Pre-Bronze category and doing only the International Standard dances. The two dances in this category are Waltz and Quickstep. We receive our membership cards and are ready to register for a competition.

The first competition we select is a relatively small one, strictly for amateur couples and located in Toronto. We register for an adult competition for couples where each partner is over eighteen years old and for an Adult II category where each partner is over thirty-five years of age. This being an out-of-town competition for us, we drive to Toronto the day before. After a restless sleep and nervous preparation, we drive to the competition hall in North York to arrive at around eleven a.m. On arrival, we pick up our entry passes and competitor number, then wander inside to assess the venue. The hall is large and has a good-quality floor. There is a small practice room separate from the main dance floor. Four large speakers sit on pedestals at each corner of the floor, and I appreciate the quality of the excellent sound system, since it eases my fears of losing the beat in my head. At one end of the hall is a raised podium for the master of ceremonies, who will announce the events and results. There is seating for spectators at dozens of small, round tables with white tablecloths along three sides of the floor. The evening events are when the best dancers compete, and the spectator entry tickets will be sold out. For the competitive events, judges stand at various places around the dance floor holding a clipboard full of papers. They determine the ranking for the dance competitors after each dance in a category. The score sheet is picked up from each of the judges after every dance and the numbers compiled to see who has the best score.

Jill attaches our competitor number to my back with four small safety pins, being careful not to stab me. The schedule, along with an estimated start time for each event, is listed in the program, so we know when to be ready. In spite of our nervousness, we admire the organizers for managing to maintain such a well-organized and well-run competition. As it turns out, the events are on time, and the organizers do a fine job of making sure competitors are lined up at the right time. After a brief warm-up, we follow instructions to enter a queue at a place slightly off the side of the dance floor and wait for the previous event to finish. The men are all on the left side and the women to their right. It is at this point that all the women nervously dash away for a final washroom break, hoping to return before the event is announced. Miraculously, a few minutes later, all couples are ready, and the category is announced by the master of ceremonies along with the number of each couple competing. We watch the couples in the event scheduled immediately before ours walk with a nervous confidence onto the floor, all hoping to start at the same spot along the beginning of the long wall. Some are disappointed. Each couple takes a position facing each other about a body length apart. The music begins, and the partners step into each other's arms, trying to attain that perfect dance hold. The man searches his brain for the beat and when to start.

When our event is announced, we walk across the floor, select a starting position, and move into a closed dance hold when the music starts. I am nervous, trying to remember the starter step. The first dance is a Waltz, and I notice that another couple has already started to move. My brain picks up the beat quickly, and we begin to dance. I strain to remember the steps and put together some semblance of order to our movement along the first long wall. Surveying for potential navigation problems, I smile and try to maintain posture. I feel that my frame is sagging. We complete a Natural Spin Turn, smile, and think about not leaning into each other. I take a short step to avoid a couple coming across the floor and finally get to the first corner and make the turn. I think to myself that the short wall is our good wall; and, *How much longer will this music continue?* It seems like an eternity. We finish moving along the length of the short wall and turn to the second long wall, continuing for another fifteen seconds, and finally the music stops. We shuffle to the nearest corner of a long wall along with half of the other couples to set ourselves up for the second dance.

The next dance is the Quickstep. The music starts and my brain grabs the beat. Suddenly we are off and moving across the floor with an unidentifiable frame and posture, but at least we have some semblance of closed position. Navigation is challenging, although there are no collisions. We finish the Quickstep, move to the edge of the floor, and bow. I take Jill's left arm in my right and walk off. We nod our heads and politely congratulate other couples then run frantically for water. Our mouths have dried up during the dance with our attempt to smile for the judges. Jill's upper lip became glued to the top of her teeth. That was one solid smile. The next event is a few minutes away, and we repeat everything in a different age category.

We discover that competitors at our level are friendly and probably know each other from the Toronto area. This is a competition, but it is really about doing the best that we can; the results are decisions made by the judges. Our goal is to dance as well as we dance in practice and then continue to improve with each practice. With effort, every successive competition will be an improvement over the previous one. Anyway, that is our thought process, but we soon discover there is a lot more to it than that. How naive we are in this first attempt.

My nervousness increases for the second event, and my navigation skills decrease. We have no routine, and I try to move around the floor as if it were a student practice party. We have huge smiles on our faces, which make our pathetic efforts all the more noticeable. Couples move around us on the floor with a fluidity and grace that instantly raises alarm bells. Our confidence sinks as we sense that there is something intrinsically incorrect in our steps and movement. A short time after our event is over, the awards ceremony begins, and for each event the master of ceremonies announces the results. It starts by naming the lowest-ranked competitor and moving to the highest-ranked couple. We place last in both events.

It is a long, five-hour drive home from Toronto, and our competitive spirit sparks and flares. After a brief interlude of feeling bad, of being discouraged and upset, we go into problem-solving mode and list the facts. On the positive side, we had good smiles, two pretty trophies, and had the fortitude to get through our first competition. On the other side, we were executing dance steps that were not appropriate for an International style competition and were far too unbalanced and sluggish on the floor.

We create a four-part plan of action. First, we need to find an experienced teacher, preferably a former competitor in International style. Second, we need to increase our practice time. Third, we need a preplanned routine to perform for each dance. And finally, we are not going to quit. Our confidence is shaken but not shattered, and developing an action plan would become a recurring pattern after each competition. On the long highway heading east toward Ottawa at 110 kilometres an hour, we analyze the results and develop a clear plan of what to do next.

On our return to Ottawa, we put our plan into action. We thank our current teacher profusely, and, being the total professional that she is, she understands that we are now headed on a different path and wishes us well. We approach the owner of the Let's Dance Studio in Ottawa. She is a former International style dance champion and a certified judge for International style competitions.

Our next competition is in two weeks, and there is not much we can do other than to gain more experience and control our nerves. Josée, our new teacher, points out the American Social steps that I am doing that are inappropriate for an International style competition. My forehead crinkles in despair at the loss of what I use as an important navigation step. We have to enter the second competition not only without an International routine but knowing that what we are doing is wrong. We work on making the steps we know better, and it is only after we return that we will start working on the first International style competitive routine that is created for us.

In general, competitors dance a routine in order to avoid using incorrect steps that could be grounds for disqualification. A good routine will include most or all of the figures that are listed at a level as defined by the published International style syllabus and included in the ISTD (Imperial Society of Teachers of Dancing) list. It will also be created to adhere to the criteria for which steps should precede and follow other steps.

A choreographed routine may reduce stress because the competitors know what the sequence of steps will be along each wall and in the corners and how they plan to move around the dance floor. A routine can allow the dance couple to feel the music and express it in their movement.

The Mississauga Open is our second competition, and our preparation at the hotel is an adventure. Washroom counters are never long enough, and the rooms are too small for a decent practice dance. At the first competition, Jill had someone else put her fake eyelashes on for her. This time she tries to do it herself while I wait outside the washroom, pacing beside the queen-sized bed. She does not admit to her hand shaking with nerves, although she pronounces success loudly when the first set of eyelashes is on.

"I got one on!" she declares as the first of the oversized eyelashes is stuck securely to her eyelid.

Half-dressed, I erroneously conclude that her preparations are proceeding well and I try to enter the washroom, only to see Jill with her second set of fake eyelashes half on, with the other half hanging loosely in front of her eye.

"Not now!" she exclaims while staring into the mirror unflinchingly as she struggles with the loose end. I retreat quickly. She gets it on but has to trim off an end without putting the scissors into her eye. We finish getting ready, load up the car, and drive off.

We no longer have any expectations after our first dismal rankings at the previous competition. This hall is a good size, and we arrive an hour prior to the evening program, which offers the adult events. The program is scheduled to start at 6:00 p.m. Since we are one of the lowest levels, we expect to be finished competing by seven or seven-thirty p.m. and drive the five hours back to Ottawa that night. When we arrive, it is obvious that the competition is a daylong event and has started much earlier in the day. It fact, most of the day is for children's competitive events. In addition to numerous age categories and selection of dances, there are odd events, such as a mother and daughter Cha-Cha. As well as competitors and parents at this competition, the spectators include entire families, relatives, and numerous younger siblings.

We enter the hall. The floor in the spectator area is covered in candy wrappers, empty potato chip bags, plastic juice containers, and children. It is like walking through a pile of freshly fallen leaves in the autumn, and we have to be careful not to step on anything that could scream. We carefully watch for a wandering limb in the process of making a snow angel in the debris on the floor. After purchasing the program of events, we make two observations. First, the event is severely behind schedule, and second, the events are divided by age groups, not level of experience. Instead of dancing our two events within minutes of each other—similar to the previous competition—they will be separated by two hours. Our Adult II competition is listed for 8:30 p.m., with the award presentation at 9:30 p.m. Considering the schedule delay, we now anticipate being finished around 10:30 p.m. We have not booked a hotel room and mentally prepare ourselves for another long and late night drive back to Ottawa.

There is no practice room in this hall, so people are creative in finding warm-up space. Some are dancing on a tiled floor outside the washrooms. Although the hall itself is large, it looks like the organizers have sectioned off a smaller area for the competitive dance floor and a larger one for paying spectators. In fact, the floor looks more like a square than a rectangle. Which wall is the long wall? Our nerves are frayed again but we need the experience. At least, that is what we try to tell ourselves. We have two events to get through and two dances in each event. We know our flaws and hope that the experience will provide incentive to improve.

If this train of thought was meant to alleviate some of the stress, it was not successful. Our Waltz is a mess again as I try unsuccessfully to stay with International steps and not look terrified by the faster-moving traffic as the other amateur couples whiz by. In the Quickstep, Jill catches her heel on a ridge while doing a back step along the short wall and almost falls over completely on her backside. In true partnership spirit, I grab her as she manages to get her other foot under herself and she stays up.

We finish last in our first event. They announce the placements from last to first place and it is gut-wrenchingly awful to hear our number called first for that last-place award. People are friendly toward us, and one of the Bronze level couples from Toronto tells us we look really good and ask where we are from. If we look good, it must be from the waist up, and the lovely Jill deserves all the credit.

The second event is a close copy of the first, and our names are announced once again as the last-place couple. While we drive home, Jill watches for clusters of deer, which signifies a need to slow down on the highway, and finally, around three a.m., our car turns the final corner close to home with our two last-place trophies tucked in our bags.

Competitions are more than dancing a routine and getting judged. The competitors are a small, exclusive club of people who almost torture themselves to achieve their goals. We meet people and make friends. There is something special about meeting another competitor who is going through the same struggles as we are. There is a common bond of knowing that this is not easy. We are gracious in any placement and polite to other competitors and the organizers. We are really competing against ourselves, wanting to do a personal best in whatever dance is next. The road has many obstacles and our job is to recognize and defeat them. We return to our lesson determined to improve.

17
AMATEUR COMPETITIVE STRUCTURE

There are several organizations, sanctioning bodies, and rules in DanceSport, as in any other major amateur sport. There are also competing organizations, differences in opinion on how organizations should be managed, and inconsistency across provinces.

The amateur levels for competition in Ontario are:

- Beginners
- Pre-Bronze
- Full Bronze
- Silver
- Gold
- Pre-Champion
- Champion

Most of the people that I know start at the Pre-Bronze level, although some dance studios hold their own informal internal competition. This can be an early opportunity to evaluate interest in competing and perform a self-readiness check. Dancers who feel confident after a studio competition may try moving to open competitions. We also meet couples who take many years of lessons then enter a competition at a Silver or higher level.

In Canada, dancers who want to compete register with their provincial organizations. These provincial organizations belong to a national organization, usually the Canadian Amateur DanceSport Association (CADA). The Ontario Amateur DanceSport Association (OADA) is the organization for amateur competitive dancers from Ontario. It is a member organization of the CADA, which in turn is a member of the International DanceSport Federation (IDSF). The

OADA works with the Canadian Dance Teachers Association (CDTA) and develops the official rules for amateur competitive dancers from Ontario and the criteria to hold a sanctioned competition. The OADA also has rules and guidelines on behaviour for their members, as well as the proper dress code for each level of competition. It is important for members to verify that a competition in or outside of Canada is sanctioned by the CADA/OADA or they could be suspended or risk losing amateur status. Jill and I are registered members of the OADA. They organize two events a year and identify sanctioned dance competitions for their members.

In Quebec, the sanctioned organization is the AADSQ (Association Amateurs de Danse Sportive du Quebec), although the requirements for competitors are slightly different. In Pre-Bronze, the standard dances in OADA are Waltz and Quickstep while in the AADSQ the Pre-Bronze dances are Waltz, Tango, and Quickstep. In Ontario, Tango is not added until the Silver level. Learning a Silver-level Tango in order to compete in Ontario would be a significantly different requirement from learning a Tango routine for competing in Quebec at Pre-Bronze. This adds to the confusion in the number of routines that have to be memorized and what steps are allowed at the level. In Latin for Ontario, the dances at Pre-Bronze are Cha-Cha and Jive. In Quebec, the same level requires Cha-Cha, Rumba, and Jive. We have a Rumba routine but it is a Bronze-level Rumba and includes steps that would not be permitted at Pre-Bronze. The result for people who compete mainly in Ontario is confusion and some frustration at the complexity of being able to compete in Quebec. Perhaps someday this will get resolved, or maybe we should simply learn to enjoy the differences.

The Canadian DanceSport Federation (CDF) was created to represent dance professionals in Canada including teachers, coaches, adjudicators, organizers, and trainers.

Ballroom dancing as a competitive sport is now referred to as DanceSport. International-level ballroom dancing has common rules, steps, and technique used for competitions around the world. It is like FIFA (Federation Internationale de Football Association), the international organization that governs football and soccer and uses a standard set of rules for every match. The rulebook for ballroom dancing is generally considered to be the ISTD Ballroom Technique. Originally founded in 1904, the present-day organization is recognized as a dance teaching institute and examination board training and certifying teachers.

There is also a single governing body known as the IDSF (International DanceSport Federation), which is recognized by the International Olympic Committee. Organizations around the world tend to start at a local level that belongs to a larger body, say a country organizing body that in turn is recognized by the IDSF. At last count, there were 4.5 million members registered in these amateur dance organizations.

American Social style also has a set of rules and a governing body based in the United States. There is the National Dance Council of America, which publishes a syllabus for its member organizations.

CHILDREN AND YOUTH BALLROOM DANCING

Greater numbers of younger people are getting involved in ballroom and Latin dancing. Unfortunately there are far fewer males than females at this level, similar to the representation in the adult world. For parents who find a good partnership arrangement for their children, it will be rewarding as the progress is witnessed. The path to success is not much different than for adults. The children need to have a good teacher and put time into practice. It is like any other sport and requires focus and dedication. From a social aspect, knowing how to dance will most likely outlive any other sport in a person's life.

Competitive ballroom dancing also includes children up to the age of eighteen. The categories in Ontario are:

- Juvenile I—9 years old and under during the competition year
- Juvenile II—10 and 11 years old
- Junior I—12 and 13
- Junior II—14 and 15
- Youth—16, 17, 18

The age category is assigned based on the age of the older partner. The other partner must be the same age or younger (OADA rulebook, 2008).

I always enjoy watching children learn to dance. It is fascinating how quickly they absorb instruction, and their bodies somehow adapt more quickly to the requirements of engaging the correct muscles. The key to success for young people competing as an amateur couple is similar to what it takes for adults to succeed. It starts with finding a great partner who is willing to work hard and requires both partners to enjoy dancing as much as possible.

It may be difficult for children to learn together when they are not living in the same household. Like many other activities, there needs to be a responsible adult to help coordinate travel and schedules. Parents have to arrange for both partners to take lessons at the same time, as well as schedule practice time together. Practice also helps the development of the partnership in terms of communication and expectations without the intervention of a teacher. When a competitive couple walks onto the floor, they are on their own. Whatever happens, they have to deal with it. If they forget the routine, get bumped by another couple, or tear a piece of clothing, they will learn to continue—which is nothing less than a good lesson for dance and for life. As they mature in dance and in years, they develop better skills to deal with unforeseen challenges.

Unless the parents have personally been through a competitive experience, they will be reliant on the teacher to make most of the decisions. When will they compete next? Are they getting enough practice time? When will they be ready to move up a level? Should they perform in shows to boost their confidence, or will that make them more nervous? Dance skills development is an uneven learning curve that is rarely straight. There are plateaus and backsliding, with dancers developing quickly then stalling. It takes patience and persistence to keep going.

OUR PRE-BRONZE PREPARATION

Our lessons continue in International style, and after much practice, we finally learn our Pre-Bronze Waltz and Quickstep routines.

This is what our Pre-Bronze Waltz routine looks like.

(Start by facing diagonal wall; beginning of long wall)

Natural Turn

Outside Change to Promenade Position (PP)

Chasse from Promenade

Natural Spin Turn

4-5-6 of Reverse Turn

Forward Change Step

Hesitation (in corner of long wall; end facing diagonal centre of short wall)

Reverse Turn

Whisk to PP

Chasse from PP

Natural Turn into

Impetus Turn

4-5-6 of Reverse Turn

(Start over at beginning of next long wall)

(Created in May 2007 by Josée Lepine)

Here is our Pre-Bronze Quickstep routine.

(Start facing diagonal wall, beginning of a long wall)

Quarter Turn to Right

Progressive Chasse

Natural Spin Turn

Progressive Chasse

Natural Turn with Hesitation

Progressive Chasse to Right

Back Lock

Closed Impetus (turn corner to short wall)

Progressive Chasse

Forward Lock

Natural Pivot Turn (3/8) (turn corner to long wall)

Chasse Reverse Turn

Repeat from Progressive Chasse (per line 2 above)

(Created in 2007 by Josée Lepine)

Our first competition where we have a solid International routine is a Canada DanceSport competition in Kingston. Rather than risk not being ready for the 10 a.m. start time, we drive from Ottawa to Kingston the night before and stay overnight. This proves to be disastrous. We book a higher-end motel that calls itself an Inn and is a short drive from the venue; we are feeling good that it has an attached restaurant where we can have a decent meal and retire to our room early for a quiet evening. We discover late into the night that the walls are paper thin, and there are two men and one woman in the room next to us. "They might have been drinking," I think to myself as the loudness increases and Jill phones security. Security, in turn, phones the offending room, and we hear the phone ring as if it is in our own room. It changes nothing. Security calls us to see if anything improves. Jill holds the phone up in our room and lets the noise fill the receiver. There is another call to the next room, and we hear it ring again. There is vociferous denial by our noisy neighbours, and we hear every word spoken in a loud, slurred voice. This motel allows pets, and this is what we hope the woman is talking about when we hear her say, "Now, aren't you a big boy!" and "Oh my, he's so cute." Sleep is important before a competition even if we don't get much, and it is past three a.m. when it finally comes.

The Kingston competition area is spacious and easy to move around. The event this year is held in the gym at the military sports facility near Fort Henry Heights. We arrive and prepare for our event and we notice there are several other competitors from our studio. We dance our Waltz routine with no less nervousness than the previous two competitions. When there are eight or more couples, the first event is considered a heat from which the bottom couples are dropped for the next round. I like heats, as long as we get recalled, because it gives me a chance to thoroughly warm up and stretch my muscles; we do get a recall after the heat. It is still too early to rejoice at not finishing last.

Our teacher watches us with support and encouragement, although, as it turns out, our dancing performance in the final does not improve. For the final, which is held a short time later, I am so eager to dance better and improve every step that I lose the start. When the Waltz music begins, we move into closed position and I fail to realize that my weight is on the wrong foot for the starter step. After two steps into the Waltz, I have to stop and start over from the closed position.

Something is not working but Jill's amazing pasted white smile does not waver as she stands in perfect form waiting without saying anything. I try it a second time, have to stop, and get confused about why the first step doesn't work. Once again, it is an aborted false start. On the third try, my weight is on the correct foot, the first step is correctly placed, and off we go, moving along the long wall to the music.

In the next dance, I find that the Quickstep is now more challenging, with the pre-set pattern, and there are fewer options for navigating around the other competitors. My misadventure results in a dichotomy of marks for the Waltz, divided between judges who saw the initial missteps and those who missed them. We have three judges place us second and two judges place us fifth for the Waltz. Combined with the Quickstep, we finish fourth. In the second event, we place third overall and leave with some confidence that we are on the right path to improving our dances. It is a good feeling not to finish last, especially with the amount of work we are doing.

There is a dance couple from the Niagara area who tell us that we look great and should have registered for the Latin dances. We had heard that before and thank them politely for the compliment and suggestion. We know the importance of taking our time to learn a good International routine rather than jumping into an event and placing last.

At the same competition, one of the young dance teachers from our studio dances in the Silver category with her partner. She dances a Jive without realizing that she forgot to wear dance underwear instead of her colourful thong. It made the spins more exciting for the spectators but the organizers are less impressed. Dance associations and competition organizers try to manage the dress code to avoid overly exposed dancers, but there are no guidelines yet to cover this kind of incident.

While in Kingston, Jill and I drive through Fort Henry Heights looking for the house my parents lived in when I was born. Lundy's Lane is easy to find, although I have no memory of anything about the house. I had been back to Kingston before and visited Fort Henry to watch ceremonies and tour the fabulous reproduction of nineteenth-century military life. We also visit the famous iron lion statue near Murney Tower on the shore of Lake Ontario. The lion statue is a precious memory for me because I still have a black and white photo of me sitting on the lion at an early age being supported by my father. The lion has a calm, fiercely proud and determined look, something I need to emulate for dance competitions.

LOOKING LIKE A COMPETITOR

People told us before we started competing that were great dancers, and we believed them. We did not realize that we look good at a studio level, not a competition level. Competing involves a whole new higher standard of being evaluated. We are competing against the best couples from all the studios in Ontario, and in the open competitions, couples come from Quebec and New York State to test their skills. It is difficult, requires amazing commitment, and takes a ton of practice time, since nothing feels natural for us.

Compared to social dancing, competitive dancing requires much more precision. The feet and body have to be in a specific position for each step, which the ISTD calls "figures." For every figure there is a proper alignment, foot position, amount of turn, rise and fall, foot rise, footwork, contrary body position (CBM), and sway. All this is performed with the proper posture and dance hold. One of the most challenging aspects is maintaining the dance posture and hold through an entire routine. There are people who do it very well and they place high at competitions. For the Latin dances, good posture is still required, but there is a slightly different dance hold and definitely more hip motion. This is only the start of understanding the complexity and knowledge required to learn competitive dance. If it looks easy to a spectator, then the dancer is doing a superb job.

Becoming a competitive dancer requires:

- Determination
- Ability to improve
- Money

While being talented and athletic are certainly important aspects to doing well in a dance competition, it takes more than that to succeed. There are many obstacles to overcome, and we discover that frustration and stress are common along the way. Determination and a willingness to push your limits despite anyone or anything that is not helpful or supportive is a key to being a good competitor.

To be great at anything, It takes more will than skill.

Dance is a continuous learning process, and performance or adoption of that learning is not linear. There are plateaus, setbacks, and distractions. Injuries can slow a dancer's development. Poor scores from the judges can be frustrating and demoralizing, especially when they seem contrary to a particularly good performance. A series of lessons and good instruction can sometimes result in no visible improvement. This is a plateau. It can last a short time or way too long, but with continued effort and persistence, improvement will undoubtedly follow.

There are times when we check with good friends, because other people can see improvements where we see none. Also, we have ourselves video recorded while doing a routine to see if that will help. We see mistakes or ways we should be doing a step that are not otherwise noticeable. Some new complex steps take longer to internalize. It takes practice and more practice, and we cannot give up. A setback often occurs when dancers stop dancing for a period of time, for example, due to injury or a vacation. When the couple returns to the dance floor, it may feel like they have forgotten the technique. Skills get rusty without practice but the good news is that with more dancing, they will return quickly.

Without the desire and ability to improve, it will be difficult to move to higher levels. Both partners need to make a commitment to working on improving their skills, and it requires good communication and hard work. It can be especially challenging when abilities do not improve in a linear fashion—and they usually don't. Another challenge is the difference in the rate of learning for each partner. Couples have to work together and understand the meaning of empathy when the path forward is littered with impediments.

It is also important to have a teacher who knows the rules and the steps of the dance at each level of the competition. Some competition organizers assign a marshal to watch for inappropriate figures at each level, and the couple may be disqualified after they dance if they perform a figure that is higher than the level they entered. When the competition is over, we check our detailed marks from the judges. Most competitions now post the marks on a wall or on the

Internet, and we are excited at one competition because we receive three second-place rankings from judges in our Waltz, even though we placed poorly overall. It was a sign that we are heading in the right direction.

Competitive dancing can be a financial challenge, and at some point it becomes more than a hobby. For us, it is a passion, and we need to feed that passion. If a couple is competing in both Latin and standard dances, there is usually the cost of two lessons a week as well as one or two coaching lessons every month. Add to this the cost of using a practice floor. For the competition itself, you need clothes that meet the rules. For men competing at the Pre-Bronze and Bronze levels, this usually consists of good black dress pants, a white shirt, black tie, and black vest. I had my pants custom-made so the fit would be perfect and the cuffs higher than normal so they don't rub on the floor. My vest is also custom-made. At higher levels, such as Silver and beyond, the man normally wears a tuxedo or a dress suit with tails, known as a tailcoat. In Latin, there are special men's shirts and Latin pants. Women need appropriate dresses and may have them custom-made. At higher levels, women will think about purchasing a specifically designed dance dress or having one made. For standard dances, these will be flowing gowns, and for Latin, sleek, sexy outfits. We have observed that in both cases there are a lot of rhinestones or sequins.

The cost of the competition itself includes registration on top of our annual provincial membership fee. Some competitions also charge the competitors an admission fee, although many do not. They realize that they are lucky to have competitors at any level. For an out-of-town competition, there are travel costs, food, and hotel. Money should not be an impediment to competing, but everyone needs to be aware and plan for it.

WHAT TO EXPECT

It seems as if every competition is different, always with an unknown factor waiting for us. It becomes easier in some ways when we return to a familiar venue. On the other hand, there are always obstacles. In some cases, it is the size or shape of the floor. It might be two events run back to back because of scheduling changes. Often, organizers try to combine events that have fewer participants in order to keep the competition on schedule. In that situation, we walk off the floor then immediately back on again.

In one competition, the standard and Latin events were not planned well, no thought having been given to age category or level separation. We performed our standard event and ran to a nearby spectator's table to change into our Latin shoes while the next event began. Jill hid behind someone and changed into her Latin skirt, then we lined up for the Latin event, which was scheduled next. After completing the Latin event, we did the reverse to get ready for another standard dance entry. Usually the standard and Latin events are scheduled to run at separate times. In this case, they were scheduled together, leaving competitors little time to change.

The music can make you cringe with a poor beat or exhaust you by playing far longer than normal. In some cases, such as a Quickstep with eight or more competing couples, there are unavoidable collisions. Regardless of circumstances, at the end of the event I give Jill a spin, and both of us bow to the nearest wall of spectators. The key is to be ready for anything and deal with it with a calm confidence that says we have the ability to excel in all situations, and that is why we are here. Every competition builds experience for the next one.

Travelling to a competition always seems to involve an unpredictable factor. We meet a couple that stay overnight at a hotel very close to the competition. They successfully cope with a morning devoid of electricity and hot water. One competition posted a timetable on the Internet, then started to combine the events in which there was a small number of entrants. The result was that competitors who arrived thinking they were over an hour early actually ended up with only fifteen to twenty minutes to prepare for their event.

Here are some tips for new competitors:

- Maintain good posture and hold throughout the routine.

- Try to relax and enjoy the routine—dance as if it were practice but make it your own personal best.

- Feel the music and make your dancing a natural expression of the music; extend the 2's in Waltz, keep your feet under you and enjoy each step.

- Always appreciate your partner. No matter what happens, you have a partner who was willing to come this far and put in this much sacrifice.

- Dance as if you mean it.

It may seem simple to exhort someone to "dance as if you mean it." It really consists of many aspects. The couple needs to maintain focus through the entire dance, ignoring any extraneous noise or distraction. There should be a focus on personal performance, the partner, the music, the routine, and remembering the technique that has taken so many hours to improve. Finally, it includes dancing the dance seriously for what it is. If it is a Waltz, then it should look like a smooth Waltz. A Cha-Cha needs to look like a well-controlled but energetic Cha-Cha.

Here is a list of items that, as competitive dancers, we need to remember to bring to a competition.

- Proof of registration (in case the organizers have lost it)

- Dance Association membership card

- Vaseline (for lips, teeth, and sides of patent leather shoes)

- Baby powder (for bottoms of shoes)

- Safety pins

- Bobby pins (for hair)

- Hairspray

- Fake eyelashes

- Extra glue for lashes in case they become loose or fall off

- Dance shoes

- Dance outfits

- Dance underpants (for women who wear a dress; full briefs for Latin)

- Imodium (for you-know-what)

- Spare shoelaces (men)

- Back-up shoes

THE JUDGES

How can judges be objective? How do they know which dancer is better than another dancer? Isn't it all subjective? Of course dancers have concerns about the fairness of judging. In a ballroom dance competition, the dancers are competing against each other, so the rankings have a comparative value. Did this couple perform better than the other couple? In support of the ability to be objective, there are some basic elements that have to be performed properly to get higher placements. Is the couple moving to the beat of the music? Also, if one couple executes the proper heel and toe leads in every step of a standard-style dance and another couple does not, then it becomes fairly obvious what the ranking should be. It is subjective as to what criteria the judge looks for when there are only ten seconds to look at each couple on the competition dance floor. There are many factors to consider, and with eight or ten couples dancing at the same time, it might be that the judges look for good frame and footwork at lower levels and smoothness or strong movement at a higher level. When all the couples are fairly close in skill and technique, then obviously it becomes difficult for judges to decide and they pick whatever makes the most sense to them. In our competitions, we have great moments dancing along one wall then I forget the routine and we fall apart for a few steps before I recover. How can we fault a judge for not looking at us when we are doing our best?

On the other hand, it is obviously unfair when a judge who teaches at a particular dance school ranks a couple that he or she knows from that school much higher than the other competitors, regardless of their performance. For most competitions, the judge's marks are posted at the end of the competition, and this makes it public. We occasionally notice one couple that receives a first- or second-place ranking from a judge who happens to be a teacher at their studio, and a sixth place from all of the other judges. The important task, as truly competitive dancers, is to make it impossible for the judge to rank our dance anything less than what we deserve. Regardless of marks, rankings at competitions can vary. Judges are human and have personal biases. It is important that competitors take the good efforts from a competitive event and feel proud of the success. There is no need to worry about poor placement, since a low ranking often provides far greater motivation to improve.

There are some very good, qualified, and objective judges. After all, judges have to go through a certification process. In fact, when our Latin dances get poor marks, we arrange for a lesson from one of the judges we know who is also a teacher and find her input is precise and insightful. After the lesson, we know what needs improvement and we know exactly why our performance resulted in lower scores. She points out specific aspects that should change, and, realizing this, we see that our previous rankings were appropriate.

There are many times when a competitor should ask for a second opinion and, in some cases, hearing the same instruction explained in a slightly different way or from a different person reinforces what one already knows needs to be improved. In other cases, the basic steps and technique may be off track for the dance and level. For example, a Natural Spin Turn is more than just a turn. There are ways to do it properly, where to place the feet, how to hold the body, and when to move the arms. Looking at two couples in a dance competition, one couple that does most of the technique properly and one that does not, it is easy for judges to determine rankings. Proper technique also helps dancers move to the next level. Dance figures are placed in each level to provide a progression to a higher level, and competence at one level builds and propels you to be successful at the next level. Dancers should not be reluctant to ask for a coaching lesson or a second opinion from someone other than your regular teacher, as it is your entitlement as a competitive student or couple in order to improve.

Ranking

A more recent feature of competitions is publishing the scores from all judges. In some cases, the results are posted at the dance competition site, and in some cases they are posted on an Internet site. The score from each judge is included for each dance. This is very useful in order for a dancer to know his or her strengths and weaknesses. Although they are comparative rankings, it still helps to know what dances are better or worse, and how consistent the marks are in any given dance.

Dance judging is carried out by ranking each couple in each dance and is based on the Skating System, which was generally adopted in 1937. In preliminary rounds, judges decide which couples are to be recalled for the next round. For example, there might be eight couples, with six to be recalled. In this case, the judges each identify the couples to be recalled, and the total number of recalls are added up to calculate the result, with the higher number of recalls contributing to a good score. For a final round, the couples are ranked in placements depending on how many couples are in the round. For example, with a final round of six couples, the judges will rank each couple from one to six, with no ties.

The rankings are collected after each dance and summarized, and a system of eleven rules determines the results. When there is a tie, a complicated, and therefore sometimes controversial, tie-breaking system is used, although there are situations that result in an unbreakable tie. With the results for all dances in the event calculated, the couple with the lowest total places first, the couple with the second-lowest total places second, and so forth. The bible for calculating results is a manual entitled *The Skating System: Scrutineering for Ballroom Dance Competitions* (ISTD, 1986).

Heat 18: Adult Pre-Bronze Standard (W/Q) Final

Waltz

No.	B	C	D	E	F	G	H	1	1-2	1-3	Result
168	1	2	2	2	1	2	1	3	7		1
202	3	3	3	1	2	1	2	2	4		2
206	2	1	1	3	3	3	3	2	3	7	3

Quickstep

No.	B	C	D	E	F	G	H	1	1-2	1-3	Result
168	2	1	2	1	1	2	2	3	7		1
202	3	2	3	2	2	1	1	2	5		2
206	1	3	1	3	3	3	3	2	2	7	3

Final Result

No.	W	Q	Result
168	1	1	1
202	2	2	2
206	3	3	3

B Judge name	C Judge name
D Judge name	E Judge name
F Judge name	H Judge name

A typical score sheet from an event. For each dance, the couple's number is displayed and the ranking from each judge. The results are tallied by the standing in each dance.

18

ADVANCING AS
COMPETITIVE DANCERS

COMPETING IN PRO-AM

A person who does not have a regular dance partner can compete by entering Pro-Am events in competitions that include Pro-Am categories. The teacher is the "Pro," or professional, and the student is the "Am," or amateur. There are Pro-Am competitions for both American Social and International styles. The couples dance in a selected number of dances at their level, and the amateur dancer is ranked by the judges. For each level, the men are rated in one ranking and the women amateurs are rated in a separate category. There are many women without partners, so the Pro-Am events are normally overflowing with women competitors dancing with their male teacher. Most competitions will also have a category in which amateurs compete against each other regardless of gender. This can be a set of three or more dances with their instructor, and the judges will rank the amateurs together regardless of whether they are leading or following. I am not sure how the judges make their decision on this one. It has to be a tough task.

Many competitions include both Pro-Am and amateur couple events and these tend to be much larger competitions, often spanning three days. The teachers frequently have several students competing in many events, and it can be very challenging for the teacher to remember all the routines as well as which student is to perform which routine at what time. Therefore, the students need to make sure they know what event they are dancing in and when it takes place. I watched a Pro-Am event in Gatineau, Quebec. A male teacher had five female students in several categories and he was dancing with them one after another. When each single dance entry was over, he came back to the table where the five students waited and then walked onto the floor with the next one. In all the excitement of the event and conversations around dancing, the women became a bit distracted, and for two events, the male teacher took the wrong student into the category. This was not noticed by the organizers or the judges, since the competitor's number is on the man's back. The students should have paid closer attention to the schedule.

Dancing with an instructor can be very satisfying, as there is an expectation that the "Pro" will perform at a high level without mistakes. On the other hand, it might be more difficult to get regular practice time before a competition if the teacher has many other students. The practice time has to be paid for like any other lesson. It needs to be discussed with the teacher and scheduled in advance to avoid disappointment. The disadvantage of having a "Pro" partner is that it is expected that all the competitors sharing the "Pro" will divide up the expenses and pay for their teacher's costs, such as travel, hotel, and meals. When the teacher is attending a competition, it takes away from time spent at the studio earning money.

Another concern with dancing with a teacher all the time is that it can be challenging for the student to dance socially. The student becomes accustomed to having a perfect or near-perfect partner, and therefore dancing with other people in general may be approached with apprehension and not be as satisfying. Many people are fine with all the limitations and love to compete in Pro-Am events. The music, movement, and personal development are all just as rewarding as it is for an amateur couple.

The difference between a professional ballroom dancer and an amateur starts with the assumption that the professional is dancing as a career or making a reasonable income from dance-related activities such as teaching or performing. An amateur does it as a hobby. The distinction I remember most clearly comes from my days at university when the students playing pool had an opportunity to meet Cliff Thorburn, a fourteen-time Canadian champion pool player and a world snooker champion. In answering questions after a few exhibition games, where he easily outscored every amateur challenger, he told the eager students that pool was his career and, as such, he played forty to sixty hours a week in any given week and more than that when preparing for a tournament. Similarly, most professional ballroom dancers try to make this a full-time career and are people who dance, teach, or practise around forty hours a week. As amateurs, Jill and I manage to dance around seven hours a week and, when getting ready for a competition, we move that up to nine or ten hours a week. The CADA also lists in its rulebook that an amateur is classified as a dancer who does not earn money from dancing or teaching, although there are certain exceptions. For example, an amateur is allowed to accept specific scholarships.

Blackpool

Blackpool is a seaside town north of Liverpool in England with a population of approximately 146,000. Participating at Blackpool is the dream of all serious dancers, and maybe one day we will find our way there. Known as "dance nirvana" to passionate fans of ballroom dancing, the prestigious Blackpool Dance Festival is held every year, hosting international competitors from around the world. Expect to see about 1,600 couples from sixty countries, a live orchestra, and a multitude of eager spectators. The competition has been held in the Empress Ballroom at the Winter Gardens since 1920 and is arguably the first and most famous of ballroom competitions.

Wheelchair dancing

At the Kingston DanceSport competition, we witnessed an amazing and inspiring event. They advertised a demonstration of wheelchair ballroom dancing, and we thought this might be one of the truly boring events of all time. Not only were we wrong, we were emotionally captivated by what we witnessed. It was a Pro-Am style event. The first dance was a male instructor with his female wheelchair-based partner. They performed a dramatic Foxtrot that flowed with grace and elegance. Jill was awestruck by the frame and musicality of the woman. Her face was filled with passion for the music, her head was always in perfect position, and her arms flowed effortlessly in the spin turns. The next couple was the reverse. A wheelchair-bound male performed a Paso Doble with his standing female partner. This dance was so dramatic and riveting that it seemed for a while that the wheelchair actually had legs. The man reared back in the chair then dropped the front wheels of the wheelchair to the ground in perfect timing with the powerful pounding beat of the Paso Doble. It was frightening and exciting at the same time.

We are so conditioned to expecting tragic consequences of a wheelchair's falling over that it prevents us from enjoying the true beauty of the event. I will never underestimate the ability of anyone to rise above what life has dealt him or her. Life is not about the situation in which you may find yourself. It is about what you decide to do about it. We are all given great gifts in life, and some of our abilities are only hiding beneath the surface, never obvious to anyone—including ourselves. People who challenge themselves are the ones who are truly living. People who do not challenge themselves are merely watching life go by.

Wheelchair dancing started in Europe about thirty years ago, and there are now more than 5,000 wheelchair dancers in over forty countries. In North America, the activity is fairly new but it is beginning to grow immensely in popularity. In the 2008 Paralympics Games in Beijing, wheelchair ballroom dancing was featured as a non-Paralympics sport.

COMPETITION WALTZ

Learning to compete in Waltz requires us to take our dancing ability to a higher level. To dance it properly, we try to keep the weight under our standing leg longer. Moving the feet too soon has two visual effects. First, it looks like we are falling into the next step before we finish the previous one. Without the next step, we would topple over because the weight is not over our feet, making the dance look rushed and sloppy. Second, a delay in weight shift facilitates the gradual rise needed in the Waltz. Without it, we pop up and down like a pogo stick as we move across the floor. On the other hand, moving the weight too late looks like we are reluctant to move or not dancing to the music. It is important to finish every step before starting the next one and show that there is a beginning and ending to each figure; although pausing between figures is not good either. We work diligently to ensure that the rise and fall motions consist of a gradual rise and a gradual fall. Also, we discover that dancers play with the beat a little bit, for example, extending the length of the second beat for greater musicality and to give the Waltz a smooth, floating feeling. The first time we achieve this, Jill expresses her delight with the movement.

Maintaining contact on the floor with our feet is another desired technique. In a smooth dance, when moving a non-weight-bearing foot, the feet brush the floor instead of being picked up and placed down, so that it resembles dancing instead of walking. Finally, we have been told that dancers have to bend their ankles before moving each leg and push with the leg muscles to give length to the steps. We try to make the movement look like the dance represented by the music, and in this case, the Waltz should look smooth and flowing. Our dance coach tells us a story about his brother going to watch a ballroom dance competition for the first time. He complained that he bought a ticket to see ballroom dancing and all he saw was people walking around to music. It was not until the highest-level professionals danced that he exclaimed he was now watching dancing.

While we work to improve our technique in the standard dances, we begin to memorize the routines in the first two Latin dances for competition. These are the Cha-Cha and Jive. Once we have the routines memorized, work begins on style and technique.

The improvement in our Latin dances is dramatic and noticeable every week, yet our standard dances seem to be going nowhere. Dancers talk about plateaus and growth spurts in the learning curve. It is disconcerting that we are on a plateau in standard dances and rapidly improving in Latin. At this rate, our Latin dances will be far superior in only a few weeks. However, the improvements in our Latin dances start to lag, and it becomes obvious that we will have peaks and valleys in learning these dances as well. Nonetheless, we become quite comfortable doing the Latin dances and feel that we are better at them. Our burning desire remains to avoid finishing last in any competition again.

OADA OPEN COMPETITION

We are registered for the OADA competition in October. This includes three standard events in three separate age categories and our first Latin event. In Latin, we will dance Cha-Cha and Jive.

We drive to Toronto the night before and after a restless sleep prepare ourselves and drive to the venue. The first event is adult standard, and we dance poorly. We are barely warmed up and have to deal with a strong bout of anxiety that makes this a two-Imodium event, which is the way we start to gauge our nervousness while preparing for each competition. At this event, my frame and posture are weak, and our execution of the routine is wobbly at best. Our next event is scheduled to take place several minutes later. The dance floor is sticky, and when I mention it to one of the other competing couples, they share a tip. John and Mary Jane tell us they use baby powder on the bottoms of their dance shoes for sticky floors.

In the second event, the Waltz goes much better, while the Quickstep resembles a demolition derby. There are seven couples on the floor dancing the Quickstep in what quickly becomes a multi-couple pile up. Perhaps the couples learn routines more than they learn floor craft and cannot break from the exact sequence of steps without getting lost. I am used to navigating a busy floor because Jill and I frequently dance at many social venues, but even I have problems. To avoid an impending collision, as the leader I have to take a smaller step or stop then move into the next step, giving my partner a quick weight shift to make sure that she knows which of my feet has weight and thereby communicating to her which foot I will use to take the next step. In this event, the Quickstep is so fast and travels down the line of dance so quickly that any couple that stops will be hit by fast-moving traffic behind them. My daughter is here to watch and support us. After the event, she tells me that the worst collision involved three couples that converged near a corner from three different directions. We have two collisions with other couples but they are mild. The first is where I attempt a last-second navigation correction and only make light contact with another couple. In the second incident, I nick someone's heel and manage to apologize later. Most competitors in this entry come away with bruises, abrasions, or welts. *Competitive dancing is a contact sport.*

We wait for the award ceremony for the adult category, our worst performance. I always tell people that the most difficult time for me is not the dancing but lining up for the results presentations afterward. This was a clear example. They called up the 6th-place finishers, then the 5th. When our names were not called for 4th or 3rd place, I knew that we had placed last once again, but the worst was yet to come. They called 2nd and 1st. The competitors were all lined up with their awards, pictures were taken, and people applauded. Then the master of ceremonies notices an oversight. They have a 7th-place award and call our names. It is an embarrassing walk to pick up that tiny plastic trophy for last place and standing out as we did while all other couples watched us take the slow walk to the presenters. Our placing in the other events turns out better. We receive a 4th out of five couples and a 5th place out of eight couples in the other two standard events and we feel good about moving closer to the middle of the pack in the rankings.

Between our standard events, we stretch our legs in the practice room. Several couples are practising frame and doing a step or two from their routine. One couple seems to be struggling with a complex Tango step. I turn around when I hear a thumping sound like someone pounding a fist into a pillow. It was not a pillow. It was the man's right shoulder. The woman's fist is indicating to him that his shoulder is too far forward and her face is flushed red with anger. She is standing there after the punch berating her dance partner for his mistake. He stands there quietly, showing no emotion, as if he is a five-year-old caught with his hand in the cookie jar and getting a scolding from his mother. Her anger escalates as she speaks in a high-pitched yet restrained tone. They are face-to-face, nose-to-nose. He does not move an inch as her voice shows more signs of agitation. Then she pauses, seems to collect herself, and spits directly into his face. He takes it well, not moving, not wiping it off, and not saying anything. He simply stands there. Finally she takes him into dance hold, and they do the step again. Jill and I look at each other in shock, thinking that any dance issues we might have are trivial compared to the way they deal with theirs. I notice that they finish second in their category that day. As bad as you think your partner may be or as nervous and competitive as anyone may be at a competition, this sort of aggressive physical behaviour is not the way to deal with it.

We line up for our Latin dances then walk onto the floor with hopes of remembering all the figures. The Cha-Cha music begins, and at least I remember to start on the proper beat. We are thrilled to remember the entire routine. The Jive is also reasonable, although the music goes on forever. In practice, we do one complete set of the figures in the routine and then stop to fix areas that need to be improved. In this competition, we do the routine four times in a row before the music starts to fade. We are exhausted, and perspiration runs down my face. We place second out of three couples and feel like winners for not finishing last for a first-time entry. We continue to gain experience from each competition.

We arrive back at the hotel and are ready for a celebration dinner in the theatre district on King Street. Riding down the elevator to the parking garage, we see three people enter the elevator and I notice a dance figure sewn on a man's jacket.

"Are you dancers?" I ask.

"Yes," the woman replies. "There is a Swing dance workshop, and we brought in this teacher from New York." She introduces him to us, and I don't recognize the name. "Do you dance?"

"We are here for a ballroom competition in North York," I reply.

"That's great. Good for you. We are holding an open dance tonight after the workshops. If you are interested, you are welcome to attend."

It is a small world. In a chance meeting in a hotel elevator, we receive an invitation to a dance party. Although it is tempting, we are mentally and physically drained after the competition and we do not find time to attend. Following a late meal and a glass or two of wine, we get some much-needed sleep.

Our dance adventures open us up to other areas, and since we are in Toronto, we purchase tickets to see *Mamma Mia* in the theatre district. We are not disappointed with this amazing show and its talented cast. On another visit, we reward ourselves after a competition with tickets to the *Dirty Dancing* theatre show. We may struggle with nervousness before a competition but we reward ourselves after it is over. This is a good life.

COMPETITIVE DANCE ATTIRE: THE WORKS

Dance Shoes—competition

As a competitive dancer, I own four pairs of dance shoes. I have two regular soft-soled, low-heeled pairs with a standard one-inch heel that I use constantly for dances, lessons, and some practices. One pair is nearly worn out, and the other pair is new. The low heel is used for all standard dancing. My third pair is also used for standard dances. These have the same soft sole but are brilliant, shiny, patent leather. I use these for standard dance competitions and some practices, especially to break them in and make sure they are comfortable. My fourth pair is for Latin dancing and these shoes consist of leather uppers with soft soles, but with higher, one-and-a-half-inch heels. I use these for Latin lessons and Latin competitions.

The patent leather shoes are polished with special patent leather polish, Patent Care™ by Tana, which I use before competitions. I also make sure to have a jar of Vaseline, which is used on the sides of the shoes that come into contact with each other near the heel and front toe, to make sure the shoes don't stick to each other when dancing. When two patent leather surfaces touch, they act like Velcro unless they are covered with a lubricant. I also have a small Tupperware tub of baby powder. On a sticky floor, competitors use a bit of baby powder on the soles of the shoes to make them slide more easily. However, it may be more of a placebo than a true solution, since the baby powder does not last more than a few steps. For shiny and smooth floors I may also gently use a stiff wire shoe brush to rough up the sole before competing. I apply shoe polish on the other pairs before any major dance event.

Jill owns eleven pairs of dance shoes and has struggled to get ones that fit properly. She has three pairs for International standard, one for American Social standard, six for Latin, and a comfortable practice pair that resemble more of a thin running shoe. She uses the practice shoes to keep her feet from hurting during a long practice session. The American Social standard shoes are different from International standard shoes in that they are open along the side. Jill has narrow heels, which make it difficult for her to find a shoe with a good fit in the heel area for support without pinching or having the shoe move around.

Latin shoes, with their loose-fitting heels, cause the most problems, and Jill has many pairs that she can no longer wear even with heel grips that fit inside the back of the heel in an attempt to make them snug. The most comfortable pair of Latin shoes is a recent purchase from a Supadance booth we visited at one of our dance competitions. A typical woman's Latin dance shoe will have a heel from 2.0 to 3.5 inches in height. With too high a heel, it is difficult for a dancer to bend the foot so that the toe touches the floor first—the toe lead that is a requirement for Latin dances.

Some shoes are reserved for competing and when these shoes get scuffed and start to look old, a new pair is purchased, and the old ones become practice shoes. A teacher told Jill she could wash off the scuff marks on an old pair, but Jill soaked them in water and they shrank. Due to all the social events that we attend, she has a pair that is used for questionable floors such as interlock, concrete, or simply dirty wooden floors that can damage the sole. There always has to be a pair for dancing outside the studio at clubs or unfamiliar places where a dance shoe will get damaged.

Shoes can be purchased at a specialty dance store, but there are also other options. Most dance studios have a catalogue that you can choose from such as the one put out by Supadance. Shoes can be ordered through the studio, which, in our experience, seems to be only slightly less expensive than buying new ones from a store, but a proper fit is not guaranteed. There are also some studios that sell shoes on consignment, new or slightly used dance shoes at a highly discounted price. The least expensive and highest-risk alternative for purchasing new dance shoes is the Internet. The shoes are made and shipped from a country with low-cost labour, and with a good fit, this is a great choice. However, if the shoes do not fit, the purchaser tends to bear the cost of returning them, which is rarely worth the expense. Finally, for those who attend a ballroom dance competition to watch or compete, there will normally be vendors' booths set up nearby to sell dancewear, including shoes.

We both have small flight bags to carry around the shoes we need. One day I put my shoe bag in the front closet at home and noticed a smell. I thought about checking the bag, then forgot about it. A week later, I noticed the smell again, so I removed a couple of pairs of shoes, made sure they were dry, and sprayed them with an anti-odour spray. I paid no further attention until a month later when the smell persisted. My shoe bag had acquired a variety of contents, so I decided to clean out the entire bag and wash it out. After pulling out four pairs of shoes, a spare shirt, socks, practice CDs, a polish rag, and other assorted items, I found a rotting banana peel at the very bottom of the bag. Apparently I had eaten a banana for an energy boost while we were at a competition probably three or four months previously, stored the peel wrapped in a napkin, and intended to remove it later. It now looked dehydrated and dark brown. With the removal of the real culprit, the shoe bag ceased to smell anything but pleasant.

Dance socks

Leaving no sock unfolded in the desire to achieve comfortable dancing, it is important to consider socks. I find that many socks have a seam across the top of the toe, or in the front of the toe, that rubs and can cause blisters or simply be uncomfortable. Some socks have tight ribs that leave marks around the ankle, limiting circulation. Maybe I wash them too often? In any case, I recently discovered seamless socks as well as socks that do not pinch the ankle in order to stay up. I found them in a section categorized as "diabetic socks" and, because they are very comfortable and fit nicely in my dance shoes, I ignore the categorization.

Dancewear

The long-sleeved black Latin competition shirt that I buy is like a woman's one-piece bathing suit, with a piece of cloth under the crotch. I step into the leg openings and pull the sleeves over my shoulders. I notice there is no flap or opening for a quick washroom break. The one-piece continuous crotch is to prevent the shirt from popping out or puffing when the arms are raised while dancing. I try it on and immediately realize the body length is too small, because when I raise an arm to see how tight it is, my voice uncontrollably goes up an octave or two. I gingerly walk out of the change room bent over, exclaiming, "Eee, oh, eee."

Jill wonders what I did to myself.

"Let's make the crotch extension a tiny bit longer," I suggest in a falsetto.

I am not supposed to wear underwear with the shirt; it is important to have a smoother look with no protruding seams. I refuse to wear a thong and going commando is a tough debate. Later, a seamstress lengthens the crotch and sews two pieces of elastic on the sleeve cuffs around the thumb to prevent the sleeves from shifting. I wear it for a practice and feel like a Latin god. I am not sure who the Latin gods would be. I know the Mayans did a lot of beheading as a sacrifice to their gods. Maybe I should feel like a Roman god who is really good at Latin dancing. It is amazing what a good shirt can do for your confidence!

My Latin pants have narrower-than-normal pant legs and are especially tight fitting around the posterior. Before they were adjusted, a decision had to be made on what I wanted that backside area to look like. Is this serious? Unfortunately, yes. We visit a vendor booth at a competition in Kingston and stare at the item hanging from the rack. They are well-shaped, padded, fake bums that men use as underwear in their Latin pants to give them a more rounded look. Supposedly they also enhance the look of the hip motion. In fact, the vendor looks at me—or should I say, slightly behind me—and suggests that I could use a bit more appeal in that area. Only slightly insulted, I politely decline. Jill is unsure whether her best course of action is to encourage me or support my decision. On the other hand, I think about putting a sock down the front of the pants. I don't know what people are watching when I dance. Maybe if they look somewhere else they will not notice my understated hip motion.

Jill gets a reference for a great seamstress and has a dress made for standard competitions. It is a teal-coloured, velvet dress that goes to mid-calf and is a simple design in order to adhere to the strict criteria for allowable dress at our level. At the Silver level, amateur competitors are allowed to wear very glittery custom-made dresses. Jill loves the new dress and feels more confident in it. Next, she borrows a Latin dress from a fellow competitor and asks the dressmaker to create one similar to it but in a different colour. She picks out a mauve-coloured fabric and has it made. The dress looks amazing, and so does Jill when she does the Latin hip motion. She is eagerly looking forward to having new dresses made for the higher levels (if we ever get there). One of her goals is to continue improving until we reach the Silver level, so that she can have two stunning dresses made. At that level, rhinestones are allowed, as well as flesh-coloured or see-through patches of cloth, as long as they don't reveal too much. We compliment one of the young competitors who dances at the championship level and ask her where she had purchased her lovely dress. She replies that her mother made it for her.

Hair

For men, hair needs to be neat and trim. Not only is it good for impressing the judges with your commitment to look good, but someone is always taking photos. Normally, I have my hair cut or trimmed the week before a competition. When getting ready, I use some light gel to keep down the stray grey hairs that want to stand up vigorously at a couple of places on my head. It is a good idea to get help from your partner in checking that everything is in place. For one competition, I did not realize that I had a tiny rooster tail behind my head and so much hair spray that it did not budge during all the dances. I noticed it a month later as I browsed the Web site of the professional photography company that took photos at the competition. Serious male competitors will dye their hair to ensure nothing grey or white is visible, something that I consider when I check my hair in the mirror. In Latin dance events, some male competitors go to the point of creating the "whole look" and grease their hair straight back with no bangs.

Women can do a bit more, and of course Jill books an appointment with her hairdresser before a competition. The general guideline for women is that no hair should be on the forehead. Jill normally has bangs and struggles with this. She is a good sport, though, and before we arrive for a competition, her hair is up and the forehead is clear. I wonder if this has to do with the Waltz, since one teacher told us to raise our eyebrows in the Waltz to show how much we liked the rise and fall. From my experience, I understand that it is also important for women to use an entire container of hairspray before every competition. Any loose strands of hair should be deliberately secured and not whip into the mouth during a spin. Spitting hair ends out of the mouth is not likely to present an appealing image.

Spray tanning

Serious competitors at higher levels want to look stunning, especially in Latin dances, and for many people this involves getting a spray tan. Spray tanning is also popular at lower levels with both adults and children who compete. I have seen some very tan, brown, and sometimes orange-coloured faces in place of their natural skin tone. For one of our competitions, Jill decides to go for a spray tan that is offered by our Latin teacher who used to manage a tanning salon and now offers it in the basement of her home.

Jill's spray-tanning story

"I take off all my clothes except my underpants. I am standing there naked, which is not easy for me. My skin is getting goosebumps from the cold, and my hands cover my naked breasts. As the spraying starts on my back, my eyes are tightly closed. I am instructed to hold my arms away from my body and to turn around. For the front, I have to hold my hands up and out in order to get sprayed all around my body and arms. It goes on fairly dry because it must contain an amount of powder. When it is finished, I have to think about getting dressed again. I don't want to rub it off on the inside of my clothes, so I soon realize that I should have worn a skirt and loose clothing instead of a tight top and jeans. The spray has a distinct odour, and I ask how long it takes for it to dry, or how soon I can take a shower. I am told that it takes four hours. The stinky odour lingers with the tan, so after counting down four hours I hop into the shower before going to bed. As the warm water hits me, streaks of orangey-brown tan flow off my body until I look like a tiger with alternating beige and brown stripes. Tiny streams of brown are flowing down my body. Shocked, I quickly get out of the shower and watch rivulets of bronze spray tan go down the drain. There goes $25."

We also hear about the time a very cocky man went in for a tan and in spite of warnings to keep his underwear on, he appeared completely naked and proud of it. In response, the female spray tanner found the coldest bottle of solution and used that while watching his pride shrink smaller and smaller.

Some competitors are thoughtless and spray themselves bronze in the washrooms or any secluded area, leaving a sticky mess everywhere. Competition organizers and hall owners are not very patient with this kind of behaviour. It is not appropriate to do it the day of the competition and leave someone else with the residual mess.

Tanning beds

Another method of tanning is the use of tanning beds such as those in a tanning salon. Critics who discourage this believe repeated exposure of the skin to ultraviolet rays can increase the risk of skin cancer. Tanning articles indicate that the lamps used in tanning beds emit two types of radiation, similar to that of the sun: shorter ultraviolet B (UVB) rays, and the longer rays, ultraviolet A (UVA).

Jill's experience with a salon caused her to rethink the tanning salon strategy. After a short tanning session where she lay on a tanning bed, she came home with itchy skin. Soon the itch developed into a heavy red rash and welts that appeared up and down her legs and back. An emergency call to her doctor revealed the cause to be chemical and it was treated as a chemical burn. She phoned the tanning salon and told them what had happened. After talking her way through a few people and finally reaching the manager, it was explained that the tanning beds are cleaned with a bleach-like solution after being used by each customer and on rare occasions an employee might forget to clean the solution off completely before the next customer arrives.

Teeth Whitening

For the serious competitor, having whiter teeth only makes the spray tan look better. Jill encourages me to improve my look because my affection for drinking red wine has taken the dazzling white sparkle out of my smile. There are many options, and I find the best place to start is with my dentist. It seems the main ingredient used is bleach and the risk is that the teeth become more sensitive to hot and cold. I decline for now and have not given any thought to the more expensive alternative of one millimetre-thin porcelain veneers glued to the front surface of the teeth.

PORTABLE MUSIC

We have all sorts of music devices, from a portable CD player to MP3 players. I add dance songs to a sport-style MP3 player with a headphone splitter for two sets of headphones. I clip it on my belt, and we are free to do standard dances in the studio to avoid distraction when other music is playing. I also have some CDs burned with practice music in case there is a chance to use the studio's sound system. When that happens, it is much more representative of a typical competition. Some couples have a mobile phone with MP3 that plays music and is wireless enabled for a couple of Bluetooth headsets. Sometimes we simply pretend there is music playing and move in unison to an imaginary song. It starts off slowly, and as we move around the floor, the tempo accelerates in my head so my dancing speeds up. It is always better to dance to actual music.

When we use the studio's CD player, the Waltz and Quickstep songs feel faster than what is played at competitions. I receive advice that the beat is slower at competitions and to use the pitch control to slow down the music. This works well.

INTERNATIONAL TECHNIQUE BOOKS

There are many important technique books that teachers use and that serious competitors might want to acquire for reference. ISTD describes in somewhat decipherable code how each step is to be performed, and I find this particularly valuable for Waltz, Foxtrot, Quickstep, and Tango. There are also separate guides for the Latin dances, including Jive, Cha-Cha, Rumba, Samba, and Paso Doble. Teachers use these guides to make sure that a competitor learns all the nuances of a step correctly. It is only from that solid base of exact technique that adding flair and pizzazz in the movement combines to give a great overall result.

EXERCISE AND NUTRITION

Physical fitness and exercise

As we go overboard in our competitive nature, Jill and I consider how to improve our fitness level. Unlike the fun side of ballroom and Latin dancing, where people use dancing itself to stay in shape, serious dance competitors need a degree of conditioning similar to that maintained by athletes in other physical sports such as hockey and football; dancers must train ahead of time and outside of the actual dance time in order to be in the best possible shape, avoid injuries, and perform their best from the start of the season to the end.

With dances such as the Quickstep in standard style and Cha-Cha and Jive in Latin, some aerobic conditioning is essential. It is not necessary to run a ten-kilometre cross-country race, but there definitely is a need to stay fresh and energetic and to be able to complete all the dances with the same level of energy from start to finish. When a dancer becomes tired, everything deteriorates—the posture, the frame, and the movement of the feet, which slows down and is not as sharp. For aerobic conditioning, I like to swim, cycle, and rollerblade. These are all activities that are easy on the joints yet provide the sustained effort required for conditioning. We also push our dance practices to two hours a couple of times a week, with limited breaks. It builds muscles and stamina.

In addition to aerobic conditioning, the development of strong muscles helps a dancer perform all the steps well. Strength begins with the torso, so basic sit-ups, leg lifts, and push-ups are great. I start with a small number of each and build up to a significant daily workout. Good aerobic training will also help with leg muscle development and toning. Strong muscles provide the base for steady and controlled rise and fall in the Waltz. We notice that one competitive couple will bring yoga mats to the dance studio and do Pilates before every practice. After a year of competing and training to compete, Jill is pleasantly surprised when she receives compliments on the definition of her calf muscles. I find her at home with her back to the mirror, turning her head to see her legs.

Here is an exercise we both use to strengthen the inner thigh muscles that are used to keep legs tight in spins and turns. "Squeeze those thighs," says our teacher.

Inner thigh exercise

Start with a few and build up to more.

- Find a wooden or tile floor—it does not work well standing on a rug. Make sure you are wearing only socks on your feet.

- Stand up tall with legs slightly more than shoulder width apart, hands at your sides.

- Without moving any other part of your body, squeeze your inner thighs as tightly as possible to bring your feet together underneath you. If you find this too easy, move your feet farther apart to start. Don't jerk the movement.

- Tighten and slowly pull the feet together.

My exercise regimen outside of dance consists of the aerobic workouts as time permits, which is usually more frequent in the non-winter seasons. My daily morning routine is to do seventy-five sit-ups and twenty leg lifts. For sit-ups, I hook my toes under a furniture ledge, cross my arms over my chest, and make sure all the muscle contraction comes from my abdomen. It sounds like a lot but I started with only ten sit-ups a day many years ago and worked slowly to increase it. The leg lifts are something I learned from the soccer coach of my daughter's team. The girls on the team loved this exercise because they believed it was the best exercise for a lean stomach.

Leg lifts

I lie flat on the floor on my back with my hands above my head then wrap my hands around something solid like the leg of the bed (providing it does not have casters). From this flat position, I keep everything straight from the waist down and slowly pull the legs up to a ninety-degree angle from the floor. I slowly lower them until the heels are about an inch from the floor, then pull the legs up again. The key for me is to do it slowly, and I never let my heels touch the floor. This exercise is great for abdominal muscles. I do twenty of these every day; once again, I started off with a few and built them up over time.

Next I do some side stretches, which are also good to use as a warm-up before a dance practice.

Side stretches

I stand tall with my feet together and place the arms straight above my head with palms facing each other. I slowly bend at the waist to the left and hold that position for ten to twenty seconds before moving my body back to centre. Next, I slowly bend at the waist to the right and hold that position for ten to twenty seconds, then move back to the centre.

This is a simple exercise, yet it is good for strengthening the muscles supporting the rib cage that are used for a good upright posture. As with all stretching, I do it very slowly to avoid any muscle pulls.

Another popular dance warm-up is to stand on a spot with the feet together and slowly rise and fall by stretching the ankles. This mimics the rise and fall used in the Waltz. We also stretch our thighs, calf muscles, and groin gently before getting into serious practice—and always before competing.

For my knee problems, I use knee lifts to strengthen the thighs and the muscles that support the knees. I sit in a chair, hang a bag or purse containing weights around an ankle and lift slowly one leg at a time.

Jill has taken yoga classes and finds that the stretching and movement improves her flexibility, strength, and balance. In addition, she does sit-ups and arm curls at home.

For serious competitors who have lots of time, there can be workouts beyond the basic exercises for muscle development and fitness. There is work that is done solely for a dance look, such as making the man's physique more appealing with chiselled muscle definition. This is more visible in Latin dancing for both partners when wearing a lot less clothing. Some men work with free weights, and I added that to my workout, including arm curls and bench presses. I do not want to look like a body builder or risk straining my muscles, but a bit of toning makes me feel more confident. When a man wears a low-cut, V-shaped top in a Latin dance, having some pectoral definition adds to the macho look, but it is not necessary.

Nutrition

Why is a ballroom dancer concerned about nutrition? First of all, dance is a sport, regardless of how entertaining and effortless it might look. Second, all the people I see doing well in a competition appear to be in great shape. Finally, there is an overwhelming amount of literature citing a correlation between what we eat and how our bodies perform. I do not have a detailed dietitian-approved, all-encompassing food intake recommendation, only some tips on what seems to be successful for us.

Good nutrition is important to us, and there are plenty of books on nutrition, diet, cooking, and healthy eating. It is important for us to find something we can live with and that works for our body and lifestyle. My basic philosophy is to lean heavily on fresh fruit and vegetables with quality meat cooked from a raw state. Although I am not a vegetarian, I try to limit my meat intake, especially processed meats. I like salads, raw carrot sticks, and raw vegetables, and Jill makes some incredibly delicious salads. I cook with basic ingredients and as much as possible, using a slow cooker in the colder months and a barbecue in the summer. An egg is considered the perfect meal, although I avoid eggs, as I am unable to digest them without pain. I like nuts, especially almonds and walnuts, and they are packed with nutrients. However, the quantity is important, and I do not eat more than half a dozen nuts a day. I also try to eat plenty of fresh fruit. When my weight starts to increase, I double my intake of fresh fruit, and somehow things seem to balance out and guide me back to my natural weight.

Everyone seems to have some dietary challenges; mine are lactose and egg intolerance. I read about what is known as a Stone Age diet or Caveman diet, both having a focus on raw ingredients, and I choose those aspects that I like the best. I do not follow either of these plans, carving out my own dietary path. In order to manage my intolerance to certain foods, I prefer to select simple, fresh foods. I know what I am eating when I cook food from the raw state. I also eat grains, mainly granola, which I combine with berries for breakfast. Preprocessed foods have too many additives and preservatives for me to trust. There are also some ingredients that are not required to be listed on food packaging in Canada, which makes me nervous. Given my intolerance and sensitivities, I try to avoid anything that I have not prepared myself.

Pre-competition meals

On the morning of a competition, our nerves go into overdrive, and it is not easy to eat much. I stick to granola and fruit, which rest in my stomach easily. Jill prefers toast and some tea. Bananas are excellent for an energy boost during the competition. Another quick energy boost is a small amount of chocolate, which Jill enjoys. We drink plenty of water the night before in order to stay hydrated. If we travel and arrive at a hotel the night before the competition, our evening meal tends to be a simple, small, steak dinner with a fresh green salad and baked potato. There are a lot of theories about what you should eat on the evening before a big event. When I was getting ready to run a marathon and doing 10K races, the literature talked about carbohydrate loading. The popular meal was pasta. I avoided that choice, because my stomach is too sensitive to the high acidity of pasta sauce, and for me, too much stomach acid results in a few too many trips to the washroom. My evening meal before I ran the marathon was two pieces of baked chicken, boiled long-grain rice, and steamed mixed vegetables. I managed to finish the marathon, although I was not attempting to break any records. At the Pre-Bronze level, a dance competition is not like running a marathon, although it feels like it when you are in several events and they all have heats or semifinals.

Dietary supplements

There are numerous dietary supplements, energy products, and natural health products for sale. Health Canada licenses natural health products after checking for safety and quality and whether they actually succeed at what they claim to do. Before using any, I check the list of ingredients as well as checking the Licensed Natural Health Products Database available on the Health Canada Web site.

INJURIES

Dance injuries are incurred in many forms, and, of course, the feet tend to be the most susceptible. It is common to have blisters, sore toes, aching arches, or sore heels. To avoid problems, a good start is to have well-fitted dance shoes and seamless socks. There are insoles, half-sized insoles, and gel inserts that might be useful. Heel grips and heel guards are also available. Sore muscles or strains are not uncommon, although dancing is a low-impact activity compared to most other active sports. There are the usual bruises and abrasions from getting kicked, hit, or spiked. These heal in reasonable time, unlike the more chronic problems.

A common problem for dancers is blisters that form from friction and rubbing of the skin. There are numerous ways they get started. They form on the toes from overworking the feet or on the ankles from the curve of the shoes. I use Vaseline to try and prevent problems or to reduce friction when an area of skin is already irritated. I wear clean, dry socks to avoid moisture and use my seamless socks when possible. If it is too late and a blister is starting to appear, I add a Band-Aid and put Vaseline over top of that.

The problem that concerns me the most is sore knees. After a life of jogging, running, and a variety of sports, I have roughness under the kneecap and thinning cartilage. I take liquid glucosamine, not the glucosamine/chondroitin tablets. It is a shellfish extract that helps rebuild cartilage and is used to treat osteoarthritis. It should be avoided by anyone with shellfish allergies, although I have seen a synthetic version as well. The findings of medical studies vary as to the effectiveness, but it works well for me.

When Jill gets sore feet after a full week of long practices, she runs cold water and sits on the side of the bathtub with her feet in the water. She swears it works very well to reduce the swelling, reduce any pain, and to generally help her feet feel much better. I have less concern about whether or not it works—I enjoy seeing the look of contentment on her face while her feet are in the water.

A visit to my family doctor confirms what I already suspected by checking on the Internet. Two fingers on my left hand are curling inward and cannot be completely outstretched. It has been occurring slowly and relatively painlessly over the past three months. A small lump is forming under my ring finger in the palm of my hand and is starting to enlarge. This is known as Dupuytren's Contracture. The tissue under the palm becomes abnormally thick and restricts the tendons. After six months, the condition stops developing any further, and my fingers can freely move again. That is good news. I kept dropping things held in my left hand and was running out of drinking glasses. A visit to a specialist surprises me with the finding that the disease has also started in my left foot. It takes a year to develop and leaves me with a swollen knuckle on one of my toes. It is not a dangerous disease, and generally no treatment is required. From a dance perspective, it is an annoyance but luckily not an impediment. It reminds me every day of people who have far more serious health problems and cannot move the way I can. It fills me with determination to continue to challenge myself and find a way to be the best ballroom dancer that I can be.

Dancer's Prayer

Dear Angel, ever at my side
Be there today, my feet to guide
Help me dance high, and light, and free,
So everyone will be proud of me.
May the judges be fair and the stages be spacious.
In winning and losing let me be gracious,
So that every dance I'll remember with pride.
And Angel, please keep my shoelaces tied.

—*Anonymous*

19
"GOOD BALANCE AND CALM NERVES"
(Our new slogan for every dance competition)

CRYSTAL LEAF

The Crystal Leaf competition is a large competition in Toronto that holds both Amateur and Pro-Am events. It is held at the Doubletree Plaza International Hotel near the airport, and we decide to stay there overnight. Once again, we have bad luck with a hotel room, and the Crystal Leaf competition becomes notable for our lack of sleep the night before. At midnight, the room next to us has a noisy party underway. We don't have to phone anyone, as a local security person walking the halls knocks on the door of the room next to us and asks for less noise in consideration of other guests. It sounds as though a few people leave. We lie awake knowing that it is already after one a.m. The party continues on and off, quiet then bursting loud, in fits and starts until after two a.m. At six a.m., Toronto's Pearson International Airport comes alive as huge, noisy aircraft take off and fly directly overhead.

It seems like we always have bad luck with hotels. Some of them have smelly rugs; others have no counter space to prepare for a competition, and there is always the potential for noisy nights or mornings. There is a great Holiday Inn on Bloor Street in midtown Toronto that is quiet and has a huge bathroom counter. However, it is an arduous forty-minute drive north through Toronto to get to the competition in North York. On this day at the Doubletree, we drag ourselves out of bed shortly past six in the morning and begin to prepare.

Since the competition is in the hotel ballroom, we don't have to go outdoors and risk a stray hair being blown out of place. We collect our number from the registration table and enter the dance hall. It is a grand ballroom and looks magnificent. However, the competition dance floor resembles a bowling alley, long and narrow. Our routine will never fill the long wall, so we find our teacher and ask for some advice. She nonchalantly tells us to start farther down from the corner and just let it happen. There is nothing we can do.

We dance a fairly average performance for the standard dances, although it is not uneventful. The dance floor is crowded, and we are involved in a big collision in Quickstep. I have to stop, but smile and nod to the other couples as if to apologize, regardless of who is at fault. I am at a complete stop. I shift from one foot to the other then back again and I hope Jill understands which foot is going next. We cannot stay too long at this spot, because another couple is bearing down on us. Jill is an excellent follower. We step together and move along the floor again. The good news is the smooth restart. The bad news is that I have no idea where I am in the routine, what figure comes next, or how to complete this wall and get to the corner. I perform extra basic steps and finally make a turn in the corner to begin along the short wall and I am now once again following the routine. It is always possible to forget the routine. (In a later competition, we will see a couple stop, and in complete frustration, walk back to the start of a long wall to begin the routine again. They received no sympathy or recalls from the judges for that dance.) Although we do not dance our best, it is a reasonable facsimile of how we perform in a practice, and we hold our heads up when walking off the floor. There are people who would love to be doing what we are doing, so we have to be proud of getting this far. It is a learning experience. In the standard dances, we place in the middle of the rankings and feel some satisfaction that we are moving up.

The highlight of our Crystal Leaf competition is our Latin dances. We finish first in the senior age category, with only two couples entered, and third in the adult category. Finishing first is always nice but offers little feedback or satisfaction when there are so few competitors. One of the higher-ranked couples performs unsanctioned kicks during their Jive routine in the adult event. We are not resentful, but it would be nice to know that they won because of better style and not because they performed a more complicated figure that is officially only allowed at a higher level. Some competitions have marshals that watch for this and call the couple aside at the end of the event. The severest punishment is disqualification, although in most cases it goes unnoticed.

Crystal Leaf competition, Latin
(GSR Studio, Inc., Toronto)

This is the first competition for the two pre-teens that we know from our studio in Ottawa, and they are understandably nervous. There are at least three tables full of parents, local relatives, siblings, and friends of parents who are all anxious to see them dance. The small couple looks great walking on the floor but struggle from there. One of them forgets the sequence in Cha-Cha and they toil to get back on the routine. They move to the opposite side of the room for their next dance and move through it well. When it is time to hear the results, the family is unrealistically hopeful, but the kids finish in last place. This is only the first step, and at least they had the courage to compete. It is certainly something to be proud of, and they have to use this to strengthen their resolve to keep improving. We know how they feel, and it is gut-wrenchingly difficult. Jill and I support and encourage them, since we have been there ourselves.

The organizers give away very nice coffee mugs to all the amateur competitors who place in the top three, and we end up with four mugs. When we return the following year expecting to get more coffee mugs, we are disappointed that none are given away.

MISSISSAUGA DANCESPORT

The Mississauga DanceSport competition is another adventure. Instead of risking a bad night in a noisy hotel, we wake up early and drive from Ottawa to Toronto during the day. When we arrive at the competition, we discover that they did not receive our previously mailed registration. The organizer apologizes, even though it is impossible to know where our papers have gone. He takes our details, hands us a competitor number, and immediately adds us to the program. This is typical of the nice people we meet along the way. He is an organizer, entry coordinator, and a dance teacher who is dancing Pro-Am that day with numerous students. Yet, in the midst of a busy event, he still has time to politely make sure we can participate.

The dance floor is a bit unique for a competition in that it has a wooden post in the middle. This location is also used for a local dance studio that is hosting the competition, and I presume the studio's students are more familiar with the post than the competitors. I have danced around posts previously but not in a competition. For the standard dances, I rely on sound navigation skills to move around the outside of the floor. We compete against one other couple in two standard events and receive one second place and an unbreakable tie for first. It is their home studio, and we do not dance our best after the long day of travel. We resolve to improve our dances to a point where we are easily the best in this category and commit to each other that we will elevate our level of ability and improve our technique.

When only a few dancers register in each category, the organizers usually combine events to streamline the schedule. When events are combined, couples are still judged in their own level and leave the floor for any specific dances that the higher levels include. In a combined event for us at this competition, we dance during a Bronze and a Silver event where the music is played much longer. We are ready for forty-five seconds of music, which sounds short but feels quite long when you are dancing a Quickstep in front of an audience. Dancing for ninety seconds seems like an eternity.

In Latin, we are the only couple registered in each of two events, so they combine us with a higher level for the dances, although we still receive first place for our level. I don't mind dancing as the only couple in a category. It allows us to be in front of the judges and not have the pressure of thinking about mistakes. Some competitions don't hold an event unless there are at least three couples, and in that situation we have to move to another age category or level in order to dance. Even though we know the result when we are the only couple, it gives us the chance to dance in front of spectators and gain valuable experience. We think of it as winning against everyone who did not have the ability, energy, motivation, or determination to compete. We win because we have the courage to enter. Our first Latin event is scheduled to start at seven p.m., and the next one is around nine-thirty p.m. We are exhausted and barely make it through the routine. We dance with the Gold and Silver level entries, and the music seems to play forever. During the Jive, perspiration flows in tiny streams down my face.

After the competition, we drive to the Holiday Inn in Mississauga, arriving around eleven p.m., just as the kitchen is about to close for the night. We are famished, having avoided imposing food on our nervous stomachs for most of the day. After explaining our situation to the manager of the bar, he vows the kitchen will not close until we are served and rushes through some swinging doors to make sure. There are so many nice people in this world. It is always both a surprise and a pleasure to meet them. After making quick decisions on our food order, we finally relax and sip some red wine. A short time later, the manager delivers two delicious entrees, and we clink our glasses at having survived another competition.

The reception back at our home studio is humbling. Regardless of where we finish in the standings, people congratulate us and offer support. People encourage us to keep working and ask when the next competition will be. Our teacher puts a photo of us on the wall from the latest competition showing us wearing competition clothes and medals around our necks. Jill and I look at each other and commit to work harder.

At a practice party we try to perform our routines when the floor is less crowded. Jakki sits in her regular chair and beams. I ask her for a smooth dance, and she exudes encouragement and pride at how far Jill and I have progressed. We are surprised to discover that Jakki also used to compete, in the Pro-Am category with her teacher a number of years ago. In this Foxtrot, Jakki smiles and hums the tune as we move effortlessly across the floor. She seems frail today, and I am very cautious to avoid traffic or any incidental contact with other dancers. It is three years since I met Jakki, and she is still taking dance lessons, a private one and a group lesson per week. Her timing and footwork are proficient. She dances with so many different men who have different styles she has adapted to everything. My steps are now confident and technically far better than ever before. She soaks up the music and movement, dancing in her shoes with bows on the tops. When Jill and I line up to compete at events, we try to hold a thought of Jakki in our minds. She has become our angel of good fortune.

BEYOND ENTRY-LEVEL COMPETING

Competitive posture

The importance of good posture increases when a couple is being judged at a competition. Some people have naturally good posture but have difficulty in other areas. For me, my chest needs to be raised and remain this way throughout the dance. My rib cage has to stretch as it would if both arms were extended high in the air, hands outstretched to touch the sky, but keeping the shoulders down. The left arm from the elbow to the shoulder is to be parallel to the floor. My hip muscles have to be flexible, and my weight has to stay longer over my feet. This stable posture needs to be maintained throughout the dance. When the leg is extended properly and the weight shifts are done at the right time, it looks like a smooth, effortless flow of partners across the floor.

Many competitors look like they are falling over from step to step because they move too quickly to the next step before finishing the one they are doing. When the weight is too far forward, the body resembles a leaning tower, which leads to a dance that looks like a series of toppling dominoes instead of a pattern of beautiful steps with a natural beginning and completion. It may also look like the woman is being pulled around the floor, something that judges are sure to notice.

We are told that shorter people have to dance "bigger." If a man is six foot six inches tall, the size and movement will easily catch the judge's eye. For a shorter couple, it becomes important not only to dance the proper steps, but to appear bigger and have greater movement to attract attention.

The head

The placement of the woman's head is critical. A person's head is a significant amount of his or her total body weight. In the standard dance hold, the woman has to bear the weight of her head, yet let its weight be felt by the man's right arm. If the woman stretches out to the left or back too far, it throws off the man's balance. The rule I use with Jill is to remove my right arm and see if she begins to fall over. If she falls over, she is not supporting herself enough, and we will struggle to maintain balance around the floor. The most concerning problem with both partners' heads is the windshield wiper effect. When the head moves to one side then goes to the other side, the balance and look of the dance will be odd. For the man, similar rules apply. The head needs to stay looking over the woman's right shoulder. My head tends to move to the centre for a number of figures, and the challenge is to keep it to the left. A good teacher will show the proper placement, not too far to the left and not too close to the centre.

Evolving lessons

We add a few coaching lessons to our learning program, and are lucky to get former Canadian Champion dancer Danny Quilliam, who is selected on Canada's first season of *So You Think You Can Dance* to do choreography for a number of smooth routines. We are now moving beyond the basic technique of having the right figure and doing it on the proper diagonal. We need to improve the look of our partnership on the dance floor and give it more feeling for the dance than simply moving around robotically. It is difficult technically, and we learn that dancing is an evolving sport. Changes by elite competitors stay within the rules of dancing but exhibit greater movement and drama on the floor. The way they achieve this becomes the basis for the next level of teaching. How do they move their feet so well? How does the woman's role change from simply following to being an active participant in movement? We get good instruction and sound advice, although it takes time and practice to implement it.

Practice

If there is a formula that says after a certain number of lessons or practice hours a couple can achieve a specific level, then I would like to see it. There is no formula and no guarantee. Of course it depends on how quickly a person picks up and internalizes the steps and learns to perform them well. Young people tend to adapt more quickly than older people.

At some point, dance learning will level out and feel as if nothing is improving, a complete sideways detour in the normal upward arch of the learning curve. For a competitor, this is not acceptable. There are many options that are available to try and change this. Sometimes more practice time can help us work through it or there may be a need for a coaching lesson from another teacher. When a different teacher gives the same message from a different perspective, the instructions might sink in this time. It is not unusual for a difficult piece of advanced technique to take several months to really gain a foothold and become evident in our dancing. Then there are times when more is required, and we are stumped. When we get stuck in Latin, we seek out a different teacher and ask for some feedback. The feedback is incredible, completely accurate, and helps move us up to the next level. Some information is identical to what we already know and have been told, while other information consists of valuable tips and a new perspective on mastering a number of techniques.

When we started entering competitions, there were other couples from our studio preparing to compete. Over time the number dwindles, and perhaps we claim a measure of victory by persistence and through attrition.

Do couples argue on the dance floor? We see it all the time, and yes, it happens to us too. We are competitive and we have difficulty taking what we learn in a lesson and incorporating the improvement into our dancing. Even when we remember a change in a figure from the last lesson, our bodies might fail to help us do it properly, which leads to frustration. Conflict is not necessarily bad, because it validates the desire that people have to be successful. It is how the conflict is resolved that creates problems between couples. There is a better way than raising your voice in the middle of the dance floor, scowling, pointing, stamping on the floor in disgust, and waving your arms. The best place to deal with issues is in practice, so we always make sure that we have practice time. Making mistakes in practice is good because they can be fixed there instead of being surprised when they show up later, probably in the middle of a competition. It is helpful to always talk politely to your partner and never use insults.

Here are my tips to achieve better positive dialogue.

First, be specific. It doesn't help by saying that the figures danced along the whole long wall were dreadful. What was the exact issue? Was the posture too far forward? Were the steps off beat? Was the right hand too tight? Try to pinpoint something that can be addressed.

Next, analyze the point to see if it really is the problem or whether it is a symptom or an outcome of something else. Being off balance in a natural spin turn might be what is happening but could be a result of something else. Was it posture, frame, or foot position?

Work on something that can be fixed. If we don't know how to fix something, then that is a good place to start at the next lesson. Sometimes we ask a competitor from a higher level who might know the answer to our problem or even give us a good suggestion. It is surprising how easy it is to recall something from a lesson when focused on the correct issue such as a foot position, the direction of movement, or the frame.

Finally, it always helps to be constructive. "That was a terrible step" doesn't work as well as "Let's try that again and focus on timing and frame." With the latter type of message, it is easy to follow up with, "I did not feel comfortable with that either." Our best practices involve correcting each other in some aspect of a step. "We need our hands to be here at the same time. I noticed yours because mine did not get there in time either." Remember that both partners are responsible for the problems. It is rare for one partner to be absolutely perfect, with the other making all the mistakes. Anyone who has a good dance partner has to make it a good relationship, too, whether it is professional or personal, and work through it in a positive way.

Floor craft

Floor craft is the ability for a couple to navigate around the floor avoiding all other couples on the floor gracefully, yet still look as if they are dancing by themselves with no one else on the dance floor. I find that American Social style dancing is more suitable to achieving better floor craft due to its hesitations, on-the-spot spins, and a variety of other helpful figures.

International style requires a dancer to develop good floor craft because no one wants to collide in the middle of a competition. International dance figures seem to have more backward movement by the man, which makes it a bigger challenge for me, and astute observation and warning by Jill.

At the beginner level, floor craft means that the couple keeps moving along the line of dance and they take any complex steps toward the middle of the floor, where it should be less crowded.

Unfortunately, floor navigation is mainly up to the man (or whoever is leading) and it takes a lot of practice. At the intermediate level, men have to keep good surveillance of the other couples, the patterns of other dancers, and predict what space will be open for the next sequence. It becomes a true challenge when there are dancers from many different dance studios and styles on the floor at the same time because it is less likely that the man will be able to forecast the patterns and know what space will be available at any given time.

Mirrors

All dance studios have mirrors, and it is not simply for the teachers to admire themselves. There are times when a dance figure is better illustrated with the two partners facing the same direction, looking into the mirror together. Also, in Latin dances, mirrors help show if the hip motion is being performed properly and consistently. I use mirrors to make sure my shoulders remain steady when doing hip motion. In a Cha-Cha New York figure that is executed toward the mirror, I check my posture and make sure my connecting hand looks good. Sometimes I practise keeping my head up by looking at myself directly in the eyes when facing the mirror. I also turn sideways to make sure my shirt is tucked into the back of my pants after a vigorous dance. In standard, I might look in order to check on the size of my step or amount of sway.

My friend Juergen moves to a new house. He removes all the furniture from the dining room, which already has a wooden floor. He installs full-length mirrors along the long wall of the dining room. That's when you know you are a serious dancer.

A student-centric model of learning

Receiving dance instruction at a competitive level is a challenge because the student needs to be sure that he/she is always improving. Many teachers cling to their students and try to make them dependent. Students feel as if they cannot leave the teacher or feel comfortable seeking advice from anyone else, because they fear they will miss the next important piece of information to make them so much better; or they feel it might be an insult to the teacher, and their relationship will sour. It boils down to control and who is at the centre of the learning model. For me, the student pays the money, so it has to be a student-centric model for adult competitors. We are so conditioned from years of public schooling that we see ourselves as subservient to a teacher. In fact, we need to be equals in charting a path to better ourselves. Good teachers promote the student's ability and skill development. They will always have some credit for that. They may bring in coaches or people who have a different perspective on dance. It is that level of professionalism that makes them special. A competitive dancer needs instruction from several different perspectives to allow the knowledge to soak in and turn that verbal infusion into physical evidence. That evidence is greater dancing ability and visibly better results.

20

MOVING UP

"A life lived in fear is a life half-lived."
(Fran in the movie Strictly Ballroom, *1992)*

Minor injuries seem to be an essential part of a competitive dance experience. The second toe on my left foot hurts and takes the shape of a bowling pin. The first knuckle below to the toenail is slightly puffed out, the middle one between the two knuckles is cinched tight and skinny to the bone, and the knuckle at the base of the toe is flared out bigger than the top knuckle. My toe looks like an asymmetrical hourglass. It is Dupuytren's Contracture that seizes my toe, and there is soreness, exacerbated by the weight of my foot in contact with the dance floor. A friend speculates that it could be a bone bruise and suggests that I need to rest it. I purchase gel foot protectors for the toe and ball of the foot area. I continue dancing with pain that sometimes is a distraction and then at times is not noticeable. It takes more than this to stop me from following my passion for dance.

My pain is insignificant to the next news that we receive. Jill has been bravely dancing and living through varying degrees of pain in her lower abdomen and abnormally heavy menstrual bleeding. She finally manages to get a doctor's appointment and she is sent for an ultrasound scan. The tests reveal that her fallopian tube is swollen to twice normal size, and there are cysts. At a follow-up visit with a specialist, the doctor takes a tissue sample from a cyst and sends it for a biopsy to determine if these are malignant tumours. We are understandably anxious and know there is a lengthy waiting time for results, since the symptoms are not considered serious at this point.

We take lessons, practise our routines for the next competition, and attend the dance parties. Two weeks pass, but it is too soon to expect any results on Jill's medical condition. The worry continues to invade our thoughts; we ignore any negative possibilities while we enjoy the wonderful life that we have and the amazing friends with whom we share time in the dance world. However, there is always an amount of added stress when someone's health is in question.

Outside of dance, Jill continues to search for decorating ideas for our home. There is a lot to do. I release some energy by swimming laps at a local indoor pool, and we both take the time to visit my parents to make sure they are doing well. My father is eighty-seven years old and still in good health. My mother makes sure they have healthful, home-cooked meals. My dad plays harmonica in a band with other senior citizens, performing songs from the forties and fifties at retirement homes in the area.

CANADA DANCESPORT, KINGSTON

For our second Canada DanceSport competition in Kingston, I have a firm resolve and determination to do well. This is the first competition where we are asked to sign an anti-doping form agreeing to be tested for prohibited substances if required. Now I realize that this is getting to be a serious sport. The competition this year has moved to the K–Rock Centre on Barrack Street. It is a hockey rink with the ice surface covered with a wooden dance floor and hard, flat, plastic covers that fit together like puzzle pieces. The ice remains intact beneath the surface, so the floor is cold and in some places wet from condensation. We arrive the night before the competition and are invited by good friends to the officers' mess for dinner. We have a wholesome meal while overlooking the easternmost tip of Lake Ontario.

Following another normal pre-competition morning of nerves and preparation, we arrive at the competition site and pick up our competitor number and package. The number of volunteers and their positive attitude is both impressive and calming. We warm up for the Waltz and Quickstep. Our numbers are called for the International standard event, and the couples walk onto the floor. This time my determination and confidence win out, and I overcome most of the nervousness. We move into dance hold for the Waltz, start beautifully, and move around the floor like we were always meant to be there. Our steps are smooth, synchronized, and technically sound. In my head I pretend to be my friend Juergen, who will be competing later at the Silver level, and try to imitate his great posture and frame. My confidence allows me another benefit. I decide that I am going to

Canada DanceSport competition, Standard
(GSR Studio, Inc., Toronto)

complete every figure without fail and only stop or react to traffic at
the end of a figure—a Natural Turn, for example.

We dance so big and move so well around the floor that people
move out of our way. This is not something that I have experienced
before and is totally opposite from our very first competition efforts.
In the Quickstep, I am so sure-footed along the short wall that
I survey the audience to see who is cheering for us. Two teachers
from our studio, Alex and Valerie, are in the stands with arms raised
wildly cheering us on. Looking at them is not the smartest diversion as I subsequently draw a blank on the next long wall, forgetting the routine. I invent a new sequence to the routine, which Jill
follows flawlessly, making it look natural, and then the music stops.
We dance again a few minutes later in another age category with less
energy but more confidence.

An hour later, we line up with all the competitors and wait for the results. The dancers' numbers are called out at the award ceremony, and we have no time to be surprised that we are no longer called for last place or second last place. Next, the couple that finishes fifth is called and it is still not our number. The fourth place couple walks up to receive their medals and now I hear short loud bursts of cheering as our supporters in the hockey stands exhale from holding their breath as each number is called. Couple number three is not our number either, and more cheers ring out. There are only two couples remaining on the dance floor in front of the medal table and there is a tie for first place. We lose the tiebreaker, settle happily for second place, and congratulate the winners. In our second event, the results are almost the same with one exception. We stand waiting to hear our number and when the second-place number is called and it belongs to another couple, we realize that we are going to finish first. There is no tie, and for the first time, throwing off our previous series of last-place finishes, we emerge solely in first place.

We go to the area reserved for competitors and sit quietly at a table by ourselves, mentally and physically drained. Our medals hang around our necks. I look at Jill and tell her how proud I am of her, of our solid partnership, and for having the perseverance and determination to finally achieve this. No one knows the effort we put in to get here after all those discouraging last-place finishes. The endless practising at all hours of the day and night, at the studio, in the kitchen, in the washroom at work, and by the rattan footboard in the bedroom have paid off. It is through

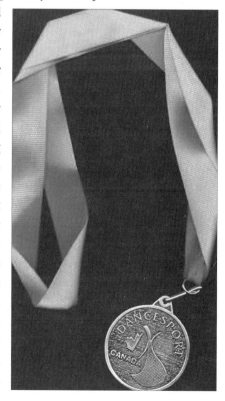

perseverance that we started with so little ability and knowledge of how to achieve this result, and now we end up at the top of our category. We feel proud and we have to acknowledge that this moment is the culmination of the passion we have for dance and for each other. We sit quietly, heads drooping down in a moment of contemplation, holding hands across the table, and then slowly raise our eyes to look at each other. Jill raises her head and looks at me as tears well up in her eyes. It is our unbending effort and strength that got us here. It is an emotional moment.

"I was always afraid to compete," she says quietly. "It was too difficult to overcome the nervousness."

"But you deserve this," I say. "We deserve this. We earned it."

"Yes, we did."

There are tears of joy in her eyes seeping out and rolling down her cheeks. I put my arms around her in a warm embrace and now tears roll down my cheeks. We savour our triumph. There are many more adventures ahead. For now, we acknowledge a very small but significant achievement for us and we are proud of it.

A gruelling six weeks pass before we finally receive the results from Jill's biopsy. We know that regardless of the outcome we have each other and we have the spirit and energy to commit to any course of action. It is a relief when the results are reported to be benign. We are grateful and thank the universe for our health when so many others are not as fortunate.

Throughout any stressful period, our dance friends provide comfort, support, and good counsel. We are blessed to know such an amazing group of people. We take some time off in order to fully heal our bodies, cancelling several lessons and practices, then finally return to both. Dancing re-energizes us and provides intellectual challenge that overcomes emotional worries. Dancing sustains us and provides comfort and peace. It invigorates us and provides a sense of belonging and calm. Beyond that, it is my partner who supports me and inspires me to be better in every way. I strive to be a better dancer, a better partner, and a better person.

OADA OPEN

At our next OADA Open competition in Toronto, we confirm that the previous results in Kingston are no fluke. We dance below our ability in the first standard event but recover and dance strongly in the second, where we place first. In the Latin entries we are energized and finish the routines with flair. We place first in both Latin events. Our Latin events don't have a lot of participation at this lower level, and we decide it is time to move up to the next level.

Although we have success in our competitions, it is a difficult year. Jill's father suffers a massive heart attack in the fall, and she travels overseas to the Azores to be at his bedside as his body begins to visibly deteriorate in a state of unconsciousness. The trip is a long one, beginning when I drive from Ottawa to Toronto and drop her off at the airport. The flight leaves in the evening, arriving the next morning in the city of Ponta Delgada on the island of Saõ Miguel. From there, SATA Airlines provides small aircraft service to a number of islands. Jill travels to the town of Horta on the island of Faial, where her father had his heart attack while on the way to an appointment with his doctor.

Jill's father remains in a coma for the entire week she is there. She finds it both shocking and sad to see him attached to so many tubes and wires. Jill stands by his bed, takes his hand and strokes it and talks to him every day during her visits in hopes that his spirit is still alive and he can hear her soothing words. She asks the angels to take care of him and, whatever his fate, to ensure that it is a painless journey.

After a few days, she travels with her mother by ferry to their home island of Pico, arriving in Magdalena then proceeding by car to the small village of São João. They must return to the hospital with clothes for a burial in the event that her father does not recover, because there are no embalming services on the island. It is a short day of rest in the house on the hillside overlooking the port below and the beautiful blue ocean waters beyond, where dolphins and whales are the major tourist attraction. They return to Faial the next day for more time with her father, whose condition shows further signs of decline. Jill does her best to look hopeful and calm. She has her final visit and says goodbye.

After an emotional week, Jill returns to Ottawa but relives the intense sad feelings one week later when life support is no longer effective at keeping her father alive. Word arrives that he has passed away. It brings back a flood of memories about a man who had the courage to leave the poverty of his home and travel to Montreal where a strong work ethic gave his children the chance for a better life. As worries about her mother's mental and emotional well-being intensify, Jill's stress level increases.

MOVING UP

We move up the competitive ladder to the next level, request Bronze routines for Waltz and Quickstep, and add another dance, the Foxtrot. We decide to move up in Latin as well, this time due to lack of competitors, and start work on our Bronze level routines in Cha-Cha, Jive, and Rumba. It feels as if we are starting over as we struggle with each new step. How can it be so difficult? We feel inadequate and incompetent. Then, slowly, with continued practice, the routines become familiar. The patterns become clear, and we work on technique. Our teacher repeats herself on key aspects of each dance, and it sinks in far more slowly than we wish.

International Foxtrot

Ready to move to the next level where a new dance is added, we start an International Foxtrot routine. International Foxtrot is not like American Social. The two basic figures in the syllabus consist of all three steps forward for the man. They are the Feather Step and the Three-Step. The count is different as well. Instead of a slow-slow-quick-quick in the Social, we do slow-quick-quick, slow-quick-quick. At first it is brutally difficult; then as our muscles internalize the steps, we move more gracefully across the floor. International Foxtrot feels far smoother than the American Social version and covers more floor space in a shorter time. I find the International style Foxtrot more difficult to do in a social dance setting because it lacks the hesitations, stops, and quick turns that can be deployed in American Social to navigate around objects and people. Once the International style is mastered, the navigation becomes easier, and the incredible feeling from the flow of the dance takes hold of me. I become passionate about dancing the International style Foxtrot.

International Rumba

We also start International style Rumba, and once again it is dramatically different than American Social. Instead of a box, the basic step is similar to the Cha-Cha without the Cha-Cha steps. The timing is different in that the movement is often held during the first beat in order to allow the hips to develop. The New York figure and back breaks are danced on the second and third beats. The count becomes 4-1, 2, 3, with steps taken only on the 2, 3, and 4, and a pause on the 1, although there are exceptions. The hip motion is performed after landing on a straight leg. Over time, we feel the increased romantic intensity of the International Rumba.

Jill works hard to improve the Latin dances, where it is usually the woman who draws the attention of a judge. We work on the Rumba closed hip twist and will bring it into a lesson to work out the subtle technique to make it better. Also, Jill wants more help on proper arm movement. Our practices go well, and we are both pleased and exhausted. We know our technique is not good enough to rank high in the competitive international bronze level, but we continue to work. When we dance well, it is extremely rewarding.

For the first time, we have a practice that lasts as long as two and a half hours. Our stamina and muscles are improving. We review each dance carefully and review every troubling section several times. We check our posture and try to maintain it through every figure. We make note of the Switch Turns to bring back to a lesson for more work.

The finale—it's just a beginning

It is December 31 as we dance in a slow cuddle to the soaring tenor of Montreal-based Perry Canestrari. He is walking around the huge dance floor at Tudor Hall in the south of Ottawa, weaving his way between couples and releasing emotional vocals into the wireless microphone. What an amazing way to end the year. We hold each other with a warm, loving touch as any semblance of dance technique melts away. Our bodies move in unison captivated by the music felt deep inside. I look at Jill and we smile at each other.

Dancing continues to fill our lives with positive energy and incredible friends. The grand hall where we dance holds over eight hundred people for the New Year's Eve dinner and dance. The table of ballroom dance friends has grown to twenty-eight this year, and we know at least as many more at other tables. Knowing how to dance certainly opens up a lot of fun and party possibilities on New Year's Eve. Most big parties will have a live band, which is far too unique nowadays. Dancing to a live band or a live performance is special, even though it might not be possible to move around a crowded floor very well. We tend to soak up the music and atmosphere, feeling the music and dancing in tiny steps until people get tired, and space on the dance floor opens up. Our dear friend Jakki is here, of course. Someone makes sure to pick her up from her house and drive her home at the end of the evening. We call her a party animal, because she never wants to be the first person to leave.

Earlier in the evening, while getting ready for New Year's Eve, Jill glued on some fake fingernails that had a beautiful deep crimson polish. Being the first time she tried this, it took concentration, since each nail required a slightly different amount of glue to secure it. As the night moves along, one of the nails pops off, and she laughs, looks around for it, and re-glues it. At one point, Jill becomes exasperated when yet another one falls off and she shouts over the music across the table to Judy, who is experiencing the same problem with her own nails, "Judy! Look!" and holds up her right hand to show her the single finger that no longer has a fake nail on it. Unfortunately, it is her middle finger that is extended upwards, and she suddenly realizes that it has a different meaning than intended. Judy joins Jill in some laughter.

Our dancing has changed as we have moved along in our competitive journey. It is difficult to dance our routine on crowded floors, and we cannot take the larger steps that we are accustomed to in practice. There are numerous backward steps for the man in International style and they don't work well in a social dance setting. We dance for fun at galas, charity events, and other dance venues. Jill is frequently asked to dance by men who want to try out their new dance steps. They see she is an advanced dancer, so they try different patterns, thinking she knows them all. In most cases, she doesn't have any idea what is coming next, but her posture and frame are so good she does well. Jill smiles and does her best.

Our story does not have a Hollywood ending where we turn into champion dancers. We are students of dance, we enter competitions, we do not know where the judges will rank us, and we continue learning every day. It is not the outcome but the journey that is important. Our journey is filled with love. We continue to work on our new routines, which slowly start to feel good as we move around the dance floor. Jill notices that when we do a good Quickstep it feels like we are moving too slowly, yet we are still on the beat. When we struggle with a figure, it feels like we don't have enough time to complete the steps and stay in time with the beat. Our steps are so large that we run out of floor space along one wall in the Foxtrot routine. The Waltz is challenging, with the tough-to-master Double Reverse Spin Turns. Our footwork, body movement, and balance have to be excellent or we notice the difference. In Latin, we become competent in performing the rondes in the Natural Top, although my hips don't want to adapt to the Cucarachas.

Dancing makes me feel alive. It challenges and stimulates me, and every single day I feel blessed to be with my wonderful dance partner, Jill. We have a common passion for life, for each other, and for dancing. Moving our bodies together in a closed hold to intensely passionate music fills our souls with happiness. There is truly no other feeling like it. We feel it from the top of our head through our entire body to the tips of our toes. Looking into each other's eyes in a Latin dance or gliding across the floor, painting the floor with our feet in a smooth dance, we feel so alive. It is the essence of life. We challenge ourselves to be the best that we can be, express and exude love, and share that with others. It is an interesting world, yet life can be dragged down by so many negative events. It does not need to be that way. For us, it is dancing that fills our lives with positive energy. We have so much more to do and so much more dancing to experience.

There is nothing to wait for and nothing better to do. Go dancing!

FINAL WORDS

We are at the Crystal Leaf competition in Toronto at the Doubletree Airport Hotel. The ballroom floor is huge, and the dazzling room is packed with spectators. We hold hands in line waiting to be called to the dance floor for our first attempt at a Bronze-level competition. Nervous energy fills my body and I feel the same effect through Jill's trembling hand. We walk on the floor, part of a contingent of ten couples in this preliminary heat, and select our starting position on the floor, which is a corner at the beginning of a long wall. I move away from Jill, and we stand facing each other a few feet apart waiting for the music to start. A surprising calm settles over her lovely face, those sparkling brown eyes look at me, and without making a sound she moves her lips so that I can clearly read her words.

A calmness settles around me as well, and as I let her words sink in, I contemplate how far we have travelled together. Maintaining my grand dance posture, I look deeply into her eyes and move my lips, repeating her words:

"I love you."

PART FOUR

THE DANCES

21

THE MOST COMMON STANDARD DANCES FOR INTERNATIONAL COMPETITION

WALTZ

Waltz is a slow, smooth dance that is usually accompanied by great flowing music. The Waltz is often referred to as "slow Waltz" to distinguish it from the faster-tempo Viennese Waltz. The Waltz is a dance that moves counterclockwise around the floor along the line of dance.

History

The origins of the Waltz can be traced back as a couples dance to 1750 in Europe. It became popular in Vienna in the late 1700s and moved to England in the early 1800s. Faster versions of the Waltz in Vienna became known as the Viennese Waltz. In International style Waltz, the couple remains in closed position for all the steps. In the American Social style Waltz, the couple may break the closed position to perform spins or turns. Dance schools using American Social style will typically teach new students the basic Waltz box, a forward change step and a woman's underarm turn. That is usually enough to get a dance couple around the floor. For navigation purposes, the extremely useful hesitation step is also great to know.

Feel

If you are doing the Waltz properly, it should feel like you are floating on a cloud. A Waltz glides across the floor with a lightness that belies the intense work of the muscles below the waist.

Count

The music is in 3/4 time. The feet normally move to the beat of 1-2-3, 1-2-3.

Tempo

28 to 30 bars or measures per minute, referred to as measures per minute (MPM) for International style. This translates to 84 to 90 beats per minute (BPM). Note that very few popular songs actually fit into these criteria, resulting in remixed versions being used for dance competitions.

Basic steps

American Social	International
• Left Closed Box (Reverse) Turn	• Reverse Turn
• Forward Progressive/Change Step	• Natural Turn
• Lady's Underarm Turn	• Natural Spin Turn

Music

- "Fascination"—Nat King Cole (88 BPM)
- "Could I Have This Dance"—Anne Murray
- "Around the World"—Nat King Cole
- "Three Times a Lady"—Lionel Ritchie
- "Come Away with Me"—Nora Jones

QUICKSTEP

Quickstep is fast-paced, swing-like music that is danced to make it look slow and controlled. The basic steps can be made very simple for a beginner, as long as you are comfortable with stepping "outside partner." Doing a solid International routine is a lot more complicated and involves serious collisions for those with weak floor navigation skills. Ouch.

The Quickstep is a dance that moves along the line of dance clockwise around the dance floor.

History

The Quickstep has origins in England, evolving from the Foxtrot in the early 1900s. Over the years, it evolved into a fast-paced, line-of-dance, smooth dance to bouncy Jive music. The Peabody is considered by many as the American Social style counterpart, although the older, original style associated with ragtime music might not fit neatly into modern ballroom dancing.

Feel

It feels like you are floating along, similar to the Waltz, but your feet are going crazy.

Count

The music is in 4/4 time. The feet move in various combinations of slows (two beats) and quicks (one beat).

Tempo

50–52 MPM; 200–208 BPM

Basic steps

- Natural Turn
- Progressive Chasse
- Forward Lock
- Natural Spin Turn

Music

- "Too Hot to Hold"—SDR Big Band and Les Brown
- "It Don't Mean a Thing If It Ain't Got That Swing"—Herman Brood
- "Snowbird"—Anne Murray

FOXTROT

The Foxtrot is a lovely, smooth dance that is easy for beginners to learn, yet can become a challenge to the point of obsession for more advanced dancers. The Foxtrot is a dance that moves counterclockwise around the floor, following the line of dance.

History

This is a dance with American origins named after Vaudeville actor Harry Fox, who created the Foxtrot and first danced it publicly in 1914. It was popular during the 1940s and over time and with the emergence of Rock 'n' Roll music in the 1950s, it split into two versions, a slower dance, Foxtrot, and a faster dance, the Quickstep. Nowadays, dance instructors shudder when people think they are similar. In International standard vocabulary, the Foxtrot also became known as the Slow Fox. In terms of the music for Foxtrot, I think of singers like Frank Sinatra, Dean Martin, and Ella Fitzgerald at the height of their popularity.

Feel

The Foxtrot is the dance that feels like a snappy walk in the park. The smooth flow of the rhythm in a good Foxtrot almost makes a dancer's feet move without any effort. It has a happy, comfortable feeling like well-fitted shoes or a nice fluffy pair of new gloves.

Count

The four beats in the bar are normally broken into steps of slows and quicks, with the slows being two beats and the quicks being a single beat. At the beginner level, the pattern of slows and quicks are danced differently in American Social versus International style, resulting in a very different look. At advanced levels, the timing and look may be quite similar.

Tempo

28–30 MPM; 112–120 BPM

Basic steps

American Social
- Forward Basic
- Back Basic
- Hesitation
- Box
- Grapevine

International
- Feather Step
- Three Step
- Weave

Music

- "Fly Me to the Moon"—Frank Sinatra (120 BPM)
- "How Little We Know"—Frank Sinatra
- "I've Got the World on a String—Michael Bublé (I know Sinatra did this one too, but I love the Michael Bublé version).
- "Orange-Colored Sky"—Natalie Cole

TANGO

The Tango is a sultry, suggestive dance with flowing movement inter-rupted by sharp staccato head and hip turns. It is probably most noted for quick head turns, where dancers try to snap the head in

another direction so quickly that it looks as if they are giving themselves a concussion. The Tango is a dance that moves along the line
of dance clockwise around the dance floor.

History

Tango originated in Argentina and Uruguay.

Feel

Tango is the ultimate macho smooth dance for a man. The look and
feel should be an air of confidence that seduction is about to take
place—or will it?

Count

The music is in 4/4 time, although the instruments often play around
the beat.

Tempo

31–33 MPM; 124–132 BPM.

Basic Steps

American Social	International
• Forward Walk	• Tango Walk
• Promenade Chasse	• Rock Turn
• Hesitation	• Reverse Corte

Music

- "Hernando's Hideaway"—Adler & Ross, from the movie *Pajama
  Game* (128 BPM)
- "Objection Tango"—Shakira (Tango version, not the Salsa
  version)
- "Cell Block Tango"—*Chicago* Broadway Revival Cast Recording
  (128 BPM)

VIENNESE WALTZ

The Viennese Waltz is one of the most difficult of all dances, probably due to the fast tempo and lack of technique in new dancers who
love the music and try to dance it. If it is not done properly, there is

a high risk of injury from falling over. I have witnessed at least three tumbles due to this dance, resulting in slightly twisted ankles and bruised ribs. The Viennese Waltz is a very beautiful, flowing dance when properly performed. Even those with good technique can catch a heel on an uneven piece of floor and topple. At least two of the falls I saw resulted in the man landing on top of the woman. It is embarrassing to both partners, although it is its potential for injury that scares me the most. To avoid stumbles, some studios teach it as a higher-level dance to be learned once the basics of slow Waltz are mastered. It is also a lot easier to perform in closed position, due to the turns. People in open position may have to take tiny steps to stay on beat.

The Viennese Waltz moves along the line of dance, around the floor moving counterclockwise, with a strong requirement for excellent navigation skills.

History

Literature claims that the Viennese Waltz is the oldest of the ballroom dances still performed. It is considered to have evolved from the Waltz, which became popular in Vienna in the late 1700s then moved to England in the early 1800s. Faster versions of the Waltz in Vienna became known as the Viennese Waltz.

Feel

When danced properly, the Viennese Waltz has the most incredible feeling of movement and smoothness. The music tends to play longer than an average song. It is a true workout for the thighs, and after dancing two Viennese Waltzes in one evening, my legs feel like they are falling off.

Count

The music is in 3/4 time. The feet normally move to the beat 1-2-3, 1-2-3. Some instructors consider it to be 6/8 time, in which the first three beats receive greater emphasis than the second three beats.

Tempo

58–60 MPM; 174–180 BPM

Basic steps

American Social	*International*
• Basic Left Turn	• Reverse Turn
• Basic Right Turn	• Natural Turn
• Left Hesitation Turn	• Closed Changes

Music

- "I'll Always Be There"—Roch Voisine
- "Mr. Bojangles"—Jerry Jeff Walker
- "Kiss from a Rose"—Seal
- "Ice Cream"—Sarah McLachlan

22

THE MOST COMMON LATIN DANCES FOR INTERNATIONAL COMPETITION

CHA-CHA

The Cha-Cha is a playful Latin dance with great footwork. When a good Cha-Cha is playing, my feet automatically start to tap, my leg swings away from my body, and then my whole body starts to move. The songs are famous for endings with the obvious lyrics, "cha-cha-cha," although sometimes it is a significant instrument that does the three notes. This is a required dance for weddings and parties, since a lot of pop songs still use this basic rhythm.

History

The Cha-Cha—or Cha-Cha-Cha, as it is sometimes called—has its roots in Cuba, and around the 1950s was brought to England and formed into a ballroom Cha-Cha. It started as Mambo, and dancers added the triple step to make it flow more easily with the music. Cha-Cha is danced to bouncy Latin music with high energy and some suggestive, flirtatious teasing. There is a lot of hip motion.

The Cha-Cha does not move around the floor like a line-of-dance smooth dance. It is performed in a small area, although as the level of expertise increases, the movement is big and the dance will take up a larger amount of space.

Feel

The Cha-Cha music forces you to get up out of your chair and dance. It has a lively feeling with lots of energy. The movement and turns should be sharp and the "one" in the beat is emphasized. The dancers need to begin on the correct beat in order for the steps to align properly with the music. For example, the Cha-Cha-Cha step (4-and-1) is done for a basic side step and the lock steps.

Count

The music is in 4/4 time. The count is 4-and-1, 2, 3, with the 4-and-1 being the Cha-Cha-Cha step.

Tempo

30–32 MPM; 120–124 BPM

Basic steps

American Social	International
• Basic	• Basic
• Cross Body Lead	• New York
• Woman's Underarm Turn	• Alemana
• Crossover Break	

Music

- "Smooth"—Santana, featuring Rob Thomas (at 120 BPM, this is a favourite of many dance teachers)
- "Save the Last Dance for Me"—Michael Bublé
- "Escape"—Enrique Iglesias
- "Sex Bomb"—Tom Jones
- "Walkin' on the Sun"—Smash Mouth

RUMBA

The Rumba is known as the dance of love. This is the dance where men look for their special woman to be a dance partner, especially after a long evening of faster-tempo dances. For those with no dance training, it is an opportunity to cuddle and sway to the music. The Rumba is danced in a confined space with bigger movements at the advanced levels but it does not move around the floor.

History

The Rumba developed as a slow Latin dance in America and Europe through the 1930s, although it has origins much earlier in Spain and Cuba. It evolved as a dance from a music style known as "*son*" in Cuba.

Feel

The Rumba is a dance with slow, sexy movement and lots of hip action. The connection between partners can be sizzling hot and steamy. It is also a dance where the couple can be playful and playfully teasing with each other.

Count

The four beats in a bar are normally broken into steps of slows and quicks, with the slows being two beats and the quicks being a single beat. The pattern of slows and quicks is used differently in American Social versus International style, resulting in a very different look.

Tempo

25–27 MPM; 100–104 BPM

Basic steps

American Social	International
• Box	• Basic
• Cuban Walks	• New York
• Woman's Underarm Turn	• Spot Turn

Music

- "Te Queiro"—various artists
- "If I Were a Boy"—Beyoncé
- "You're Beautiful"—James Blunt
- "Underneath Your Clothes"—Shakira
- "Whatever Happens"—Michael Jackson (100 BPM)

JIVE

Jive resembles a very fast Triple Swing with some critical differences. In International style, the man's left hand is usually held upright as in a Latin dance, whereas in the Triple Swing, the hand is held in a lower, waist-high position. For Jive, the knees are lifted higher, the toes point down, and the steps have some bounce at the performance level. Jive is considered an International Latin dance and is found in International style competitions.

Jive is danced in a confined space and does not travel around the floor, although dancers with a higher level of skill will tend to use a much larger space.

History

Jive originated in the United States in the early 1940s, evolving with similar dances such as the Jitterbug and other Swing dances of the era.

Feel

Bouncy, sassy, lively Rock 'n' Roll.

Count

The music is in 4/4 time. The basic step is performed in a pattern of six beats. The basic back steps are 1-2 and the basic side steps are 1-a-2, 3-a-4.

Tempo

42–44 MPM; 168–176 BPM

Basic steps

- Basic in Place
- Fallaway Rock
- Fallaway Throwaway
- Hip Bump

Music

- "Crazy Little Thing Called Love"—Michael Bublé
- "Jailhouse Rock"—Elvis Presley
- "Jump, Jive, and Shake"—Dr. Zoot
- "Wake Me Up before You Go-Go"—Wham (168 BPM)

SAMBA

The Samba is a distinctive, very rhythmical, and showy Latin dance. It is included in the International Latin syllabus and danced competitively at International style competitions. Samba music is characterized by heavy beats on 2 and 4. It has been referred to as the Latin version of Waltz, although I have never tried to make sense of that. The Samba is considered a travelling dance and moves around the floor along the line of dance. Beginner steps are usually taught to be in a confined space, but with more advanced steps, the Samba has grand movement.

History

The Samba appeared as a distinctive music and dance in Rio De Janeiro, Brazil, in the early 1900s.

Feel

This is a lively dance with great movement and hip motion. It is tempting to add bounce but this has to be controlled. Many dance instructors teach the basic forward and backward steps with the metaphor of stepping over a stick lying in your path, and this leads to adding a bit too much up and down bounce to the Samba as the dancers move on and learn other steps.

Count

The music is in 4/4 time. Overall, the count runs to eight beats and it is considered to be 2/4 tempo because the basic dance steps are danced as 1-a-2 with a slight delay on the first beat. The three steps taken in most movement make it similar to 3/4 time.

Tempo

50–52 MPM; 100–104 BPM

Basic steps

American Social

- Basic
- Side Basic (fifth position)
- Lady's Underarm Turn

- International
- Basic
- Samba Walks
- Voltas

Music

- "Ain't It Funny"—Jennifer Lopez
- "Suerte (Whenever, Wherever)"—Shakira
- "La Isla Bonita"—Madonna (104 BPM)
- "I'm Alive"—Celine Dion (104 BPM)

PASO DOBLE

The Paso Doble is common in Southern Spain and is noted for being a simulated bullfighting dance with stomps and drama. The phrase *"paso doble"* means "double step." The music sounds like an uneven march. It is mainly danced as a competitive routine or for dance show purposes and is not danced socially (with some exceptions).

Although it falls in the category of an International Latin dance, it probably has more similarities to a normal standard dance. There is less hip movement and lots of posturing. The music has breaks in it, and the dance is usually choreographed to highlight the breaks or pauses.

History

Although many think the Paso Doble began in Spain, it is purported to have originated in southern France and is based on music played at Spanish bullfights during the entrance of a matador.

Feel

There is high drama and tension in this dance.

Count

The music is in 4/4 time, but the tempo is measured in 2/4.

Tempo

60–62 MPM; 120–124 BPM

Basic steps

- Basic Movement
- Sur Place
- Chasse to Right and Left
- Drag

Music

- "España Cañi"—Pascual Marquina Narro
- "Amparito Roca"—Jaime Teixidor

23

MORE DANCES TO ENJOY

SALSA

For many people, Salsa is the ultimate Latin dance. It is fast and sexy with lots of spins, turns, and twisting arms. It is a dance for everyone to have fun, and the basic step is easy to learn. For a better understanding of Salsa, we go for a full immersion by going to a Salsa club after eleven p.m. and watch the young men and women energize the place with this dance. Listen to a good Salsa tune; it should reveal how a cowbell got to be such an important instrument.

The Salsa is danced in a confined space and does not move around the floor. It is well suited for crowded clubs where the patterns have to be danced in a small space.

History

Give credit to Cuba and Puerto Rico for the dance we now call Salsa. There is no consensus regarding its exact origins, although many believe the Salsa grew from Swing, Hustle, and Mambo. There is a lot of evidence that it was the Cuban populations of Miami, Los Angeles, and New York that developed Salsa as we know it today. The only link to the food called "salsa" is that the dance is also referred to as saucy and spicy.

Feel

Salsa is light and free movement on the floor unlike the heavier Mambo. It is high energy, smooth and sexy. The women love it for suggestive hip motion, lots of spins, turns and arms twisted every which way.

Count

The music is in 4/4 time. There are many variations that result in the same rhythm: 1-2-3-pause (every count is a beat, the pause is a hold with no steps); quick (one beat)–quick (one beat)–slow (two beats);

1-2-3-pause-5-6-7-pause. There is often a distinctive cowbell on the first beat. Listen for the tinny sound of the cowbell and time the man's forward step to hit the floor on the "one," which corresponds to the timing of the sound made by the cowbell.

Tempo

Generally danced anywhere from 40 to 55 MPM, 160–220 BPM.

Basic steps

- Salsa Basic Forward Break and Back Break
- Woman's Underarm Turn
- Cross Body Lead or Side Break

Music

- "La Salsa Vive"—Tito Nieves
- "Caridad"—Gloria Estefan
- "La Vida Es un Carnaval"—Celia Cruz
- "No Me Hace Falta"—Victor Manuelle
- "Me Libere"—El Gran Combo

SWING
(EAST COAST SWING OR TRIPLE SWING)

Swing is the dance of good old Rock 'n' Roll music. Think of Elvis and the 1960s. A lot of Swing music is played at balls, parties, fundraisers, and weddings, so this has to be a basic staple in any dancer's repertoire. The Swing is performed in a confined space with bigger movements at the advanced levels but it does not move around the floor.

History

Swing dancing started somewhere in the United States around the 1940s. East Coast Swing emerged as a stripped-down version of the Lindy Hop and had similarities with the Charleston.

There are various forms of Swing, with Triple Swing arguably the most common. Swing is different from most ballroom and Latin dances because the dance partners often move away from each other in a basic step by dancing a back break. This is different from smooth dances and other dances where the partners move in the same direction.

Feel

When I have an overwhelming desire to nod my head up and down to the beat of a song, it is likely a Swing. The music is bouncy and high energy with a heavy beat. Since the partners often separate, it is important to have a good handhold to be able to lead and follow the steps. This is normally the man's left hand connected to the woman's right hand.

Count

The music is in 4/4 time, with emphasis on the one and three beats. The basic dance count is beats of six, not eight.

Tempo

Generally danced at around 36 MPM, 144 BPM.

Basic steps

- Swing Basic
- Woman's Underarm Turn
- American Spin

Music

- "All Shook Up"—Elvis Presley
- "Cry Just a Little Bit"—Shakin' Stevens
- "Old Time Rock 'n' Roll"—Bob Seger
- "Help Me Rhonda"—Beach Boys
- "Don't Stop"—Fleetwood Mac
- "You Belong to Me"—Taylor Swift

MERENGUE

Merengue is very fast-sounding Latin music normally played with numerous instruments that produce a resulting variety of sounds. It is loved by beginners for its simplicity and disliked by many advanced dancers for the same reason. Dancing a Merengue is a good opportunity to develop hip muscles as well as a great dance for chatting with a dance partner. The Merengue is danced in a small area and generally does not move around the floor.

History

There are numerous versions of how the Merengue evolved, but it was declared the official dance of the Dominican Republic.

Feel

The music is a simple 1-2 beat that makes you want to march in a parade, but when the hip movement is done properly, it has a different look and feel. When we were in the Dominican Republic, we saw people dancing it in closed position with a lot of closed position contact, making it a very suggestive dance.

Count

The music is in 4/4 time. The count is 1-2, 1-2, although with progress there are patterns for a sequence of 4 beats and 8 beats. We lower the hip then step. If the music is fast, we take smaller steps.

Tempo

Generally 29–32 MPM, 116–128 BPM, but could be much faster.

Basic steps

- Chasses
- Walks
- Basic Left or Right Underarm Turns

Music

- "Suavamente"—Elvis Crespo
- "Enamorado"—Elvis Crespo
- "En Este Momento"—Manny Manuel

MAMBO

It is the Americanized version of the Mambo that we dance to today and is taught by ballroom dance instructors. The Mambo can be difficult to learn, due to the timing and stepping on the two count. Patience and persistence are required to learn to dance the Mambo properly. The Mambo is performed in a confined space and does not move around the floor.

History

The Mambo traces its roots as a dance to Havana, Cuba, somewhere in the 1930s but was changed in the United States around the 1970s.

Feel

Mambo has many similar steps to the Salsa, but the feeling is quite different. There needs to be a heaviness of the feet on the floor, pushing and using the floor to move. The pause is more pronounced.

Count

The music is in 4/4 time. The feet move to quick-quick-slow, or 2-3-4-pause. The man's forward step in a basic is danced on the two count, or it is not a true Mambo.

Tempo

Usually around 47 MPM, 188 BPM.

Basic steps

- Mambo Basic
- Cross Over Breaks
- Open Break with Underarm Turn

Music

- "Mambo Number 5"—Lou Bega
- "Mambo Italiano"—Rosemary Clooney
- "Tequila"—The Champs

ARGENTINE TANGO

The Argentine Tango is the slow and sultry version of the regular Tango. It has a number of similar steps but is danced much differently. The most common understanding is that the Argentine Tango is from Buenos Aires, Argentina, where it was a bordello dance used to help men find a partner and pique their interest before taking the woman to a room. As a dance of the lower class, it was frowned upon and remained underground until Eva Peron brought it into mainstream acceptance.

History

The Argentine Tango originated in Argentina and Uruguay in the 1900s, although its roots can probably be traced further back into Spain and Cuba in the 1800s.

Feel

Argentine Tango is danced in a closed position with full body contact; often the head of the dancer looks at the floor and the couple's heads touch. It is a claustrophobic dance. The man performs a heavy lead, moving the woman carefully but solidly into whatever position she should be in. It still has heel kicks and swivels like Tango, but adds a more sultry feeling.

Tempo

Most Argentine Tango music does not follow a strict tempo throughout the entire song.

Basic steps

I learned what was called the "basic step" at various times with three different teachers, and each one taught a different pattern; this led me to believe that there is no common basic step and that there is a variety of styles.

Music

- "A La Gran Muñeca" — Carlos Di Sarli
- "Tango un Amigo" — Carlos Di Sarli

WEST COAST SWING

The West Coast Swing actually does come from the West Coast of the United States, California. It is a partner dance that is completely different from East Coast Swing. It has roots in the Lindy Hop and Jitterbug but developed its own unique flowing style. It is danced along a line or slot and takes on the appearance of two people pulling on a big elastic band. The basic step has the man going straight back and the woman coming forward. West Coast Swing does not travel around the floor.

History

There were many dances spun off from the Jitterbug that became popular around the 1940s and 1950s in the United States; the West Coast Swing was one of them. It was originally known as Western Swing, and elements of it appeared in movies such as *Hot Rod Gang* (1958).

Feel

This is laid-back Swing that you would do on a warm day when you want to dance but also want to look and feel cool. Soulful Blues music is ideal for West Coast Swing, although it is now danced to nearly any slow music in 4/4 time.

Count

The music is in 4/4 time.

Tempo

28–32 MPM; 112–128 BPM

Basic steps

- Basic Back and Forward
- Sugar Push
- The Whip
- Underarm Pass

Music

- "Mustang Sally" (the unofficial anthem of West Coast Swing)—The Commitments
- "Be Bop a Lula"—Stray Cats
- "One Drop of Love"—Ray Charles

BOLERO

The Bolero is a slow-tempo Latin dance that is similar to the International Rumba. The Bolero is performed to very slow Rumba rhythms in a confined space and does not move around the floor. When the music is so slow that you are finding it a struggle to do a Rumba, switch to Bolero.

History

Bolero was originally a Spanish dance in 3/4 time and, when it moved to Cuba, the rhythm changed to 2/4 time and then finally into the 4/4 time danced in the modern Bolero.

Feel

The feel is very slow, smooth, and romantic.

Count

The music is in 4/4 time. The count is similar to International Rumba.

Tempo

20–25 MPM; 80–100 BPM

Basic steps

- Basic
- Open Break
- Fifth Position Break
- Cross Over Break
- Cross Body Lead
- Lady's Underarm Turns to Left and Right

Music

- "Unchained Melody"—The Righteous Brothers
- "Breathe"—Faith Hill
- "Beautiful Maria of My Soul"—Mambo All Stars (with Antonio Banderas)
- "Truly Madly Deeply"—Savage Garden

BACHATA

The Bachata is a sexy dance from the Dominican Republic based on guitar music. If done with a grinding hip motion in a closed dance hold position, the Bachata is as intimate as any couple can be without being arrested for dancing in public. The Bachata is danced in a confined space and does not move around the floor.

History

The Bachata has origins in the Dominican Republic, and when we spend a week there on vacation we wake up in the morning, turn on the radio, and listen to Bachata music.

Feel

This is like an intimate encounter with clothes on.

Count

The music is in 4/4 time. The basic step is danced with one step one each beat and a tap step or touch with no weight transfer on the last beat, as in 1-2-3-tap.

Tempo

Modern Bachata is generally around 32–36 MPM, 128–144 BPM.

Basic steps

- Basic steps left and right
- Basic steps forward and back
- Basic steps on the spot
- Natural Top

Music

(Get CDs from the Dominican Republic or go on-line and get a good compilation CD.)

- "Amor Eterno"—Nueva Era
- "Perdido"—Yoskar Sarante
- "Intentalo Tu"—Joe Veras
- "Que Te Vayas"—Frank Reyes

HUSTLE

The Hustle reached celebrity status in the 1977 movie, *Saturday Night Fever*. It is a dance linked to disco music and was popular in the 1970s. This fun dance can also be performed to any Cha-Cha music. Watching John Travolta in the opening sequence of the movie swing his lunch pail precisely back and forth to the beat of the Bee Gees opening music is priceless. If your foot involuntarily starts to tap to the swinging beat then you will be great at the Hustle.

There are several versions taught. Some instructors make it very simple by using four basic steps. The one I learned has a syncopated step. You can do most Swing figures in the Hustle.

The Hustle is danced in a confined space and does not move around the floor.

History

Hustle is associated with the 1970s disco era in the United States and originated in that era in the Latin communities in New York and Florida.

Feel

The Hustle is high-energy and has a lot of showy movement. It is great for extroverts.

Count

The music is in 4/4 time. Think Disco.

Tempo

28–30 MPM; 112–120 BPM

Basic steps

- Basic—in place, turning left or right, closed or open position
- Left or Right Underarm Turns—Man and Lady
- Wrap/Cuddle/Sweetheart
- Pretzel/Hammerlock

Music

- Almost any classic disco era song.
- "Bad Girls"—Donna Summer
- "Staying Alive"—Bee Gees
- "The Hustle"—Van McCoy and the Soul City Symphony
- "Funkytown"—Lipps, Inc.
- "Upside Down"—Diana Ross

24
SAMPLES OF INTERNATIONAL STYLE COMPETITION ROUTINES

INTERNATIONAL STANDARD

Pre-Bronze Waltz

Start facing diagonal wall, at the beginning of a long wall.

1 Natural Turn
2 Outside Change to Promenade Position (PP)
3 Chasse from Promenade
4 Natural Spin Turn
5 4-5-6 of Reverse Turn
6 Forward Change Step
7 Hesitation (in corner of long wall; end facing diagonal centre of short wall)
8 Reverse Turn
9 Whisk to PP
10 Chasse from PP
11 Natural Turn into
12 Impetus Turn
13 4-5-6 of Reverse Turn

Repeat from #1 at the beginning of the next long wall.

(Created in May 2007 by Josée Lepine, Let's Dance Ottawa)

Pre-Bronze Quickstep

Start facing diagonal wall, at the beginning of a long wall.

1 Quarter Turn to Right
2 Progressive Chasse
3 Natural Spin Turn
4 Progressive Chasse
5 Natural Turn with Hesitation
6 Progressive Chasse to Right
7 Back Lock

8 Closed Impetus (turn corner to short wall)
9 Progressive Chasse
10 Forward Lock
11 Natural Pivot Turn (3/8) (turn corner to long wall)
12 Chasse Reverse Turn

Repeat from Progressive Chasse (from #2, above).

(Created in May 2007 by Josée Lepine, Let's Dance Ottawa)

Bronze Waltz

Start facing Line of Dance (LOD) 1/3 down the long wall.

1 Progressive Chasse to Right (3/8 turn)
2 Back Lock
3 Closed Impetus
4 Reverse Pivot
5 Double Reverse Spin x 2, end facing diagonal wall
6 Whisk and Chasse from Promenade
7 Natural Spin Turn, ending against LOD short wall
8 Reverse Corte
9 Back Whisk to new LOD
10 Chasse from Promenade
11 Hesitation Change (1/4 turn) to new LOD
12 (Check &) Basic Weave ending in Promenade Position
13 Chasse from Promenade
14 Natural Turn
15 Right foot Closed Change
16 Reverse Turn
17 Left foot Closed Change
18 Natural Spin Turn in corner
19 4-5-6 Reverse Turn
20 1-2-3 Natural Turn and Outside Change
21 Natural Spin Turn in corner and 4-5-6 Reverse Turn (3/8)

Repeat from #1.

(Created in May 2008 by Josée Lepine, Let's Dance Ottawa)

Bronze Foxtrot

Start facing diagonal wall, at the beginning of a long wall.

1 Feather Step
2 Three Step turning to Line of Dance (LOD)

3 Natural Weave
4 Change of direction
5 Feather Step
6 Reverse Turn
7 Three Step
8 1-2-3 Natural Turn
9 Closed Impetus and Feather Finish (turn corner, end facing diagonal wall of a short wall)
10 Three Step curving to LOD
11 Natural Turn (1/4 on heel pull) (corner of short wall)
12 Feather Step
13 1-2-3 Reverse Turn Check and Basic Weave

Repeat from change of direction (#4 above).

(Created in May 2008 by Josée Lepine, Let's Dance Ottawa)

Bronze Quickstep

Start facing diagonal wall, at the beginning of a short wall.

1 Natural Turn; Back Lock and Running Finish (ends diagonal wall new long wall)
2 Forward Lock
3 Natural Spin Turn
4 Reverse Pivot
5 Double Reverse Spin; end facing diagonal centre
6 Chasse Reverse Turn and Progressive Chasse
7 Tipple Chasse to Right in corner, end long wall
8 Quarter turn to Right (i.e., like a Natural Turn)
9 Heel Pivot
10 Change of direction in corner
11 Cross Chasse
12 Forward Lock
13 Natural Turn and Hesitation
14 Progressive Chasse to Right
15 Tipple Chasse to Right along wall
16 Quarter turn to Right
17 Progressive Chasse
18 Natural Spin Turn (corner); Progressive Chasse

Repeat from #1.

(Created in May 2008 by Josée Lepine, Let's Dance Ottawa)

INTERNATIONAL LATIN

Pre-Bronze Cha-Cha

Start in open position facing LOD near the middle of the floor.

1 New York (NY) in Left Side Position (LSP)
2 Solo Turn to Left
3 1-2 open basic and 3 Cha-Chas back with Underarm Turn Right (UATR)
4 Shoulder to Shoulder to LSP
5 Hand to Hand in LSP
6 Solo Turn to Right
7 Side Step to Left commencing with Right Foot (two measures and curving 1/4 Left)
8 Hand to Hand in LSP
9 Three Cha-Chas forward in LSP end facing
10 UATL
11 6-10 Open Basic
12 Solo Open Basic
13 There & Back
14 Time Steps x 2 w/Guapacha timing
15 Solo Switch to Right
15 6-10 Open Basic
16 Solo Open Basic
17 3 Cha-Chas back with Pat-a-Cake & UATR
18 Shoulder to Shoulder x 2
19 NY LSP
20 Solo Turn to Left
21 NY in LSP
22 6-10 Closed Basic 1/8 Turn to Left

Repeat from #1 (backing LOD).

(Created in May 2007 by Josée Lepine, Let's Dance Ottawa)

Pre-Bronze Jive

Start in open position facing the short wall.

1 Fallaway Throwaway
2 Hip Bump x 2
3 Change of Places Left to Right
4 Change of Places behind back and Link
5 Change of Places Right to Left Solo with Right to Right Hand Hold
6 Double Link
7 Change of Places Left to Right Solo Regain Left to Left Hold

8 Change of Places Left to Right with 1/4 Turn
9 Change of Places behind back
10 Link

Repeat from #1 (facing opposite short wall).

(Created in May 2007 by Josée Lepine, Let's Dance Ottawa)

Bronze Cha-Cha

Start in open position facing LOD near the middle of the floor.

1 NY in Left Side Position (LSP)
2 Solo Turn to Left
3 1-2 Open Basic and 3 Cha-Chas back ended backing Long Wall
4 11-15 Natural Top (end facing a Long Wall)
5 Closed Hip Twist
6 Hockey Stick
7 Alemana from Open Position ended to side
8 Shoulder to Shoulder to Left side
9 Hand to Hand in LSP
10 Solo Switch Turn to Right
11 Side Step to Left commencing with Right foot x 2 bars 3/8 Turn Left
12 There and Back
13 Time Steps w/Guapacha timing x 2
14 Solo Switch to Right
15 6-10 Open Basic
16 Solo Open Basic
17 Alemana
18 Natural Opening Out Movement into Fan Position
19 Hockey Stick to Open Promenade Position

Repeat from #1.

(Created in May 2008 by Josée Lepine, Let's Dance Ottawa)

Bronze Rumba

Start in open position facing diagonal wall against LOD

1 1-3 Open Basic into 7-9 of Natural Top
2 Opening out to Right and Left (Cucarachas)
3 Closed Hip Twist ended in Open Position (facing each other)
4 New York in Left Side Position
5 Solo Switch Turn to Left
6 1-3 Open Basic into Progressive Walks Back with 1/4 Turn Right
7 4-6 into Fan Position

8 Hockey Stick
9 Alemana from Open Position ended to side (the one-count is a Closed Touch)
10 Side Step to Left commencing with Left foot
11 Side Step to Right commencing with Right foot
12 Cucaracha x 2
13 1-3 Basic with 1/8 Turn Left
14 Hand to Hand x 2
15 Solo Switch Turn to Right
16 Alternative Basic Solo x 2
17 Solo Switch Turn to Right
18 Hand to Hand in LSP and Progressive Walks Forward
19 Solo Turn to Right
20 4-6 Side Step to Left, 1/4 Turn Left (should be facing diagonal centre)
21 1-3 Closed Basic into 7-9 Natural Top

Repeat from #2.

(Created in May 2008 by Josée Lepine, Let's Dance Ottawa)

Bronze Jive

Start in open position facing LOD.

1 Change of places Left to Right (1/4 turn) to wall
2 Stop 'n' Go x 2 (first one is Left to Right; second one is solo)
3 American Spin, end with Right to Right Hand Hold
4 Double Link
5 Change of Places Left to Right solo
6 Double Whip (or could be a single Whip)
7 Walks (8 Quicks)
8 Fallaway Throwaway and Hip Bump x 1
9 Change of Places behind the back
10 Link
11 Mooch
12 Change of Places Right to Left solo
13 Change of Places Left to Right (1/4 turn)

Repeat from #1 (should be backing LOD).

(Created in May 2008 by Josée Lepine, Let's Dance Ottawa)

25

BALLROOM LINE DANCES

Ballroom line dances begin with a basic dance such as Samba or Swing and consist of a repeated routine or a sequence of steps that are danced by all dancers at the same time in unison, all facing the same direction and with no partner required. They are created to help people learn to move well to the beat of the specific ballroom or Latin dance, as well as being great practice for learning specific figures and techniques. Line dances also allow people who don't have a regular partner an opportunity to dance more frequently. This is especially important for the women, who generally outnumber the men and love to get on the floor and move around instead of sitting and watching others. Ballroom line dances are usually not choreographed to a specific song, although the music needs to have the appropriate rhythm. The songs listed with the line dances in this sections are examples of popular songs that are played where Jill and I dance on a regular basis. All the line dances listed below begin with the group of dancers facing the long wall.

There is another genre of line dances that are choreographed to a designated song, may have over 100 counts (beats) before they repeat, and include numerous movements for both steps and arms. They are a great mental and aerobic workout. One example is included: the Electric Slide, which is a very popular choreographed line dance.

SAMBA

This is the first line dance I learned. It is very simple and popular. As a dancer advances in experience, there are opportunities to practise good Samba technique, including footwork, hip movements, and upper body posture.

Description: Four-Wall Line Dance, 24 Count, Novice/Beginner Level.

Music: Usually any Samba is fine.

Styling Tips: (Beginners) Never let your arms dangle lifelessly. Practise the Samba syncopated steps. (Advanced). In Section 2, practise hip thrusts on beats 2 and 4.

Section 1   Counts 1-8   Walking forward and walking back.
1 Step LEFT FOOT forward
2 Step RIGHT FOOT forward
3 Step LEFT forward
4 Kick RIGHT forward; keep weight on LEFT
5 Step RIGHT backward
6 Step LEFT backward
7 Step RIGHT backward
8 Step LEFT FOOT directly to the left side; keep weight on RIGHT

Section 2   Counts 9-16   Doing the Copa walk.
1 Step LEFT directly in front of and slightly ahead of RIGHT
2 Step RIGHT to the right side; shift weight quickly RIGHT then back to LEFT (1-a-2)
3 Step RIGHT directly in front of and slightly ahead of LEFT
4 Step LEFT to the left side; shift weight quickly LEFT then back to RIGHT (3-a-4)
5 (Repeat from 1) Step LEFT directly in front of and slightly ahead of RIGHT
6 Step RIGHT to the right side; shift weight quickly RIGHT then back to LEFT (1-a-2)
7 Step RIGHT directly in front of and slightly ahead of LEFT
8 Step LEFT to the left side; shift weight quickly LEFT then back to RIGHT (3-a-4)

Section 3   Counts 17-24   Syncopated Steps sideways.
1 Step with LEFT foot to the right side, crossing in front of RIGHT
2 With LEFT still in front of RIGHT take a small step right with RIGHT foot, then another small step right with LEFT, both on 1/2 beat (1-a-2)
3 Repeat (a-3)
4 Repeat (a-4)
5 Step with RIGHT foot to the left side, crossing in front of LEFT
6 With RIGHT foot still in front of LEFT take a small step left with LEFT foot, then another small step left with RIGHT, both on 1/2 beat (1-a-2)
7 Repeat (a-3)
8 Repeat (a-4)

Start back at the beginning, but do a 1/4 turn left as you step forward on the left foot in the first sequence. The whole pattern repeats with a 1/4 turn each time.

mAmBO

This is a great Four-Wall line dance that has a mix of Mambo and Samba patterns.

Description: Four-Wall Line Dance, 56 Count. Beginner Level. Many repeated movements.

Music: "Sex on the Beach," Vengaboys

Styling Tips: Hip motion; Turn-out

Section 1   Counts 1-16   This is a basic Mambo step.
1 Step LEFT foot forward, with weight on LEFT foot
2 Shift weight back to RIGHT
3 Bring LEFT back so feet are together
4 Hold
5 Step RIGHT foot backward, with weight on RIGHT foot
6 Shift weight back to LEFT
7 Bring RIGHT back so feet are together
8 Hold
9–16 Repeat this sequence (Section 1).

Section 2   Counts 16-32   Mambo basic to the side.
1 Step LEFT foot to the left side, with weight on LEFT foot
2 Shift weight back to RIGHT
3 Bring LEFT back so feet are together
4 Hold
5 Step RIGHT foot to the right side, with weight on RIGHT foot
6 Shift weight back to LEFT
7 Bring RIGHT back so feet are together
8 Hold
9–16 Repeat this sequence (Section 2).

Section 3   Counts 32-40   Turns and Cha-Cha steps.
1 Step LEFT foot forward
2 Keep both feet on the ground and turn right so that you are now facing the opposite direction
3–4 Step LEFT forward into a forward cha-cha step (3-and-4)
5 Step RIGHT foot forward
6 Keep both feet on the ground and turn left so that you are now facing the opposite direction
7–8 Step RIGHT forward into a forward cha-cha step (7-and-8)

Section 4   Counts 40-48   Travelling sideways.

1 Step LEFT foot forward and to the left at a 45-degree angle, step RIGHT foot to the left, keeping it behind the LEFT foot (both are 1/2 beats: 1 and, 2 and 3, and 4)
2 Repeat
3 Repeat
4 Step LEFT foot forward and to the left at a 45-degree angle
5 Step RIGHT foot forward and to the right at a 45-degree angle, step LEFT foot to the right keeping it behind the LEFT foot (both 1/2 beats)
6 Repeat
7 Repeat
8 Step RIGHT foot forward and to the right at a 45-degree angle

Section 5   Counts 48-56   Walking in circles.

1 Step LEFT foot straight forward
2 Step RIGHT foot forward directly in front of the LEFT foot
3 Step LEFT foot back and slightly to the left side
4 Step RIGHT foot back and to the right side at a 45-degree angle
5 Step LEFT foot straight forward
6 Step RIGHT foot forward directly in front of the LEFT foot
7 Step LEFT back and slightly to the left side
8 Bring RIGHT foot beside LEFT, but in doing so turn on LEFT foot 1/4 turn to the right.

Repeat from Section 1.

CONTINENTAL #1

The Continental is a basic line dance that is a good one for beginners. More advanced dancers add optional turns to any directional steps.

Description: Four-Wall Line Dance, 16 Count. Novice/Beginner Level. Simple, with an interesting turn.

Music: Any Hustle with a good heavy beat (Examples: Shakira; "Ready for the Good Times," from the CD Laundry Service; Donna Summer, "Bad Girls"; Michael Jackson, "Billy Jean"; or any good disco music).

Styling Tips: Keep your head up—don't look at your feet!

Section 1   Counts 1-8   Stepping sideways right, then sideways left, crossing feet in front.

1 Step RIGHT foot to the right side
2 Step LEFT to the right side, crossing in *front* of RIGHT
3 Step RIGHT foot to the right side
4 Keeping weight on RIGHT foot, bring LEFT together and tap floor with LEFT foot beside RIGHT
5 Step LEFT foot to the left side
6 Step RIGHT to the left side, crossing in *front* of LEFT
7 Step LEFT foot to the left side
8 Keep weight on LEFT foot, but bring RIGHT together and tap floor beside LEFT

Section 2   Counts 9-16   Walking forward, turning and walking backward.

1 Step RIGHT foot forward
2 Step LEFT foot forward
3 Step RIGHT foot forward
4 Keeping weight on RIGHT, bring LEFT together and swivel 1/4 turn to the right, tap LEFT foot on the floor beside RIGHT
5 Step LEFT backward
6 Step RIGHT backward
7 Step LEFT backward
8 Keeping weight on LEFT, bring RIGHT together and tap RIGHT foot on the floor beside LEFT

Start again at Section 1.

Technique options: On the movement right or left, you can do a full turn instead of just stepping sideways. Try pointing with the toe (ballroom) or kicking (street swing) with your foot instead of doing a tap.

CONTINENTAL #3

This line dance moves a good distance along the dance floor and has elements of Foxtrot, Swing, and Mambo.

Description: Two-Wall Line Dance, 32 Count. Beginner/ Intermediate Level.

Music: "Jenny from the Block," Jennifer Lopez

Styling Tips: Use arms to style through the turning grapevine sequence. Keep head up during swerve steps (and at all other times). Swerve motion is a styling option used in women's basic forward steps in West Coast Swing.

Section 1   Counts 1-8   Stepping to the side.
1 Keeping weight on LEFT foot, step to the right side with RIGHT foot
2 Bring feet together
3 Keeping weight on LEFT foot, step to the right side with RIGHT foot
4 Bring feet together
5 Keeping weight on RIGHT foot, step to the left side with LEFT foot
6 Bring feet together
7 Keeping weight on RIGHT foot, step to the left side with LEFT foot
8 Bring feet together

Section 2   Counts 8-16. Swivel Turn.
1 Step RIGHT foot forward
2 With equal weight on both feet swivel to the left so you are facing the opposite direction
3 Step RIGHT foot forward
4 With equal weight on both feet, swivel to the left so you are facing the opposite direction
5 Step forward with RIGHT foot into a Cha-Cha step forward (5-and-6)
6 Finish Cha-Cha
7 Step forward left into Cha-Cha step (7-and-8)
8 Finish Cha-Cha

Section 3   Counts 17-24   A Turning Grapevine.
1 Step RIGHT foot forward and land with foot and frame 1/4 turn to the left
2 Step LEFT foot sideways to the right, crossing behind the LEFT
3 Step RIGHT foot sideways to the right side and shift all weight to the RIGHT foot
4 Swivel 1/2 turn right on the RIGHT foot and step sideways to the left with LEFT foot
5 Step RIGHT foot sideways to the left, crossing behind the LEFT
6 Step LEFT foot sideways, close to right
7 Kick RIGHT foot waist high (Kickball change step)
8 Bring feet together, shifting weight LEFT then RIGHT again on 1/2 beat. This could be tiny steps on the spot

Section 4   Counts 25-32   Swerving steps.

1 Step forward with RIGHT foot in a swerve motion. Foot makes a half-circle motion, starting to the left then curving away to the right. Hips move correspondingly if possible.
2 Step forward with LEFT foot in a swerve motion. Foot makes a half-circle motion, starting to the right then curving away to the left. Hips move correspondingly if possible.
3 (Repeat 1) Step forward with RIGHT foot in a swerve motion
4 (Repeat 2) Step forward with LEFT foot in a swerve motion
5 Step RIGHT foot forward and land with foot and frame 1/4 turn to the right
6 Step LEFT foot forward with weight on left foot
7 Shift weight to RIGHT foot
8 Bring feet together, stepping back with LEFT beside RIGHT

Repeat from Section 1.

CHA-CHA

This Cha-Cha line dance is a bit more challenging until you get used to it. It helps train the body to stay in sync with the rhythm.

Description: Single Wall Line Dance, 16 Count. Novice/Beginner Level.

Music: Any Cha-Cha with a good heavy beat

Styling Tips: Keep your head up. Don't look at your feet! When doing the travelling Cha-Cha, keep your hands at waist level.

Section 1.   Cha-Cha basic—a starter step only.

1 Step LEFT foot to the left side
2 Step RIGHT foot directly behind LEFT
3 Shift weight back to LEFT foot
4 Step RIGHT foot to the right starting a cha-cha step. Move LEFT foot beside RIGHT at the half beat
1 Step RIGHT foot to the right side

Section 2.   Quick Steps shifting weight on half beats.

2 Step LEFT foot in front of RIGHT, shift weight back to RIGHT on the half beat
3 Step LEFT back to position beside RIGHT in normal standing position, shift weight back to RIGHT on the half beat

4   Step LEFT foot in front of RIGHT, shift weight back to RIGHT on the half beat

1   Step LEFT back to position beside RIGHT in normal standing position, shift weight back to RIGHT on the half beat

2   Step RIGHT foot in front of LEFT, shift weight back to LEFT on the half beat

3   Step RIGHT back to position beside LEFT in normal standing position, shift weight back to LEFT on the half beat

4   Step RIGHT foot in front of LEFT, shift weight back to LEFT on the half beat

1   Step RIGHT back to position beside LEFT in normal standing position, shift weight back to LEFT on the half beat

Section 3.   Three Cha-Cha steps back and forward.

1   Step LEFT foot directly ahead of RIGHT foot

2   Shift weight back to RIGHT foot

3   Step LEFT foot behind RIGHT starting a cha-cha step. Move RIGHT foot directly in front and touching LEFT at the half beat

1   Step LEFT foot behind RIGHT

2   Step RIGHT foot behind LEFT starting a cha-cha step. Move LEFT foot directly in front and touching RIGHT foot at the half beat

3   Step RIGHT foot behind LEFT

4   Step LEFT foot behind RIGHT starting a cha-cha step. Move RIGHT foot directly in front and touching LEFT at the half beat

1   Step LEFT foot behind RIGHT

2   Step RIGHT foot behind LEFT

3   Shift weight back to LEFT

4   Step RIGHT foot in front of LEFT starting a cha-cha step. Move LEFT foot directly behind and touching RIGHT at the half beat

1   Step RIGHT foot in front of LEFT

2   Step LEFT foot in front of RIGHT starting a cha-cha step. Move RIGHT foot directly behind and touching LEFT foot at the half beat

3   Step LEFT foot behind RIGHT

4   Step RIGHT foot in front of LEFT starting a cha-cha step. Move LEFT foot directly behind and touching RIGHT at the half beat

1   Step RIGHT foot in front of LEFT

2   Step LEFT foot in front of RIGHT

3   Shift weight back to RIGHT foot

4   Step LEFT foot to LEFT side, step RIGHT foot beside LEFT on the half beat

Section 4.   Turns

4   Step LEFT foot to the left side starting a Cha-Cha step. Move RIGHT foot beside LEFT at the half beat

1   Pivot 1/4 turn on LEFT and step RIGHT foot in front of LEFT

2   Shift weight to back to LEFT, pivot 1/2 turn

3   Step RIGHT foot in front of LEFT, with weight on RIGHT pivot 1/4 turn to face the direction at the start. This is also the start of a Cha-Cha step. Move LEFT foot beside RIGHT at the half beat

4   Step RIGHT foot to the right side

1   Move LEFT foot beside RIGHT at the half beat

2   Pivot 1/4 turn on RIGHT and step LEFT foot in front of RIGHT

3   Shift weight to back to LEFT, pivot 1/2 turn

4   Step LEFT foot in front of RIGHT, with weight on LEFT pivot 1/4 turn to face the direction at the start. This is also the start of a Cha-Cha step. Move RIGHT foot beside LEFT at the half beat

Start again at Section 1.

HEY BABY

This is a sassy number that is great for learning turns and making your feet accept different patterns than normal.

Description: 2 Wall Line Dance, 32 Count. Beginner/Intermediate Level.

Music: "Hey Baby," DJ Otiz dance remix of 1962 hit by Bruce Channel

Styling Tips: Keep turning steps small; practice squeezing thighs together for a crisp turn.

Section 1   Counts 1-16   Turning right (8 beats), then turning left (8 beats).

1   Step RIGHT foot to the right side, landing with a 1/4 turn

2   Step LEFT foot to the right side, landing with another 1/4 turn, now facing the opposite direction

3   Continue in same direction stepping RIGHT foot with a 1/2 turn

4   Step LEFT beside RIGHT, bringing feet together, but keep all weight on RIGHT foot

5   Step LEFT foot to the left side

6   Step RIGHT foot left, bringing feet together, but keep all weight on LEFT foot

7   Step RIGHT foot to the right side

8   Step LEFT foot left, bringing feet together, but keep all weight on RIGHT foot

1 Step LEFT foot to the left side, landing with a 1/4 turn
2 Step RIGHT foot to the left side, landing with another 1/4 turn, now facing the opposite direction.
3 Continue in the same direction, stepping LEFT foot with a 1/2 turn
4 Step RIGHT beside LEFT, bringing feet together, but keeping all weight on LEFT foot
5 Step RIGHT foot to the right side
6 Step LEFT foot to the right, bringing feet together, but keeping all weight on RIGHT foot
7 Step LEFT foot to the left side
8 Step RIGHT foot to the left side, bringing feet together

Section 2   Counts 17-24   Walking steps with pendulum motion.
1 Step RIGHT foot forward
2 Step LEFT foot forward 1/2 step, landing beside RIGHT
3 Step RIGHT foot forward
4 Step LEFT foot forward past RIGHT as in a walking motion
5 Step RIGHT foot forward past LEFT as in a walking motion with weight on RIGHT
6 Shift weight to LEFT foot
7 Step backwards with RIGHT with weight on RIGHT foot
8 Shift weight to LEFT

Section 3   Counts 25-32   Swivels and Cha-Cha steps.
1 Step RIGHT forward
2 With equal weight on both feet, swivel 1/2 turn to the left
3 Step RIGHT forward into a forward cha-cha step (3-and-4)
4.
5 Step LEFT foot forward into a forward cha-cha step (5-and-6)
6.
7 Step RIGHT with a small step to the right side and clap hands loudly on the beat
8 Clap hands on the beat a second time

Repeat from Section 1.

ELECTRIC SLIDE

I first saw the Electric Slide line dance on a cruise ship. People from a wide geographical area, mainly the United States and Canada, were doing it with amazing unison. On returning to Canada, I looked it up and discovered that at one time it was the most popular dance at weddings and remained number one for three years, even ahead of the Chicken dance. Obviously, it was still very popular—voted in the top three most popular lines at weddings in the United States for the past five years—and I had never seen it before. There is always more to learn in the dance world. The Electric Slide is a form of Hustle coming out of the '70s disco era and has an interesting pause step.

Description: 4 Wall Line Dance, very simple beginner level

Music: "Electric Boogie," by Marcia Griffiths

Styling Tips: Wiggle the hips slightly when rocking back and forth at end of sequence

Section 1.   4 steps right, 4 steps left, moving feet behind; stepping back and rocking weight changes, 1/4 turn to right slide and start again.

1 Step RIGHT foot to the right side
2 Step LEFT to the right side, crossing behind of RIGHT
3 Step RIGHT foot to the right side
4 Keeping weight on RIGHT foot, lift LEFT foot slightly off the floor and tap with LEFT foot
5 Step LEFT foot to the left side
6 Step RIGHT to the left side, crossing behind LEFT
7 Step LEFT foot to the left side
8 Keeping weight on LEFT foot, lift RIGHT foot slightly off the floor and tap with RIGHT foot
1 Step directly back with RIGHT (swivel hips as you do this and the next two steps)
2 Step directly back with LEFT
3 Step directly back with RIGHT
4 Keeping weight on RIGHT foot, lift LEFT foot slightly off the floor and tap with LEFT foot
5 Rock forward and put all weight on LEFT foot
6 Bend at the waist and wiggle your behind
7 Rock back and put all weight on RIGHT foot
8 Straighten up and tap floor with LEFT on floor
1 Shift all weight to LEFT foot
2 Do 1/4 turn to the right with RIGHT foot in the air then start again back at the beginning.

2b

ISTD INTERNATIONAL STYLE SYLLABUS FIGURES LIST

ISTD International style Syllabus Figures, as listed by the Canadian Dance Teachers Association (CDTA). Note that the syllabus is open to updates, so some figures may not be current.

STANDARD FIGURES

SLOW WALTZ

Beginners
1 Closed Change
2 Natural Turn
3 Reverse Turn
4 Natural Spin
5 Whisk
6 Chasse from Promenade Position (PP)

Pre-Bronze
7 Closed Impetus
8 Hesitation Change
9 Outside Change

Bronze
10 Reverse Corte
11 Back Whisk
12 Basic Weave
13 Double Reverse Spin
14 Reverse Pivot
15 Back Lock
16 Progressive Chasse to Right

Silver
17 Weave from Promenade Position
18 Closed Telemark
19 Open Telemark and Cross Hesitation
20 Open Telemark and Wing
21 Drag Hesitation
22 Open Impetus and Cross Hesitation
23 Open Impetus and Wing
24 Outside Spin
25 Turn Lock

Gold
26 Left Whisk
27 Contra Check
28 Closed Wing

29 Turning Lock to Right
30 Fallaway Reverse and Slip Pivot
31 Fallaway Whisk
32 Hover Corte

QUICKSTEP

Beginners
1 Quarter Turn to Right
2 Heel Pivot (Quarter Turn to Left)
3 Progressive Chasse
4 Forward Lock
5 Natural Spin Turn

Pre-Bronze
6 Natural Turn
7 Natural Pivot Turn
8 Natural Turn with Hesitation
9 Chasse Reverse Turn
10 Closed Impetus
11 Back Lock
12 Reverse Pivot
13 Progressive Chasse to Right

Bronze
14 Tipple Chasse to Right
15 Running Finish
16 Zig-Zag Back Lock
    and Running Finish
17 Cross Chasse
18 Change of Direction
19 Natural Turn and Back Lock
20 Double Reverse Spin

Silver
21 Quick Open Reverse
22 Fishtail
23 Running Right Turn
24 Four Quick Run
25 V 6
26 Closed Telemark

Gold
27 Cross Swivel
28 Simba Cross
30 Tipsy x Quick Run
29 Ruto Right and Left
31 Hover Corte

FOXTROT

Pre-Bronze
1 Feather Step
2 Three Step
3 Natural Turn
4 Reverse Turn
    (including Feather Finish)
5 Closed Impetus and Feather Finish

Bronze
6 Natural Weave
7 Change of Direction
8 Basic Weave

Silver

9   Closed Telemark
10   Open Telemark and Feather Ending
11   Top Spin
12   Hover Feather
13   Hover Telemark
14   Natural Telemark
15   Hover Cross
16   Open Telemark Outside Swivel and Feather Ending
17   Open Impetus
18   Weave from Promenade Position
19   Reverse Weave

Gold

20   Natural Twist Turn
21   Curved Feather to Back Feather
22   Natural Zig-Zag from Promenade Position
23   Fallaway Reverse and Slip Pivot
24   Natural Hover Telemark
25   Bounce Fallaway with Weave Ending

TANGO

Beginners

1   Walk
2   Progressive Side Step
3   Progressive Link
4   Closed Promenade
5   Rock Turn

Pre Bronze

6   Open Reverse Turn, Lady Outside
7   Back Corte
8   Open Reverse Turn, Lady in Line
9   Progressive Side Step Reverse Turn

Bronze

10   Open Promenade
11   Left Foot and Right Foot Rocks
12   Natural Twist Turn
13   Natural Promenade Turn

Silver

14   Promenade Link
15   Four Step
16   Back Open Promenade
17   Outside Swivels
18   Fallaway Promenade
19   Four Step Change
20   Brush Tap

Gold

21   Fallaway Four Step
22   Oversway
23   Basic Reverse Turn

24 The Chase
25 Fallway Reverse Turn and Slip Pivot
26 Five Step
27 Contra Check

VIENNESE WALTZ

Bronze
1 Closed Changes
    Forward, Natural, and Reverse
2 Natural Turn
3 Reverse Turn

Silver
4 Closed Changes
    Backward, Natural, and Reverse

Gold
5 Reverse Fleckerl
6 Natural Fleckerl
7 Contra Check

LATIN

CHA-CHA

Beginners
1 Basic Movements
    Closed, Open, in Place
2 New York
    Left and Right Side
3 Spot Turns to Left or Right
    Including Switch and
    Underarm Turns
4 Shoulder to Shoulder
    Left Side and Right Side
5 Hand to Hand
    Right and Left Side Positions

Pre-Bronze
6 Three Cha Cha Chas
    Forward and Back
7 Side Steps to Left and Right
8 There and Back
9 Time Steps

Bronze
10 Fan
11 Alemana
12 Hockey Stick

Silver
10 Fan (development)
16 Open Hip Twist
17 Reverse Top

13 Natural Top
14 Natural Opening Out Movement
15 Closed Hip Twist

18 Opening Out from Reverse Top
19 Aida
20 Spirals Turns
    Spiral, Curl, and Rope Spinning
21 Cross Basic
22 Cuban Breaks
    Including Split Cuban
    Breaks
23 Chase

Gold

11 Alemana Right to Right Hand Hold to Advanced Hip Twist
    (Development)
24 Advanced Hip Twist
25 Hip Twist Spiral
26 Turkish Towel
27 Sweetheart
28 Follow My Leader
29 Foot Changes

RUMBA

Beginners

1 Basic Movements
   Closed, Open, In Place,
   Alternative
2 Cucarachas Left Foot
   and Right Foot
3 New York to Left and Right Side
4 Spot Turns to Left and Right
   Including Switch and
   Underarm Turns
5 Shoulder to Shoulder
6 Hand to Hand to Right
   and Left Side

Pre-Bronze

7 Progressive Walks
8 Side Steps Left and Right
9 Cuban Rocks

Bronze

10 Fan
11 Alemana
12 Hockey Stick
13 Natural Top
14 Opening Out to Right and Left
15 Natural Opening Out Movement
20 Aida

Silver

10 Fan (development)
17 Open Hip Twist
18 Reverse Top
19 Opening Out from Reverse Top

16 Closed Hip Twist
21 Spirals Turns (Spiral, Curl, and Rope Spinning)

Gold
7 Progressive Walks forward in Right Shadow Position (Kiki Walks)
11 Alemana with Right Hand Hold to Advanced Hip Twist Development
22 Sliding Doors
23 Fencing
24 Three Times
25 Three Alemanas
26 Hip Twists (Advanced, Continuous, Circular)

JIVE

Beginners
1 Basic in Place
2 Fallaway Rock
3 Fallaway Throwaway
4 Link Hip Bump
5 Change of Places Right to Left
6 Change of Places Left to Right

Pre-Bronze
5 Changes of Places Right to Left with Changes of Hands
6 Changes of Places Left to Right with Changes of Hands
7 Change of Hands Behind Back
8 Hip Bump (Left Shoulder Shove)

Bronze
9 American Spin
10 The Walks (Forward or Back)
11 Stop and Go
12 Mooch
13 Whip
14 Whip Throwaway

Silver
4 Flick (or Point) Ball Change Hesitation
15 Reverse Whip
16 Windmill
17 Spanish Arms
18 Rolling Off Arm
19 Simple Spin
20 Miami Special

Gold
21 Curly Whip
22 Shoulder Spin
23 Toe Heel Swivels
24 Chugging
25 Chicken Walks
26 Catapult
27 Stalking Walks, Flick, and Break

SAMBA

Beginners

1 Basic Movements
    Natural and Reverse, Side and Progressive
2 Whisks
    Also with Lady's Underarm Turn
3 Samba Walks in Promenade Position
4 Rhythm Bounce
5 Travelling Voltas to Right and Left (facing—no turn)

Pre-Bronze

6 Travelling Bota Fogos Forward
7 Criss Cross Bota Fogos (Shadow Bota Fogos)
3 Samba Walks Side and Stationary

Bronze

8   Travelling Bota Fogos Back
9   Bota Fogos to Promenade Position
    and Closed Promenade Position
10 Criss Cross Voltas
11 Solo Spot Voltas
12 Foot Changes 1 and 2
13 Shadow Travelling Voltas
14 Reverse Turn
15 Corta Jaca
16 Closed Rocks

Silver

12 Foot Change 1-2-3-4-8
17 Open Rocks
18 Back Rocks
19 Plait
20 Rolling Off the Arm
21 Argentine Crosses
22 Maypole
23 Shadow Circular Volta

Gold

12 Foot Changes 1 to 8
24 Contra Bota Fogos
25 Roundabout
26 Natural Roll
27 Reverse Roll
28 Promenade and Counter Promenade Runs
29 Three-Step Turn
30 Samba Locks
31 Cruzados Walks and Locks

PASO DOBLE

Beginner
1 Sur Place
2 Basic movement
3 Chasses to Right or Left (including elevations)
4 Drag
5 Drag Deplacement (also Attack)
6 Promenade Link (also Promenade Close)

Pre-Bronze
7 Promenade
8 Ecart (Fallaway Whisk)
9 Separation
10 Separation with Lady's Caping Walks

Bronze
11 Fallaway Ending to Separation
12 Huit
13 Sixteen
14 Promenade and Counter Promenade
15 Grand Circle
16 Open Telemark

Silver
17 La passe
18 banderillas
19 twist turn
20 fallaway reverse turn
21 coup de pique
22 left foot variation
23 spanish Lines
24 Flamenco Taps

Gold
25 Syncopated Separation
26 Travelling Spins from PP
27 Travelling Spins from CPP
28 Fregolina (also Farol)
29 Twists
30 Chasse Cape (incl. outside turn)

27
ISTD AMERICAN STYLE SYLLABUS FIGURES LIST

WALTZ

Bronze
1 Forward Change Steps
2 Left Box Turn
3 Right Turn Box
4 Simple Twinkle
5 Hesitations
6 Hesitation Combinations
7 Promenade Hesitation
8 Promenade Turn
9 Twinkle and Walk Around
10 Left Turn Cross

Silver
1 Progressive Basic
2 Open Left Box Turn
3 Advanced Twinkle
4 Progressive Twinkle
5 Left Side Rock and Spin
6 Open Right Turn
7 Twinkle and Twist
8 Twinkle and Fallaway
9 Twinkle and Pivots
10 Fallaway and Rock

FOXTROT

Bronze
1 Forward Basic
2 Quarter Turns
3 Left Rock Turn
4 Swing Step
5 Promenade Walk
6 Left Turn Box
7 Right Turn Box
8 Simple Twinkle
9 Right Rock Turn
10 Promenade Turn

Silver
1 Progressive Basic
2 Open Left Box Turn
3 Advanced Twinkle
4 Open Left Rock Turn
5 Open Swing Step
6 Open Right Turn
7 Twinkle and Twist
8 Grapevine
9 Twinkle and Pivots
10 Fallaway and Rock

TANGO

Bronze
1 Basic and Outside Basic
2 Promenade Basic
3 Promenade to Fan

Silver
1 Corte and Walk Around
2 Rock and Ronde
3 Left Turn and Fans

4 Progressive Rocks
5 Continuous Basic
6 Corte
7 Turning Rocks
8 Outside Swivels
9 Turning Corte
10 Promenade Turns

4 Promenade Turn to Corte
5 Continuous Ronde
6 Back Turning Rocks
7 Quick Change
8 Turning Rock to Same Foot Lunge
9 Double Ronde
10 Oversway

CHA-CHA

Bronze

1 Basic Cha-Cha
2 Cross Over Breaks
3 Outside Breaks
4 Back Breaks
5 Open Break
6 Progressive Basic
7 The Chase
8 Underarm Turn
9 Cross Body Lead
10 Kick Swivels

Silver

1 Underarm Turn with Spin
2 Back Spot Turn
3 Forward Spot Turn
4 Three Cha-Chas
5 Side-by-Side Triples
6 Stop and Go
7 Sweetheart
8 Fallaway Swivel
9 Promenade Swivels
10 Back Spot with Underarm Turns

RUMBA

Bronze

1 Rumba Box Step
2 Underarm Turn
3 Rumba Rocks
4 Progressive Walks
5 Outside Breaks
6 Back Breaks Right
7 Open Breaks/Underarm Turn
8 Cross Body Lead
9 Open Walks
10 Back Spot Turn

Silver

1 Back to Back
2 Side Pass
3 Forward Spot Turn
4 Side-by-Side Progressive Walks
5 Side-by-Side Rocks
6 Back Spot with Underarm Turn
7 Back Spot with Underarm Turn Left
8 Wrap Around
9 Back Spot to Spiral Turn
10 Free Turns with Breaks

SWING

Bronze

1 Swing Basic
2 Throwaway Change

Silver

1 Kick Ball Change
2 Underarm Turns with Hand

3 Closing Link
4 Underarm to Left
5 Underarm to Right
6 Four Kick
7 Change of Hands
8 Whip Throwaway
9 Windmill
10 Stop and Go

3 Hesitation
4 Back Shuffle
5 Whip and Underarm Turn Left
6 Whip and Underarm Turn Right
7 American Spin
8 Rolling Off the Arm
9 Spin Whip
10 Toe Heel Swivels

MERENGUE

Bronze

1 Chasse to Left
2 Forward Walk
3 Promenade Walk
4 Left Rock Turn
5 Separation
6 Back Breaks Right
7 Open Break UAT Right
8 Open Break UAT Left
9 Chasse to Left and Right
10 Open Rocks

Silver

1 Back Spot Turn
2 Syncopated Chasse
3 The Freeze
4 Forward Spot Turn
5 Back Spot with Underarm Turn Left
6 Back Spot with Underarm Turn
7 Promenade Swivels
8 Wrap Around
9 Pendulum and Grapevine
10 Flick Breaks

SAMBA

Bronze

1 Samba Basic
2 Whisks
3 Samba Walks
4 Simple Twinkle
5 Samba Box Step
6 Chasse Right and Left
7 Open Break Underarm Turn
8 Back Spot Turn
9 Progressive Twinkle
10 Opening Out

Silver

1 Kick Release
2 Twinkles to P.P. and C.P.P.
3 Back Samba Walks
4 Solo Turns
5 Syncopated Twinkle
6 Criss Cross
7 Shadow Twinkles
8 Rolling Off the Arm
9 Maypole Left and Right
10 Closed Swivels

MAMBO

Bronze	Silver
1 Mambo Basic	1 Forward Spot Turn
2 Passing Basic Right	2 Back Spot with Underarm Turn
3 Cross Over Breaks	3 Back Spot with Underarm Turn Left
4 Open Break with Underarm Turn	4 Side By Side
5 Back Spot Turn	5 Open Hip Twist
6 Mambo Breaks	6 Spin Whip
7 Kick Swivels	7 Advanced Hip Twist
8 Stop and Go	8 Spins
9 Cross Body Lead	9 Time Steps
10 Fallaway Swivel	10 Chase Turn to Cross Turn

28

NDCA AMERICAN STYLE SYLLABUS

This is another dance pattern syllabus. Two of the most notable members listed for the NDCA (NDCA: National Dance Council of America, www.ndca.org) are Arthur Murray International and Fred Astaire Dance of North America. This is a list of the allowable figures for the Bronze level to be used in NCDA-recognized events, although the syllabus may be open to updates.

WALTZ
1 Left Closed/Box (Reverse) Turn—Right Closed/Box (Natural) Turn
2 Forward Progressive/Change Step, right foot or left foot
3 Lady's Underarm Turn to the Right—two measures/6 beats
4 Balance Steps/Hesitations, Fifth Position Breaks (in closed hold or double hand hold only)
5 Closed Twinkles (may be danced in any direction)
6 Cross Body Lead from LF Fwd Hesitation or from 1-3 of Left Closed/Box (Reverse Turn)
7 Natural Spin Turn (same as International style)
8 Forward Twist to Left from P.P.
9 Syncopated Chasse
10 Simple Grapevine or Zigzag (no Syncopation)
11 In and Out Change Steps / Butterfly

FOXTROT
1 Forward Basic, Closed or O.P. (with or without quarter turn)
2 Back Basic, Closed or O.P. (with or without quarter turn)
3 Promenade
4 Rock Turn / Ad Lib to Left or Right
5 Lady's Underarm Turn to the Right—two measures/8 beats
6 Left Closed / Box / Reverse Turn

7 Cross Body Lead
8 Closed Twinkle, may be danced in any direction, must close feet
9 Single Promenade Pivot
10 Syncopated Chasse
11 Forward twist to left from promenade
12 Sway Step / Side Balance
13 Promenade Under Arm Turn
14 Simple Grapevine or Zigzag (8) quicks max. (no Syncopations) xxx

TANGO

1 Tango Walks—All Slows
2 Forward Basic, Closed or O.P. (SSQQS timing only)
3 Promenade turning to left or right (SSQQS timing only)
4 Corte or Simple Oversway
5 Open Fan
6 Open Fan to Same Foot Rocks
7 Right Side Fan/Outside Swivel
8 Rocks—Closed or P.P. position (may be danced w/ or w/o turn to left or right in any direction)
9 Single Pivot from P.P.
10 Linking action to and from P.P.
11 Left/Reverse Turn (Open or Closed)
12 Under Arm Turn Left or Right from Open Fan
13 Twist Turn to Left or Right from P.P.
14 Running Step/Progressive Side Step or Argentine Walks (basic w/ alternative rhythm)

VIENNESE WALTZ

1 Left Turns/Reverse Turns
2 Right Turns/Natural Turns
3 Progressive/Change Steps
4 Balance Steps/Hesitations/Fifth Position Breaks
5 Cross Body Lead/Turn
6 Underarm Turn from Fifth Position Break or Cross Body Lead
7 Closed Twinkle (may be danced in any direction or alignment)
8 In and Out Change Steps/Butterfly
9 Left Box w/Lady's Left or Right Underarm Turn

CHA-CHA

1 Basic Step (Closed, Single or Double Handhold)
2 Cross Over Breaks (single only—no timing changes)
3 Offset Breaks—O.P.
4 Open Break
5 Lady's Underarm Turn Left or Right
6 Walk Around Turns (may be danced under arm or free turn to Right or Left)
7 Chase Turns
8 Cross Over Break with Swivel
9 Fifth Position Breaks
10 Cross Body Lead—may end in Closed, Open or Open Counter Promenade Positions
11 Three Cha-Chas—chasses may be danced forward or back or side
12 Back Spot Turn / Natural Top
13 Parallel Breaks / Sweetheart / Cuddle—same foot is allowed on this pattern

RUMBA

1 Box Step
2 Cuban Walks—Closed and Open (may be danced in side-by-side position)
3 Lady's Underarm Turn to Right or Left
4 Rock Steps and Breaks (forward, side or back)
5 Cross Body Lead / Turn
6 Fifth Position Breaks
7 Open Break—may end in Closed, Open or Open Counter Promenade Positions
8 Cross Over Breaks
9 Offset Breaks O.P.
10 Walk Around Turn (may be danced under arm or free turn to Right or Left)
11 Back Spot Turn
12 Back Spot Turns/Natural Top

EAST COAST SWING

1 Basic w/ or w/o Turn Left or Right
2 Lady's Underarm Turn to Right
3 Lady's and Man's Underarm Turn to Left
4 Throwaway

5 Tuck in Turn / American Spin / Lady's Free Spin
6 Continuous Tuck in Turn
7 Back Pass/change hands behind back
8 Sweetheart/Cuddle/Wrap
9 Lindy Whip—up to four quicks
10 Hitch Kicks
11 Lindy Whip with Underarm Turn Left or Right—up to 4 quicks
12 Stop and Go / Peek-a-Boo

BOLERO
1 Basic
2 Open Break (man may use Flex Point)
3 Fifth Position Breaks
4 Cross Over Breaks
5 Cross Body Lead—may end in Closed, Open or Open Counter Promenade Positions
6 Lady's Underarm Turns to Left and Right
7 Free Walk Around Turn from Cross Over
8 Side Passes Left and Right
9 Open Cuban Walks, Open and Closed Positions—may be danced in side-by-side position
10 Rock Steps (may be danced in any direction)
11 Back Spot Turn (Natural Top

MAMBO
1 Basic, open, closed, progressive w/ or w/o turn to right or left
2 Open Break
3 Offset Breaks O.P.
4 Fifth Position Breaks
5 Cross Over Breaks
6 Lady's Underarm Turn to Right and Left
7 Walk Around Turn turns to left or right
8 Cross Body Lead—may end in Closed, Open or Open Counter Promenade Positions
9 Chase Turns 1/2 or full
10 Side Breaks
11 Promenade Walks
12 Cross Over Break with Swivel
13 Progressive Walks
14 Parallel Breaks / Sweetheart / Cuddle—same foot is allowed

SAMBA

1 Basic (Closed or box, w/ or w/o turn)
2 Side Basic (5th Position/Whisk)
3 Left or Right Underarm Turns
4 Extended Basic (Chasses)
5 Promenade / Samba Walks / Rocks (Conversas, Copas)
6 Open Counter Promenade/Samba Walks/Rocks
7 Twinkles / Bota Fogos (Single, Double, Progressive, Forward and Back, PP and CPP)
8 Open or Progressive 5th Positions
9 Open Break
10 Cross Body Lead
11 Voltas

MERENGUE

1 Chasses (Forward, Backward, Side)
2 Walks (Forward, Backward, Promenade)
3 Basic Left or Right Underarm Turns
4 5th Position Breaks
5 Left Rock Turns
6 Back Spot Turn/Natural Top
7 Wrap/Cuddle/Sweetheart
8 IBO Walks
9 Promenade Swivels
10 Pretzel/Hammerlock

WEST COAST SWING

1 Basic/Sugar Push
2 Passes and Underarm Turns Left and Right
3 Tuck In Turns
4 Wrap/Cuddle/Sweetheart
5 Basic Whip
6 Basket / Wrap Whip
7 Whip w/ Underarm Turn Left or Right
8 Hitch Kicks

HUSTLE

1 Basic—in place, turning left or right, closed or open position
2 Left or Right Underarm Turns—Man and Lady
3 Wrap/Cuddle/Sweetheart

4 Pretzel/Hammerlock
5 New York Walks
6 Lady's Underarm Spin to Left—1 1/2 turns maximum
7 Throwaway
8 Back Pass
9 Shoulder Drapes/Head Combs

PEABODY

1 Six and Eight Count Right Turns
2 Six and Eight Count Left Turns
3 Running Steps / Gallops
4 Locks—Forward and Backward
5 Twinkles—Forward and Backward
6 Right and Left Underarm Turns
7 Grapevines

APPENDIX

BALLROOM DANCE ORGANIZATIONS IN CANADA

Association Amateurs de Danse Sportive du Quebec (AADSQ)
http://www.dansesportquebec.com/

Canadian Amateur Dance Association (CADA)
www.dancesport.ca

Canadian DanceSport Federation (CDF)
www.canadiandancesportfederation.org

Canadian Dance Teachers' Association, Ontario Branch
http://www.cdtaont.com

DanceSport Alberta (DSAB)
www.dancesportalberta.org

DanceSport Atlantic (DAA)
www.dancesport.chebucto.org

DanceSport BC (DSBC)
www.dancesportbc.com

Ontario Amateur Dance Association (OADA)
www.ontariodancesport.com

REFERENCES

Books

Franks, A.H. *Social Dance: A Short History*. London: Routledge and Kegan Paul, 1963.

Moore, Alex. *Ballroom Dancing*. London: Routledge, 2002.

Richardson, P.J.S. *The History of English Ballroom Dancing (1900–1945)*. London: Jenkins, 1948.

Silvester, Victor. *Modern Ballroom Dancing*. London: Trafalgar Square, 1993.

———. *Old Time and Sequence Dancing*. London: Barrie and Jenkins, 1980.

Wainright, Lyndon. *The Story of British Popular Dance*. Brighton: Dance Publications, 1997.

Publications of the Imperial Society of Teachers of Dancing, London, England

ISTD, The Ballroom Technique
ISTD, Popular Variations—Standard
ISTD, Latin American Cha Cha Cha
ISTD, Latin American Rumba
ISTD, Latin American Samba
ISTD, Latin American Jive
ISTD, Latin American Paso Doble
ISTD, Viennese Waltz
ISTD, Argentine Tango
ISTD, Salsa
ISTD, Mambo
ISTD, Popular Variations—Latin
ISTD, The Skating System: Scrutineering for Ballroom Dance Competitions

Internet Sites

Imperial Society of Teachers of Dancing
www.istd.org

NDCA Syllabus American Style
(NDCA: National Dance Council of America)
www.ndca.org

Non-profit organization promoting ballroom dance in the United States, which serves as the National Governing Body for DanceSport
www.usadance.org

Dance Material

www.amazon.com

www.supadance.com

www.danceshoesonline.com

www.ballroomdancers.com

www.ballroomdancingdirectory.com

www.thedancestoreonline.com

www.danceshopper.com

ABOUT THE AUTHOR

Paul and Jill in 2009

Paul Boudreau was born in Kingston, Ontario, and moved to Ottawa in the 1960s. He graduated from Carleton University and received an MBA from the University of Ottawa. He has a long work history in the technology industry and currently resides in Ottawa with Jill, where they continue their passion for each other and for ballroom dancing. They take lessons together on a regular basis, enter dance competitions, and enjoy the adventure of life.

TO ORDER MORE COPIES:

GENERAL STORE PUBLISHING HOUSE
499 O'Brien Road, Box 415, Renfrew, Ontario, Canada K7V 4A6
Tel 1.800.465.6072 • Fax 1.613.432.7184
www.gsph.com